MW01257392

Biplanes and Bombsights
British Bombing in World War I

George K. Williams

University Press of the Pacific
Honolulu, Hawaii

Biplanes and Bombsights:
British Bombing in World War I

by
George K. Williams

ISBN: 1-4102-0012-4

Reprinted from the 1999 edition

University Press of the Pacific
Honolulu, Hawaii
http://www.universitypressofthepacific.com

Contents

Illustrations

Photographs

Foreword

This study measures wartime claims against actual results of the British bombing campaign against Germany in the Great War. Components of the Royal Naval Air Service (RNAS), the Royal Flying Corps (RFC), and the Royal Air Force (RAF) conducted bombing raids between July 1916 and the Armistice. Specifically, Number 3 Wing (RNAS), 41 Wing of Eighth Brigade (RFC), and the Independent Force (IF) bombed German targets from bases in France. Lessons supposedly gleaned from these campaigns heavily influenced British military aviation, underpinning RAF doctrine up to and into the Second World War.

Fundamental discrepancies exist, however, between the official verdict and the firsthand evidence of bombing results gathered by intelligence teams of the RAF and the US Air Service. Results of the British bombing efforts were demonstrably more modest, and costs in casualties and wastage far steeper, than previously acknowledged. A preoccupation with "moral effect" came to dominate the British view of their aerial offensives. Maj Gen Hugh M. Trenchard played a pivotal role in bringing this misperception to the forefront of public consciousness.

After the Armistice, the potential of strategic bombing was officially extolled to justify the RAF as an independent service. The Air Ministry's final report must be evaluated as a partisan manifestation of this crusade and not as a definitive final assessment, as it has been mistakenly accepted previously.

This study develops and substantiates a comprehensive evaluation of British long-range bombing in the First World War. Its findings run directly counter to the generally held opinion. Natural limitations, technical shortfalls, and aircrews lacking proficiency acted in concert with German defenses to produce far less results than those claimed.

Mention must be made here of the excellent appendix that concludes this study of British bombing efforts in the Great War. Prepared by Steve Suddaby, it presents a compact yet comprehensive view of British bombing raids against German targets during World War One. Both the author and Air University Press are indebted to Mr. Suddaby for his fine contribution to this treatise.

George K. Williams

About the Author

George K. Williams was born on 30 March 1944 in Lamar, Colorado. He graduated from Lamar High School in 1962 and entered the US Military Academy at West Point in 1964, graduating in June 1968 with a Bachelor of Science degree. He earned a Master of Arts in US Intellectual History from Cornell University in 1973 and a PhD in Modern History from Oxford University, England, in 1988.

Colonel Williams was commissioned as a second lieutenant in the US Army upon graduation from West Point in 1968. Following graduation, he attended US Army Ranger School at Fort Benning, Georgia. He later completed the Armor Officer course at Fort Knox, Kentucky, and the Advanced Jumpmaster course at Fort Bragg, North Carolina.

From August 1968 to August 1969, Colonel Williams was a platoon leader with 1st Squadron, 17th Cavalry, 82d Airborne Division, at Fort Bragg. From August 1969 to August 1970, he was a platoon leader and company commander with 1st Squadron, 1st Cavalry, I Corps, in South Vietnam. Upon returning to the United States, Colonel Williams completed the Armor Officer advanced course at Fort Knox and attended Cornell University at Ithaca, New York. From August 1973 to July 1975, he served as instructor of English at the US Military Academy.

Colonel Williams was an exchange officer and assistant professor of English and Fine Arts at the US Air Force Academy from August 1975 to July 1976. He then returned to the US Military Academy and served as assistant professor and course director in the English Department until August 1977, when he completed an interservice transfer to the US Air Force and entered Air Weapons Controller training at Tyndall Air Force Base (AFB), Florida. After graduation, he was assigned to 963d Airborne Warning and Control Squadron, 552d Airborne Warning and Control Wing, Tinker AFB, Oklahoma. From October 1977 to July 1981, he served as airborne weapons controller, senior director, and airborne battle staff member on the E-3A airborne warning and control system aircraft.

Colonel Williams entered Oxford University in August 1981 and completed his resident studies in July 1984. He was assigned as special assistant to the commander, Air Force Logistics Command, from August 1984 to August 1985. He then served as Deputy Air Force Historian in the USAF Office of History, Washington, D.C., until November 1996, when he was assigned as research fellow, National War College, National Defense University, Washington, D.C. He retired from active duty in June 1998.

Acknowledgments

Many fine people on both sides of the Atlantic encouraged and assisted in the convoluted development of this study. The sustained support of my family and the peerless example of Sir Michael Howard, decorated infantryman and Regius Professor of Modern History, have been particularly noteworthy and are gratefully acknowledged.

Introduction

In broad brush, this study balances wartime claims against actual results as determined after hostilities. It also documents the cost, in men and equipment, of the bombing offensive waged by 3 Wing, Royal Naval Air Service, and components of the Royal Flying Corps and the Royal Air Force—specifically 41 Wing, Eighth Brigade, and Independent Force, between July 1916 and the Armistice. The study's organization was based on the organizational scheme of Sir Charles Webster and Noble Frankland in their four-volume history of Bomber Command in World War II, *The Strategic Air Offensive Against Germany.*

Maj Gen Hugh M. Trenchard's Independent Force, the major strategic force to undertake significant and protracted bombing operations in the Great War, levered into place the cornerstone of the postwar Royal Air Force and shaped its doctrine during the interwar years. It also conditioned domestic expectations concerning the offensive potential of aerial campaigns in any future conflict. The lessons supposedly gleaned from the Great War heavily influenced the progress of British military aviation during the 1920s and 1930s, underpinning RAF doctrines, expectations, and policies up to the initial phases of the Second World War. The subject thus deserves careful study in its own right.

Fundamental discrepancies between the materials and conclusions reported in the January 1920 Air Ministry's classified evaluation of the Great War's long-range bombing offensive on the one hand, and those contained in seven volumes of evidence gathered firsthand by RAF intelligence officers who surveyed German-occupied territory immediately after the Armistice on the other, prompted an initial interest in this aspect of military history. Data from seldom-consulted records of the bombing study conducted independently by the United States Air Service complicated these differences. Subsequent examinations of RAF, Air Ministry, and other official archives brought even more contradictions to light.

Opinion of British long-range bombing efficacy during the First World War has previously been unduly influenced by two factors: (1) the laudatory judgments rendered in the six-volume official history, *The War in the Air,* by Sir Walter Raleigh and H. A. Jones, and (2) a retrospective awareness of the Anglo-American combined bombing offensive. Compared to the scale and intensity of its successor, the 1917–18 bombing effort seems to shrink into insignificance, serving merely as a slight and inconclusive prelude.

Contributing further to this neglect has been the general unavailability of definitive materials that might refute or corroborate the enthusiastic assessments of bombing promulgated in *The War in the Air.* By default, the flawed conclusions of the official history have been accepted and echoed by many later studies. Even those investigators who have delved deeper have often been led astray, most notably by the Air Ministry's classified report of January 1920, "Results of Air Raids on Germany Carried Out by the 8th Brigade and Independent Force, R.A.F."

In point of fact, the results of the 1917–18 RFC and RAF bombing offensives were demonstrably far more modest—and costs in aircrew and aeroplanes far steeper—than previously acknowledged or estimated. When other pertinent information is compiled and used, it severely undercuts the traditional view. Inordinate personnel losses and equipment wastage must be attributed to the policy of unrelenting offensive action that characterized RFC and RAF activities during the period. It impacted negatively upon aircrew proficiency and replacement programs, and on the muddled concepts of employment under which bombing squadrons in the field found themselves. Weather conditions and technical deficiencies also exacted a heavy toll.

From the outset, a preoccupation with the "moral" effects versus "material" results of bombing characterized the British view. This stance was not, however, shared by any of their major allies. By mid-1918, when Trenchard assumed control of the Independent Force, this preoccupation had evolved into a widespread obsession. It affected not only target selection—it affected the manner in which the targets would be assaulted. After the war, the alleged moral effect of aerial bombardment became the predominant justification for the RAF. Trenchard, as wartime bomber commander and later as Chief of the Air Staff in the decade following 1919 (when histories were written and doctrines formulated), exerted a pivotal influence in this regard.

When Trenchard took over the IF in June 1918, his arrangements with Lord Weir, the Air Minister, were such that he could wage his bombing program quite independently of the Air Ministry and even the War Cabinet, guided only by his own prejudices and predilections. Further, his IF headquarters staff originated and disseminated all reports, summaries, and other returns detailing the results of his aerial offensive. This exclusive control meant that any assessment of success would have to depend largely upon documentation produced by those who had waged the bombing campaign.

In the lean years after the Armistice, strategic bombardment was extolled to justify the continued viability of the Royal Air Force as an independent third service. Trenchard strove to mold opinion and was overwhelmingly successful. Wartime encounters with Zeppelins or Gothas, and memories of the protracted attrition of the trenches, had predisposed domestic citizenry toward the arguments of Air Ministry; British society developed an exaggerated consensus of bombing's potential.

The widely cited January 1920 Air Ministry evaluation of bombardment must be viewed as a partisan manifestation of an official crusade, not as a definitive final assessment. Point-by-point analysis and comparison of its assertions with those contained in the RAF field reports from which it was ostensibly derived, as well as those in the US Air Service bombing survey, lead one inescapably to this conclusion. The Air Ministry's final report, exemplifying the bombing rationale unceasingly preached during and after the hostilities, illustrates the extent to which exaggerated notions and fears quickly permeated the body politic. A ruthless aerial counteroffensive appeared to offer the only realistic future hope for home defense. The 1923 recommendations of the Salisbury Committee, confirming the RAF as a coequal—and conceivably preeminent—fighting service, endorsed and enshrined this nearly universal misconception.

In sum, this study develops and substantiates a comprehensive evaluation of British long-range bombing in the First World War that runs directly counter to more generally held opinions. Natural constraints, technical limitations, and training shortfalls combined with the impact of enemy countermeasures to create a considerable disparity between the bombing results officially claimed and those actually produced. Conversely, personnel losses and aircraft wastage rates were demonstrably far greater and more operationally significant than hitherto realized or admitted.

Finally, the misrepresentations of the January 1920 Air Ministry report highlight the extent to which the potential of strategic bombardment was touted between the two wars to rationalize and guarantee the continued existence of the Royal Air Force as a separate service.

Had the Royal Air Force and the Air Ministry critically analyzed their own files, they probably would have understood the restrictions that adverse weather, navigational precision, sighting accuracy, and the state of aircrew training and morale impose upon the conduct of any sustained campaign of long-range aerial bombardment. In fact, very little such institutional introspection occurred between the wars.

Chapter 1

No. 3 Wing
Royal Naval Air Service
(July 1916–May 1917)

Any study of British long-range bombing campaigns against Germany logically commences with the operations of No. 3 Naval Wing from its bases at Luxeuil and Ochey in France. Between July 1916 and April 1917, this Royal Naval Air Service (RNAS) unit launched 18 raids into Germany and German-occupied territory. The average formation (15 Sopwith 1½ Strutter aircraft) dropped an average of 2,500 pounds of bombs per mission.[1] By October 1916, No. 3 Wing had proved able to cooperate effectively with French air forces in a series of aerial attacks against German iron works and blast furnaces in the Saar valley, where the British Admiralty believed steel for U-boats was being produced.[2] Yet, No. 3 Wing never realized more than half its proposed strength of one hundred machines.

Examining the plans and operations of No. 3 Naval Wing during its short career reveals the divergent conclusions of the Admiralty and the War Office concerning the relative importance of strategic bombing and the practical difficulties surrounding Anglo-French cooperation. These issues were to vex British policy makers throughout the war.

The RNAS had enjoyed a somewhat greater freedom of action and diversity of function than its army counterpart, the Royal Flying Corps (RFC).[3] While the latter had developed into an air arm tied to ground elements, the RNAS independently probed the application of airpower. In large measure, the wartime increase in naval air strength beyond the immediate needs of purely maritime activities provided an operational surplus to encourage RNAS experimentation. Unfortunately, Britain's aviation industry failed to satisfy the expansion programs of both services, thus compounding RFC suspicions as to the purity of RNAS motives and generating arguments about aircraft procurement between the War Office and the

1

Admiralty.[4] On balance, the weight of advantage lay with the navy.

> The doctrinal tradition that aircraft could best defend Britain by taking the offensive against the enemy had already been established during the early R.N.A.S. raids against Zeppelin bases. Finally, the interest of the Admiralty in the more indirect application of force, as opposed to the War Office's increasing fixation with the titanic struggle on the Western Front, made the notion of striking at the German war industry with naval air forces seem particularly attractive.[5]

Thus, the navy was able to take the lead in the first strategic bombing operations against Germany. The RNAS received "little encouragement" from its army counterpart, however, or from the British Expeditionary Force in France. In the spring of 1917, No. 3 Wing was disbanded to provide men and machines for the Royal Flying Corps.[6]

On 4 April 1916, the Admiralty's director of Air Services prepared a memorandum, "Defense Against Zeppelin Raids," for the War Cabinet. In this paper, Rear Adm C. L. Vaughn-Lee argued that a purely defensive policy did not adequately respond to the growing menace of airship raids on England; he asserted that such a limited approach "cannot compare with a vigorous offensive." He emphasized that an organized and systematic attack on the enemy home front would restrict Zeppelin activities and have an immense "moral effect" on Germany itself. The naval staff officer concluded that Britain, by regaining the initiative, could then inflict both direct (material) damage and indirect (morale) casualties on her foe.

> It now appears essential that a definite policy of Retaliation be laid down and carried into effect without any further delay. A sustained offensive will have a decided effect in weakening the enemy's activities at the front by calls for defensive measures.[7]

The idea that strategic bombing could force a recall of German fighter units from the front to the homeland while damaging Germany's industrial base was seductively attractive to Admiralty planners. This notion surfaced again in late 1917, in the Air Ministry, to justify the creation and expansion of No. 3 Wing's successors.

The Admiralty Air Department had received considerable encouragement and support from the French, who also advocated bombing on a large scale. At the end of May 1916, the Admiralty received a formal request from the French naval attaché, who proposed a combined French/British bombing force to be based near Luxeuil, south of the British sector.[8] The French, who supplied engines to the British but had not yet developed a suitable daylight bombing machine themselves, emphasized that their participation would depend upon a continued supply of serviceable aircraft from the British. The Allies agreed not to initiate operations until sufficient force had been assembled, as ineffective attacks would merely alert the enemy and permit him to disperse production and deploy countermeasures.[9]

At an Anglo-French conference in London on 4 July 1916, the concept and details of the forthcoming aerial campaign were discussed at length.[10] By this time, the Admiralty had already dispatched a small advance party under Capt W. L. Elder to arrange for the arrival of the British component. The Admiralty agreed that French bombardment groups should receive one-third of the Sopwith bombing machines delivered to Luxeuil and that the French would have operational control of the English squadrons committed to the joint offensive. These concessions further damaged Admiralty-War Office relations.[11] Apart from difficulties with their army colleagues, the navy had no misgivings about allowing the French air staff to select targets based on the French bombing plan.

> This arrangement was perfectly acceptable to the Admiralty, who were able to secure the use of a French base which was within the operational range of the principal German industries. In any case, the French bombing plan was an eminently practical one and included many targets which the Navy wanted to attack.[12]

A revision of the original French plan of 1915, this plan constituted the most comprehensive scheme for strategic bombardment of German military and industrial objectives available to British authorities at the time.

In formulating their plan, the French air staff first drew up a list of critical targets in Germany and determined their relative importance. They then ascertained whether each objective lay within range and whether it was vulnerable to aerial attack. Finally, they allocated an order of priority based on operational feasibility. They did not concern themselves with the force required to destroy or severely damage their targets.[13]

From this process, the French determined that the four most important enemy industrial complexes were located in four target areas: Mannheim-Ludwigshafen, Mainz, Cologne, and Saar-Lorraine-Luxembourg. The first three were then discarded because the forces required to bomb these targets frequently and systematically were not available.

Since Saar-Lorraine-Luxembourg emerged as the only tactically feasible target area, the French defined the main task of the long-range bombing force as "annihilating the iron districts of Lorraine and Luxembourg." The blast furnaces there produced nearly half of Germany's total steel output.[14] In bowing to present constraints, however, the French air staff did not lose sight of the future.

> When the number of squadrillas will have increased, other objectives may be attacked. Then the industrial centres of MANHEIM-LUDWIGSHAVEN, on the Main (Frankfurt), of Cologne, and eventually Westphalia, may be classed as the most important objective, and it will be against the latter that the aerial forces of industrial destruction will be marshaled.[15]

This pragmatic evaluation conceded that, given the size of the force available at Luxeuil, the iron and steel industry in the Saar-Lorraine-Luxembourg area was the only vulnerable objective of importance.

One must note that the French assessment considered material damage to enemy industry primarily; moral effect was unimportant, even as a secondary consequence of aerial attack. The Allied force was authorized to bomb selected towns and cities at greater distances only as "specific reprisals" in response to particular illegal actions by the enemy. The French dissociated these attacks from the strategic strikes against German blast furnaces.

Since the British Admiralty agreed in principle with the French proposals, they set about gathering machines and aircrews. Captain Elder had been sent to Luxeuil in early May 1916 to arrange for establishing the new unit.[16] Once sufficient long-range bombing machines became available, No. 3

Wing would be able to raid German munition works and industrial centers in the Saar valley.

A key region, the Saar valley was accessible to Allied units based in the vicinity of Luxeuil and Ochey. It was hoped that the wing would be equipped with 35 bombers (mainly Sopwith 1½ Strutters) and 20 escort aircraft (1½ Strutters configured as fighters) by 1 July 1916, with steady expansion to an eventual strength of 100 planes.[17] Later that fall, this planning estimate was revised upward—to a minimum of at least two hundred bombers, with two thousand high-horsepower engines on order to support future replacement.[18]

Some evidence exists that the Admiralty attempted to assemble this sizable aerial force without consulting the War Office.[19] In fact, however, these levels for No. 3 Wing were never realized—due largely to War Office opposition and the necessity to reinforce the Royal Flying Corps in support of the army on the Somme.

The army rested its case upon the questions of strategic priorities and unity of effort on the Western Front. It adhered to the principle that strategic bombing ranked far down the scale of aerial duties, well below such missions as aerial observation and adjustment of artillery fire. In a paper presented to the Air Board on 9 June 1916, Maj Gen Hugh M. Trenchard argued that "this observation must be regarded as of primary importance to all bombing operations . . . efforts should be devoted to providing observation requirements in the first instance."[20]

Further, the War Office asserted that if scarce aviation assets were diverted from support of the army to participate in the Luxeuil sideshow, operations on the Western Front (which the War Office saw as the decisive theater) would be hampered in direct proportion. Sir Douglas Haig crystallized this position in his memorandum to the War Office on 1 November 1916.

Unless my requirements have first been adequately provided, the provision of flying machines by the naval authorities for work on the fronts of the French and Belgian armies in France amounts to very serious interference with the British Land Forces, and may compromise the success of my operations.[21]

Field Marshal Haig and General Trenchard opposed the scheme. They based their formidable dissent on the grounds that, since no surplus of aircraft existed, implementing the Admiralty plan would commit machines and crews needed elsewhere to an endeavor of secondary importance. This dissipation of resources, they said, would seriously hinder their primary effort.

The army's demands for flying machines at the expense of No. 3 Wing began in late spring 1916 and continued until the Wing was disbanded a year later. In July 1916, when the Luxeuil force had been expected to consist of 55 serviceable bombing and escort aircraft, its actual strength had been whittled to fewer than a dozen machines and pilots. On one occasion, when Brig Gen Sir David Henderson, director-general of military aeronautics for the army, needed a minimum reinforcement of 72 planes but could only comb out 12 suitable machines from the home establishment, he sought aid from the RNAS. But, as the official history notes, "The Admiralty could only respond at the expense of their new bombing wing." By mid-September 1916, a total of 62 Sopwith two-seaters had been transferred to army squadrons.[22] These War Office requests significantly delayed expansion of the Luxeuil wing and reduced its strength below that necessary to conduct effective bombing.

Even after No. 3 Wing commenced active operations in the fall of 1916, it never recouped its logistical losses. It was able to expand somewhat, but on a more modest scale than originally calculated.[23] For the period of peak bombing activity, October 1916 to March 1917, an average of 43 pilots and 35 serviceable machines were available for operations. On 25 March 1917, the Admiralty acquiesced to War Office pressure and began to disband the Luxeuil force in order to reinforce the Royal Flying Corps.

By May, the remnants of No. 3 Wing had been transferred to No. 10 (Navy) Squadron for support of the armies in the British sector of the Western Front.[24] Even during its decline, the wing managed to fly four bombing missions, including one in April with the French, before its withdrawal from action.[25]

The Admiralty planners hoped the Luxeuil wing, in cooperation with the French, could damage enemy industrial centers and depress civilian morale sufficiently to affect German combat power on the Western Front. That hope never reached fruition.

The preeminence of long-range bombing was by no means universally acknowledged. The War Office in particular looked askance at the Admiralty's preoccupation with what seemed to the soldiers to represent a peripheral mission for airpower. The army chiefs emphatically asserted that flying machines would best be employed in ground support, with squadrons tied to a subordinate, cooperative role. Additionally, the War Office argued there was no surplus of aircraft that could be committed to strategic bombardment. The struggling British aviation industry had yet to fulfill Field Marshal Haig's requirements for tactical aviation and seemed unlikely to do so in the foreseeable future.

These two interservice issues were initially aggravated by the Admiralty's attempt to organize and deploy the Luxeuil force without informing the War Office. The consequent uproar at the Air Board, combined with the necessity to reinforce the Royal Flying Corps for the Somme, kept No. 3 Wing well below its planned rate of expansion. Finally, No. 3 Wing was disbanded in order to bring RFC squadrons in the British sector up to strength. The high-level dissension over roles and priorities seriously affected the scale and pace of No. 3 Wing's operations. Even if the Admiralty had been able to carry out its original program of expansion for the unit, the Luxeuil wing would probably not have developed into a decisive strategic weapon.

The Sopwith 1½ Strutter, when configured as a single-seat day bomber, took 24.6 minutes to reach 10,000 feet. Carrying a pilot and four 65-pound bombs, it cruised at 98.5 miles per hour. Its service ceiling was 13,000 feet and it could remain in the air for three and three-fourths hours.[26] These characteristics restricted its combat radius to less than 150 miles—assuming that its pilot prudently chose to climb to at least 10,000 feet before crossing the lines. The small size of its bombs made them useless unless a direct hit could be attained. As a fighter escort, the 1½ Strutter carried a pilot and an observer/gunner to a service ceiling slightly in excess of 15,000 feet. The aircrew, in addition to the stress induced by flying in marginal weather conditions and the threat of enemy countermeasures, faced a number of physiological obstacles as well. In their open cockpits, they spent extended periods well above the level at which the average healthy individual begins to suffer from oxygen deprivation (anoxia typically commences between 8,000 and 12,000 feet). They were also subjected to ambient temperatures that varied from plus 15 degrees Fahrenheit to minus 30 degrees Fahrenheit, summer to winter.[27]

The ratio of serviceable machines to the number available stood at around 20 percent, and the average number of sorties per assigned aircraft stood at a very low 1.4 percent.[28] Even under ideal conditions of equipment and weather, No. 3 Wing would have found it extremely difficult to meet the ambitious goals set by its Admiralty advocates. The operational record of the Luxeuil force must be analyzed against this background.

Although Captain Elder's newly created unit was anxious to attack enemy industrial targets in the Saar valley, it was not equipped with sufficient machines to launch a major strike until October 1916. In the interim, No. 3 Wing cooperated with six French aircraft in a raid on the benzine stores at Mulheim on 30 July. The Wing's contribution apparently consisted of two bombers and one escort machine, or one-third of the Allied force that dropped 1,450 pounds of bombs.[29] The Luxeuil wing participated in no further operations for nearly two and one-half months.

The first large raid in October encountered spirited enemy resistance, an unwelcome phenomenon that underscored the necessity for fighter escort to protect bombers in daylight attacks. On 12 October, German fighters attacked the Anglo-French force (31 bombers and numerous escorts, including 15 navy bombers and six navy fighters), both inbound and outbound, shooting down six French and three British aircraft against no losses. The Luxeuil component dropped 3,780 pounds of bombs on the Mauser arms factory at Oberndorf, with unreported results.

On their 23 October mission against the Thyssen steel works at Hagendingen, just 25 miles behind the lines, returning aircrews claimed "direct hits on the blast furnaces" from twenty-six hundred pounds of bombs. No losses occurred among their nine bomber and six escort machines.[30]

Five raids in November and December concentrated on blast furnaces and iron works in the Lorraine coal basin, objectives of priority to the French. On 10 and 11 November, nine and fourteen bombers, escorted by eight and seven fighters, hit the iron works at Völklingen. German records collected by British intelligence teams after the Armistice list 14 air raid alarms within the Völklingen complex in November 1916, a consequent shortfall of 1,713 tons in steel production, and a total repair cost of 42,171 marks.[31] British escort pilots reported "considerable fighting," but no British losses.

Nine Luxeuil bombers escorted by seven fighters dropped 2,280 pounds of bombs on the blast furnace and iron works at St. Ingbert on 12 November. The same force configuration hit the iron works at Dillingen on 24 November and on 27 December, the last raid of 1916. Aircrews reported "many direct hits" on each mission. No naval aircraft were damaged, and the escorts claimed one enemy fighter destroyed.

This Handley Page is being hand-pushed to the runway.

The five missions conducted in the final two months of the year targeted three iron works within 10 miles of Völklingen, two of which were hit twice in successive raids. Given the marginal weather conditions and the state of No. 3 Wing's resupply, such activity indicates that the Luxeuil force attempted to concentrate its striking power in space and time.

The Luxeuil wing continued to concentrate its attacks primarily upon blast furnaces and iron works in 1917 till its official disbanding on 25 March. Four of the six raids were directed against the iron works at Saarbrücken. During the winter, freezing weather presented two problems in particular: oil in aircraft engines congealed, and targets were obscured by ground fog. Such obstacles held the wing's operational strength to that achieved in late 1916 and curtailed the number of missions flown. Nevertheless, No. 3 Wing achieved some degree of concentration with its small force.

The Saarbrücken iron works were struck on 23 January by 10 bombers with six escorts; on 25 February by 13 bombers escorted by five fighters; on 4 March by 10 bombers with five escorts; and on 22 March by six bombers with three escorts. These missions aimed a total of 10,140 pounds of bombs at the blast furnaces. The French supported this effort with missions against Völklingen in January, February, and March, and with day and night raids against Dillingen and Hagendingen during February.[32]

Two raids against other types of targets also occurred during this period. On 16 March, nine No. 3 Wing planes dropped 1,560 pounds of bombs on Morhange, aerodrome. That night, a single Handley Page dropped twelve hundred pounds of bombs on the railway station at Metz, with unobserved results. When an Admiralty telegram directed that No. 3 Wing be disbanded, its assets were transferred to the RFC.

No. 3 Wing continued to operate until mid-April, even as it was being slowly dismembered. Improving weather conditions, and the incongruous arrival of two more Handley Pages (three-man bombers carrying nearly five times the payload of the Sopwith 1½ Strutters), allowed No. 3 to mount four more missions before passing into history.

The rail junction at Arnaville was struck on 5 April. On the night of 13/14 April, the blast furnaces at Hagendingen were hit, followed by a raid the next night on the supply depot and aerodrome at Chambley. Each of these sorties was flown by a single Handley Page—perhaps the same machine—carrying approximately twelve hundred pounds of bombs.[33]

Freiburg was hit on 14 April as a reprisal for German submarine attacks in March against two hospital ships (*Asturias* and *Gloucester Castle*).[34] (The French had established a practice of launching retaliatory raids against designated German towns only when specifically provoked.) The Luxeuil wing contributed 15 bombers and eight escort fighters to the Allied force that struck the small German city. Two and one-half tons of bombs were dropped in two raids, mingled with leaflets explaining the action to the population of the town. All the French pilots returned safely, but No. 3 Wing lost three escort machines plus four crewmen killed and two taken prisoner. That these casualties could be inflicted despite an escort of 17 fighters indicates the intensity and determination of enemy opposition that day. It seems certain that this attack on Freiburg was intended solely as a reprisal and that no material damage to the war machine was intended. Aircrew reports refer to "a reprisal raid on the centre of town," and there is nothing to suggest a military objective. German records indicate that "the bombs fell in the most thickly populated quarter of the city."[35]

The French separated planned reprisals from the strategic goals of their aerial campaign against the Saar industries. The British Admiralty, hoping to undermine the will of Germany's civilian population to continue the conflict, optimistically attributed "an immense moral effect" to every bomb that fell on Germany, whether or not it hit anything of military importance.[36] But since the Freiburg mission marked the end of the Luxeuil Wing's operational career, the Admiralty's thesis could not be conclusively tested.

After the Luxeuil wing had been in operation for some months, the Fifth Sea Lord, Commodore Godfrey Paine, queried Haig concerning whether bombing enemy blast furnaces had significantly restricted steel output. He also wanted to know the extent to which naval bombing operations had forced the Germans to withdraw fighting squadrons from the front for home defense duties.[37]

In his responses, Sir Douglas Haig indicated that his earlier judgment (that strategic bombing "as a means of defeating the enemy is entirely secondary") had been confirmed and that, even when successful, "results are comparatively unimportant."[38] He answered a definite "no" to the question of whether bombing had caused the enemy to withdraw aircraft from the battle front, elaborating that a general expansion in enemy aviation units had occurred all along the front. Regarding Paine's question as to whether enemy steel production had been reduced, Haig replied, "No such information has reached me, and it would, therefore, appear highly improbable that the output has been seriously affected."[39] To the War Office, field results seemed to indicate that the Admiralty's bombing experiment had merely siphoned assets from tactical support of British ground units. Lord George Curzon's Air Board agreed with Haig's view in its final decision, which was forwarded to the War Committee.[40]

Faced with this adverse summary from the army, the Admiralty had little choice but to disband the Luxeuil wing. Whether No. 3 Wing attacks had shaken the morale of the German industrial population was a point that neither the Admiralty nor the War Office explicitly addressed at the time. The assertion that the moral effect of strategic bombardment could outweigh its material results had to wait for the Royal Air Force and 1918.

One consequence of No. 3 Wing's existence centered upon the issue of British unity of command. The affair hardened Haig's suspicions that independent operations of any sort seriously interfered with his ability to organize and control a coordinated, unified campaign. Further, it jeopardized British operations in what he considered to be the decisive theater of war.

Widespread public dissatisfaction with the conduct of the war led to Asquith's replacement by Lloyd George. The new prime minister, who had a low opinion of the military, underscored Haig's pessimism and was fully capable of withdrawing units from the Western Front to stage an operation in some peripheral theater.

The field marshal's opinion of strategic bombing was consistent with his greater concern that the politicians, with an eye toward his reassignment or dismissal, hoped to discredit his professional judgment. He objected to the existence of an independent Allied air detachment outside his control and operating from French soil, contending that "the employment of bombing machines in France is. . . . Primarily, even if not entirely, a military question." He condemned "interference by the naval authorities with the British land forces" and argued that the Luxeuil force undermined his authority as the director of Britain's effort in the field.[41]

Sir Douglas Haig's misgivings concerning independent bombing detachments and unity of command seem partially justified, since the French air staff clearly dominated the tactical conduct of No. 3 Wing's activities. Not only did the French develop the plan—they also selected specific targets for attack by the British naval aviators. The Admiralty voiced no objections to this arrangement because the plan had been discussed at the July 1916 joint conference and seemed practical.

In fact, permitting the French authorities to take charge of British squadrons created a local unity of command for coordinating the efforts of the Luxeuil force. And targets listed by the French were those the Royal Navy had hoped to bomb in any case. Throughout the campaign, the French continued to dictate specific targets for No. 3 Wing's daylight missions—even after the French began to bomb exclusively by night after the costly day raid against Oberndorf on 12 October 1916.[42]

Official reports forwarded to the Admiralty from the commander of the British component substantiate the Gallic control: "a raid on Brebach Iron Works, this being the objective assigned us by the French."[43] On several occasions, in order to maintain pressure, the French coordinated day attacks by the British Sopwiths on targets that French forces were hitting at night. Völklingen, bombed successively by No. 3 Wing on the 10th and 11th of November 1916, was also hit by a French

13

force during the intervening night. After the British raid on Dillingen on 27 December 1916, the French attacked targets in the vicinity. "Aeroplanes were around the district for 10 hours with intervals."[44] Timely execution of such joint operations was considerably assisted by a single planning staff.

Collocation of the British squadrons with their French counterparts simplified tactical cooperation. And since the French assumed responsibility for logistical support, the decision to place the French air staff in charge of flying operations was also quite logical. It is doubtful that such a degree of coordination could have been achieved had the Royal Navy refused to surrender its squadrons to French operational control. The alternative would have been to have British positions resolved miles away from Luxeuil and transmitted, with concomitant delays, to the French air staff. The effectiveness of the joint force would have unavoidably declined, even if the planners had been of like minds.

The subordination of British aviation units to a foreign authority guaranteed an effective, coordinated unity of effort, albeit under a French commander. Field Marshal Haig considered this policy to endanger his authority and the unity of effort on the Western Front. At Luxeuil, however, no one questioned the arrangement; it functioned with a minimum of Anglo-French friction.

That an Allied long-range bomber force with a workable plan could mount a systematic offensive against selective objectives seems indisputable, given the example of No. 3 Wing. The campaign, however, was hampered by weather conditions, mechanical and design difficulties, and chronic resupply problems. These factors severely limited the size of the bomber force as well as its opportunities.

Of particular note is the cumulative effort directed against enemy blast furnaces, which were attacked on 11 of the 19 raids launched and in 58 percent of the sorties flown by No. 3 Wing.[45] The French apparently adhered to their overall plan rigorously. Two other missions, on 16 March 1917, had also been scheduled to raid blast furnaces but were forced to divert to alternate targets.[46] No. 3 Wing's attentions were not only concentrated in a small, well-defined region (the iron works within the Lorraine coal basin); they were also distributed in time, other conditions permitting.

The French plan of bombardment identified targets in accordance with a system of clearly defined priorities. Raid totals for the remaining target categories, excepting Freiburg and the two diversions, indicate that they were not prime objectives of the Luxeuil force. The intensity and cadence of attacks against identified targets were largely determined by such factors as availability of machines and trained aircrews, design limitations, poor weather, and the effects of extreme cold.

The retaliatory raids on Freiburg, a joint operation in which the French returned to daylight attacks, characterize the second element of the French strategic plan: reprisals. Shortly after the demise of No. 3 Wing, the Chief of the Imperial General Staff (CIGS) in London received an elucidation of the French reprisal policy from his liaison officer at the French War Ministry.

> Bombardment of an open German town, by way of a reprisal, follows on every bombardment of a French town. This bombardment is carried out by decision of the Government.

> There exists, beyond these reprisals, a permanent plan for bombardment by aeroplanes. This plan established by the Government has solely military objectives in view. These objectives are, at present, the factories and stations of the Saar valley.[47]

Thus the two partners in strategic bombing differed fundamentally on the importance of morale within the enemy's civilian population. Based on the No. 3 Wing campaign, targeting the German population remained a moot issue. It would, like the debate over unity of command, emerge again in 1917 and 1918.

The means for estimating material damage and moral effect during hostilities were necessarily fragmentary and often contradictory. The indicators needed to evaluate the campaign's effectiveness were largely unavailable to the Allied air staffs. Without the *required* indicators, such as poststrike photographs and access to enemy industrial records, British and French planners had to rely upon *available* indicators (aircrew observations, captured letters, agents' reports, and articles/editorials in German periodicals) to judge the results of bombing programs. These latter indicators had to be used with caution.[48]

Both the Admiralty in London and squadrons in the field assumed that bombing is effective and that measuring the level of bombing effort would reflect the degree of damage inflicted upon the enemy. Official raid reports transmitted to the Admiralty from No. 3 Wing invariably featured the number of sorties flown and the total weight of bombs dropped.[49] Lacking other indicators, planners were forced to rely almost exclusively upon friendly data for evaluating the effects of their aerial attacks. In doing so, however, air staffs at Luxeuil ran the risk that their statistics would become ends in themselves.

"The utilization of these indicators did have the effect . . . of orienting operational activity to the indicators that had been designed to measure attainment of objectives."[50] In sum, flying missions and dropping bombs, tasks controlled by commanders and their staffs, can assume lives of their own. As the only reliable sources of cumulative statistics, these endeavors inevitably become goals in the eyes of the men performing them.

To the extent that this translation occurred in the Luxeuil Wing, it obscured the original purpose for collecting such information: to aid in assessing the damage caused by bombing. Appendix I of Captain Elder's final report, in which he compared the totals of his No. 3 Wing with the French No. 115 Wing at Malzeville, shows his preoccupation with numbers and bombing effort.

> It will be seen that we made 12 raids against Commandant Lefort's 12, but amongst the latter are raids of the 9th, 10th and 15th February 1917, which took place during a period of cold so intense at Ochey that all efforts to start the engines proved unavailable [sic] so that during the periods preceding and following the spell of very low temperature, we actually beat the French record by three raids or 33 1/3 percent.

> Commandant Lefort told me that to attain that number of raids he had to take more than usual risks.[51]

This focus upon activities that squadron commanders could oversee and influence seems to indicate some degree of goal displacement—a confusion of ends and means—within No. 3 Wing. In concluding, the naval commander identified a factor beyond his control (a period of extreme cold) as the cause of his difficulties. Then he rearranged the statistics in an effort to demonstrate that "we actually beat" the French wing's performance by a sizable margin. Further, he intimated that his French counterpart at times resorted to unsafe practice in order to bolster his totals. This elaborate rationalization tends to confirm the hypothesis that goal displacement was occurring at least as high as wing level in the Luxeuil bombing force.

The contrast between returning aircrew reports and data gleaned after the war highlights the optimism prevalent in London and in Luxeuil. Official raid reports forwarded from Luxeuil to the Admiralty provide extracts of the results reported for each mission. Typical of such reports is the narrative forwarded by Captain Elder to the Admiralty on 27 January, following the 23 January 1917 raid on the Burbach works at Saarbrücken.

> The pilots report that the atmosphere was clear over Burbach and that considerable damage appears to have been done by the 2,600 lbs. of bombs which were dropped . . . three Pilots, one Observer and one Gunlayer returned suffering from severe frostbite.[52]

The Admiralty subsequently summarized this mission: "16 British naval aeroplanes bombed the blast furnaces at Burbach (basin of the Saar) which appears to have suffered considerable damage."[53] Thus did results percolate through the British chain of command to the Air Department.

In addition to field data, the Admiralty collected and evaluated other intelligence via the Directorate of Aerial Intelligence. This data typically consisted of fragments, such as a quotation from a captured letter in which a factory manager in Saarbrücken complained to his clients that he would be unable to meet his scheduled deadlines. This particular executive blamed the general suffering caused by the war "and more recently from aerial bombardment, [so] that it is absolutely impossible to make promises for numerous orders in hand."[54] And this disparate data was compiled and evaluated by the same units or agencies responsible for conducting the bombing.

No direct indices of effectiveness came into Allied hands until after the Armistice, when teams of British and American air intelligence officers were able to obtain information from the Germans themselves. The British team of three experienced air intelligence officers and three of other ranks, all under the direction of Maj H. W. M. Paul, examined and catalogued the results of Allied bombs. Between 7 December 1918, just after the Armistice, and 20 January 1919, Major Paul's group visited over two-thirds of the objectives that had been attacked from the air, up to the left bank of the Rhine.[55] Their final report, comprising seven volumes of data organized by target category, was submitted through Headquarters RAF in the field to the Secretary of the Air Ministry on 26 February 1919.[56] This study of the effects of aerial bombardment systematically investigated the "material damage done" and the "moral effect caused," as well as the "organization of the enemy's countermeasures against bombing." The British team also collected information to "enable decisions to be made as to how far the Allied bombing policy was correct and effective from a military point of view."

The survey groups dispatched by the US Air Service had similar tasks. Between early March and 20 May 1919, 12 American teams (one officer, one photographer, one chauffeur) investigated bombing sites in 140 towns in the Allied Zone of Occupation west of the Rhine.[57] Surprisingly, neither British nor American teams seemed aware of the existence of the other. Their reports thus provide an independent means for cross-checking data and comparing conclusions; in fact, the American report was misplaced soon after its completion and not rediscovered until July 1974.[58]

Considering the limitations imposed by lack of time and personnel, the two bombing surveys are remarkably complete, due largely to the cooperation of the German authorities, who kept meticulous records of air raid damage and associated costs. Apparently, they hoped for Allied reparations should the Fatherland win the war. At almost every location, the air intelligence teams were able to gather information:

- A list of the air raids, giving dates and numbers of bombs dropped.

- Sketches of objectives, showing positions in which bombs had been dropped on various dates.
- An account or report of the damage caused by the bombs, cost of repairs, moral effect, and various details of interest.
- General organization and positions of all antiaircraft defenses.
- Different methods of warning and intercommunication.
- Any photographs that showed material damage caused by raids, as well as others that might be of military value.[59]

This firsthand information depicted the actual results, as opposed to the reported results, of bombardment. The low correlation between wartime claims and postwar findings emerges clearly from the case of No. 3 Wing's two raids against the Burbach Works at Saarbrücken on 23 January and 22 March 1917. After the first mission, Captain Elder cabled the Admiralty that "the atmosphere was clear over Burbach and . . . considerable damage appears to have been done."[60] The Sopwith 1½ Strutter bombers dropped a total of forty 65-pound bombs in this attack.

In its postwar survey of Burbach, the British team relied upon a large diagram compiled by the works directors. It plotted every bomb that fell on the works between 1915 and 1918.[61] On 23 January 1917, according to this map, nine bombs (out of 40 dropped) fell on Burbach, mainly in its southwest sector. The American group's findings agreed with the British data. Moreover, the American survey included a narrative description of the points of impact and the damage caused.

Raid No.	Date	No. of Bombs	Place and Kind of Damage
6	23/1/17	9	Fell near smelting furnace no. 3, in the steel works, near the foundry, in the Modeling shed and on the port on the Saar, damaging a large water reservoir, different roofs and sheds and also the tracks. 6,600 Marks.[62]

Under conditions of good visibility, British aviators could accurately observe and report the points of impact of their payloads; however, their damage assessment betrayed a tendency toward wishful thinking.

Six bombers and three escort machines participated in the Wing's 22 March visit to Burbach. "Conditions over Germany were bad, and heavy cloud banks were met. . . . On the return journey compasses froze."[63] One machine landed at Malzeville with a frozen oil pump. Many airmen sustained frostbite from the intense cold. Despite the best efforts of the British aviators, no bombs fell on blast furnaces in or near Saarbrücken that day. Local authorities recorded no attacks against the city, and managers at the Burbach works logged no air raids after the 23 January attack until October 1917.[64] Twenty-four 65-pound bombs dropped from No. 3 Wing's formation on 22 March 1917 had no determinable effect upon machinery or morale in the Saar valley.

Likewise, when missions were flown against the Burbach works on 25 February and 4 March 1917, neither inflicted any noticeable damage.[65] A force of 23 machines carrying 92 bombs comprised the total British effort on these two raids.

Similarly, the nine Sopwith bombers that raided the St. Ingbert Steel Works on 12 November 1916 went unrecorded in the local tabulation of bomb damage. This plant was hit only twice during the entire war (9 August 1915, six bombs; 11 November 1917, one bomb), according to the files of the municipal and factory officials.[66]

Of five daylight missions flown by No. 3 Wing against blast furnaces, four went completely unnoticed by the industrial and civilian populations. This meager result would not become apparent until after the war, however, by which time subsequent campaigns in 1917 and 1918 had imbued the concept of strategic bombardment with a vitality of its own. This campaign against German blast furnaces is illustrative of a chronic tendency for the advocates of strategic bombing to overestimate results. These postwar data are presented here to provide a scale for evaluating the information reported and evaluated by British airmen and staff officers during wartime, not to criticize the accuracy of their conclusions.

Nor were the disappointing results at Saarbrücken unique; Dillingen, eight miles downstream, provided a similar case in point. When No. 3 Wing first struck there on 24 November 1916, the "target was large and visibility good." Encouraging results were reported to the Admiralty.

> The majority of the bombs were seen to actually strike the objective, and it is thought that very considerable damage must have been done—the actual weight of bombs dropped being 2,340 lbs.[67]

On the 27 December mission, flown after several weeks of poor weather, Captain Elder admitted to the Admiralty that results were not observed.

> It was impossible to observe the results owing to the haze and clouds over Dillingen, but as the target is a large one it is probable that many bombs reached the objective.[68]

The Admiralty uncharacteristically waited for confirmation of this field report, which apparently was revised due to other intelligence data arriving at the Aerial Intelligence Directorate. The announcement that "no damage was done during the raid on Dillingen on the 27th December 1916" came nearly a month after the raid.[69] Satisfactory bombing seemed to depend on satisfactory visibility, though the aviators implied that some targets were too large to miss completely even when visibility was poor.

Postwar German records revealed that all the bombs dropped by No. 3 Wing in these attacks fell on the outskirts of the factory complex. American investigators catalogued only the raids subsequent to February 1918.[70] In the British survey, which summarized the effects of all Allied attacks between 25 August 1915 and 23 October 1918 on Dillingen, Major Paul concluded that "in no case has any stoppage of work resulted from the damage caused by air raids."[71] In this instance, accurately delivered ordnance, confirmed by bomber crews if conditions permitted, consistently failed to inflict serious damage. Under such circumstances in wartime, the tendency to inflate results would be inevitable, regardless of any other pressures upon the bombardment advocates to justify their expensive campaign. Contradictory information would seldom surface.

The well-documented raids on the Thyssen Steel Works at Hagendingen graphically illustrate the scale and precision of the Luxeuil wing's aerial effort. In this case, a bomb-by-bomb comparison of actual effects with reported results is possible. Both postwar survey teams collected records from the German authorities, which permits us to analyze the accuracy and influence of reported results during wartime.

No. 3 Wing's 23 October 1916 day attack by nine bombers on Hagendingen has generally been considered a successful operation.[72] On the evening of 22 October, aircraft of the Luxeuil wing moved north to an advanced base at Malzeville aerodrome while the 4th Groupe de Bombardment took off to strike the Thyssen works.[73] The next day, 23 October, nine Sopwith bombers and six escorts from No. 3 Wing also hit the Thyssen works; Wing Commander R. B. Davies reported a successful operation.

> Our aircraft kept excellent formation, moved into single line and went down to bomb in succession, and I could see the bombs bursting amongst the furnace buildings. The return journey was uneventful, with little AA fire.[74]

Captain Elder agreed, notifying the Admiralty that "only two factory chimneys were left intact after the last two bombs had dropped . . . the majority of the works will be out of action for some considerable time."[75]

The Air Department then overstated the reported results:

> Hagendingen. The results of the raid of the 25th October were very satisfactory. Three out of five blast furnaces have been completely destroyed.[76]

Both London and the field agreed that the joint bombing campaign was off to a promising start.

A widespread desire to encourage the program and silence its critics in the War Office increased the Admiralty's tendency to exaggerate damage reports—and air staffers *were* handicapped by the scarcity of reliable information concerning the effects of air raids. The results of the bombing campaign were observed, analyzed, and judged by men who had a considerable stake in the campaign's success. Under such conditions, wishful thinking would rationalize any ambiguity.

22

For the most part, the Thyssen files available to Allied investigators in early 1919 substantiated the reported results of the French and British attacks on 22/23 October 1916. In the French night raid, five bombs fell "between the central shops and the office of the machine shop," damaging the main conduit and shattering numerous windows.[77] To show the detail typical of many such records, the German report of damage caused by No. 3 Wing's attack is presented here in full.

> On October 23, aeroplanes flew over the colony at noon. Two squadrons of about 7 to 10 planes followed each other at a short distance. Part of the aeroplanes succeeded in flying over the factory. Seventeen bombs were dropped. They fell in the following order:
>
> 1) Three beside the porter of the cement factory; they formed funnels of four to 4.50 meters in diameter.
> 2) Four in the coke dump. It is here that the largest funnel was formed. It had a diameter of seven meters and a depth of 3.50 meters.
> 3) One bomb in building No. 16.
> 4) One bomb in building No. 6.
> 5) One bomb in front of the northern facade of building No. 3. This bomb did not explode and was unearthed intact.
> 6) Two bombs on the roof on building No. 1.
> 7) One bomb in front of building No. 1.
> 8) Four bombs on the steel mill.
>
> The bombs which fell on building No. 6 and 16 and on the roof of the steel mill caused serious damage to the roofing and to the windows of the establishments.[78]

This narrative, extracted from the US Air Service survey, and the bomb-plot diagram included in the British survey, permit one to ascertain the sequence and points of impact of each bomb that fell on the Thyssen works that day. The German documents largely support the wartime claims of Allied bombing accuracy, but they differ radically with respect to the actual damage inflicted upon the objective.

Further study of the bomb-plot diagram confirms the futility of Anglo-French attempts to destroy such a sprawling industrial complex with a handful of planes carrying four 65-pound bombs each. Despite appearances, vital facilities within such complexes as Thyssen were relatively few and often protected by overhead cover or adjacent structures. The small scale of the Allied aerial effort against German blast furnaces did not support a reasonable probability of damaging or destroying such key points. Planners and squadron commanders did not emphasize the need for a high degree of accuracy; they were content with designating and attacking the targets in toto, accepting the hypothesis that "bombs anywhere on Thyssen (or Burbach or Hagendingen) hurt the Hun." In fact, however, they did not.[79]

In addition to errors in navigation and imprecise bombing, design deficiencies in British ordnance also vitiated the results of No. 3 Wing raids. Interviews inside Germany after the war indicated that the Allied bombs, particularly those of 112-pound weight or smaller, lacked "any real penetrating effect" against most factory structures. In instances where such bombs struck "massive and solidly built" machinery or build-ings, the bomb casings often telescoped without detonating.[80] German plant managers also revealed that blast effects from aerial bombs were almost exclusively directed vertically rather than horizontally, so that "near-misses" had little effect.[81]

> They considered that our bombs lacked blasting effect. They pointed out that Works were very solidly built, and it required a big bomb to cause really serious damage. They did not overlook the effects bombs had had on their Works, but they considered that both the French bombs and our own were deficient both in penetrating and blasting effect.[82]

The German authorities also remarked on the persistent and perplexing problem of "bombs well made and apparently faultless" failing to explode; these "blinds," which occurred on almost every raid, were carefully recorded.[83] In the French raid on Saarbrücken on 6 September 1915, 38 of 45 bombs failed to detonate—and throughout the war, 25 percent of the bombs dropped on this industrial area were blinds.[84]

As the means for—and the goals expected from—the British strategic bombing offensive expanded, the emphasis upon moral effects increased proportionately. This preoccupation with "moral effect" (reducing the enemy population's will to continue fighting) seems to have been a peculiarly British obsession.

By the end of hostilities, General Trenchard, commanding the Independent Force, could proclaim that the importance of moral to material effect was "as 20 to 1" without much fear of contradiction.[85] Neither the French air staff nor the American Air Service attached a commensurate importance to such an intangible indicator. Nor did they acknowledge civilian morale as an appropriate bombing target.

Calculation of moral effect and its estimated impact was an Admiralty activity rather than a field concern during the tenure of the Luxeuil wing. References to moral effects from British and French attacks began to appear in Air Department communiqués in the spring of 1917. Included with reported results of material damage, under the heading "Results of Raids," these citations included agent and neutral reports as well as excerpts from German periodicals and correspondence.[86] These data, screened and published in London, supplemented the No. 3 Wing's reports and satisfied the Admiralty's desire for independent information.

Under certain conditions, the two sources served as a cross-check on the progress of the bombing campaign. Taken together, they supplied ammunition to silence War Office critics and to aid the Admiralty in competing for scarce machines and crews. In official bulletins, moral and material claims combined to justify strategic bombing and confound its detractors.

During wartime, no independent means existed for testing the reliability of intelligence coming from Germany. Likewise, that the Admiralty Air Department uncritically accepted and distributed such material lent it disproportionate credibility as a barometer of effectiveness. No. 3 Wing's efforts against industries in the Saar valley provided the impetus for developing moral effect into a major rationale for continuing to bomb.

In the course of No. 3 Wing's assault on German blast furnaces, Admiralty bulletins devoted increasingly more attention to indicators of moral effect. Initially, such indicators seemed to claim that indirect damage resulted from otherwise ineffective attacks. Although an earlier release stated unequivocally that "no damage was done during the raid on Dillingen," this assessment was followed by other intelligence data two weeks later.[87] The subsequent communiqué suggested that, though no militarily significant results had been achieved, there were some indirect benefits.

> It is reported that during the raid on Dillingen on the 27th December 1916 aeroplanes were around the district for 10 hours with intervals. People took shelter in cellars four times.[88]

The implication of this second Admiralty communiqué on Dillingen was that German morale—and hence productivity—could be impaired simply by the proximity of Allied bombers. That is, depression resulted from the *threat* of attack as well as from attacks themselves; it was independent of any actual damage caused. The bombing focus had subtly broadened to include not only German industry but also its labor force. This linkage of bombs and moral effect, largely forged by the wishful thinking of the Admiralty Air Department, was initially tentative.

Barely two months later, however, presumption of moral effect had developed to the point that it was accorded equal space with "reported military results" in the "Results of Raids" column. On 24 March 1917, the column excerpted a letter in which a German factory manager in the Saar valley regretted that he could no longer give his clients definite delivery dates due to wartime disruption "and more recently from aerial bombardment."[89] Two weeks later, under severe pressure from the War Office to abandon the long-range bombing from Luxeuil and disband No. 3 Wing, the Admiralty issued this statement:

> It is reliably reported that the Allies' recent frequent aerial bombardments of objectives in the Saar Valley have caused panic among the workmen, and they refuse to carry on their work. Nearly all of them have cancelled their agreements, fearing for the safety of their lives on account of the Allies' machines.[90]

The Admiralty assumed that deterioration of morale within the enemy populace, from initial curiosity through annoyance to eventual panic, was a feasible bombing goal; the relationship between bombs and morale was presumed to exist.

Similarly, moral effect was presumed to be a cumulative phenomenon. Its importance persisted for two reasons: (1) very little data existed that could be used to evaluate bombing results during wartime and (2) selective use of moral effects by the Admiralty could support propitious assertions of results which opponents of strategic bombardment could not definitely refute. While the war raged, the effectiveness of air attack had to receive the benefit of the doubt.

Few assumed that the German populace would eventually become habituated to bombing or that the enemy would develop effective countermeasures. Yet, some indication of this trend existed even during the war. For example, an article in the *Sarregemunder Zeitung* cautioned its readers against remaining in the open during air raids.

> One was able to notice yesterday for the twentieth time that all our warnings to the public have been useless. The streets were blocked with people, and one could tell by the number of bombs that were dropped, what would be the inevitable result of these assemblies . . . that there were no victims among the crowd, it is most certainly to be put down to the English inexperience.[91]

Apparently, the novelty of sighting enemy aircraft above one's city outweighed any fears that the average German citizen felt on such occasions. The newspaper editor argued for caution; the possibility of panic was not mentioned.

Interviews with German managers and workers at the Saar blast furnaces after the war emphasized that the British had consistently overestimated the moral effects of their raids. Material supplied to the Americans led US Air Service investigators to conclude that the main effect was insufficient rest among the workers.

> The morale of workers was affected to the extent that when they "went on" again on their next shift, their physical strength was somewhat reduced and [they] were incapable of working at their normal capacity, and would try to find someplace to steal a rest.[92]

The team of American intelligence personnel at the Burbach works reached a similar, if blunter, conclusion after their interviews: "the workmen maintained a fairly good working standard in the factory and many were glad when an alert was sounded because it meant a loaf for a while."[93] At Burbach, the Americans noted that "no bonuses were paid to employees and no strikes ever occurred here."[94] Since the bombing survey included data from the RFC and RAF raids in late 1917 and 1918 as well as No. 3 Wing raids, one can conclude that

Admiralty bombs never posed a threat to German productivity along the Saar.

Throughout the war, the morale of the enemy population was considered by British planners to be susceptible to aerial attacks. During late 1916 and early 1917, this concept received official attention as a secondary "bonus" effect resulting from air strikes against industrial targets of military importance. The utility of moral effect as one of the few available indicators of bombing progress led to its frequent use by the Admiralty Air Department to rationalize the lack of direct results and to justify strategic bombardment. This preoccupation with morale was to become an obsession later in the war; it was largely a fond hope.

Against this evaluation of the Luxeuil wing, one must set the conclusions of the official historian, H. A. Jones. In this regard, the sixth volume of the official history, *The War in the Air*, published in 1937, has set the tone for subsequent verdicts.

> With our fuller knowledge it is clear that the effect produced by the naval bombing wing was disproportionate to the number of raids, which were comparatively infrequent and are not to be judged by the material results. The British and French bombing attacks went some way to shake the morale of the industrial population and had an adverse effect on the output of munitions of war, but chiefly they compelled the Germans to divert aeroplanes, labor, and material to the beginnings of widespread schemes of home defence.[95]

Here, Jones evaluated the fortunes of the Luxeuil wing merely as a prelude to the later bombing of the RAF; altogether, he devoted eight pages (three in volume 2, five in volume 6) to this inaugural experiment in British strategic bombardment. A recent author, Neville Jones, cited the official history paragraph below in agreeing that "the bombing campaign of the naval wing was remarkably successful."[96]

> It can hardly be doubted that the removal of No. 3 Wing brought great relief to the Germans to whom the provision of an air defence system (no matter how inadequate) was an intolerable burden.[97]

This latter Jones then proceeded beyond *The War in the Air*. While he repeated *The War in the Air's* argument that civilians "compelled the German government to build up a defense system at a great cost both in men and material," he also favorably contrasted the Admiralty raids with German airship attacks on Britain in 1915.

> Whereas the Zeppelins were seldom able to locate and bomb their objectives at night, the naval bombers, operating in more favourable conditions and at a shorter range, had proved themselves capable of finding and bombing specific targets both by day and night. In consequence, these operations were far more dangerous to the Germans than the airship raids had ever been to the British.[98]

In making these pronouncements, neither author appears to have compared post-Armistice survey materials with wartime claims. The universal tendency has been to accept wartime observation reports and intelligence information. German records made available after 11 November 1918 have been largely ignored or selectively employed. Documentation contained in the postwar bombing surveys simply fails to support the wartime reports.

The widespread opinion that one major effect of the French and British air raids was to "compel" Germany to commit aviation assets to home defense makes sense only if strategic bombing is analyzed *in vacuo*. The evidence for the alleged redeployment of German fighter units to counter Allied air raids stems almost entirely from Air Ministry and RAF intelligence estimates prepared in August and September 1918, a period when British bomber losses in daylight missions were increasing sharply.[99] This support has been demolished by recent research into the surviving logs and records of the German interceptor squadrons assigned to defend the fatherland.

> In fact, the German home defense system (Heimatluftschutz) was first constructed because of French air raids which had been going on since 1915, and were to continue, albeit erratically, throughout the war. There was none of the dramatic movement of fighter aircraft between the front and the industrial arena which the British were quick to perceive in any redeployment of German Jagdstaffeln fighter squadrons along the Western Front. Until 1918 at least, German home defence squadrons (Kampfeinsitzerstaffeln) remained a separate and largely unreinforced contingent, fighting a small-scale campaign against predominantly French opposition.[100]

German archives also confirm that until late 1918, the home defense squadrons were forced to operate with war-weary machines discarded by other units. Coordinated formation attacks against British bombing machines by such a motley variety of veteran aircraft were correspondingly rare.[101] The perception of No. 3 Wing aircrews and Air Department staff officers that enemy resistance stiffened because German front-line fighters were diverted to the home front proved, in the final analysis, to be illusory.

Notes

1. Public Record Office (PRO), Air Ministry Record (AIR) 1/2266/209/70/18, "Notes on Report of Bombing Operations by No. 3 Wing, RNAS, in France during winter, 1916/1917," Capt W. L. Elder, Royal Navy (RN), Commanding No. 3 Wing, to Admiralty, 24 May 1917.

2. AIR 1/2266/209/70/18. H. A. Jones, *War in the Air, Being the Story of the Part Played in the Great War by the Royal Air Force*, vol. 6 (Oxford: Clarendon Press, 1937), 118. (A note of clarification is in order here: *War in the Air* is in six vols.; Sir Walter Alexander Raleigh wrote volume 1, H. A. Jones wrote vols. 2-6.

3. Geoffrey Till, *Air Power and the Royal Navy, 1914–1945: A Historical Survey* (London: Jane's 1979), 111–13.

4. H. A. Jones, *War in the Air*, vol. 3, 251–300.

5. Malcolm Cooper, "The British Experience of Strategic Bombing" (Oxford University typescript, 1982), 10.

6. H. A. Jones, *War in the Air*, vol. 2, 452; and Sir Charles Webster and A. Noble Frankland, *The Strategic Air Offensive Against Germany 1939–1945*, 4 vols. (London: Her Majesty's Stationery Office [HMSO], 1961), 34.

7. PRO, Admiralty Records (ADM) 1/8449/39A, "Defence Against Zeppelin Raids," in *Documents Relating to the Naval Air Service*, ed. Stephen W. Roskill (London: Navy Records Society, 1969), 342–44.

8. AIR 1/2266/209/70/18, Captain Elder.

9. Ibid.; and AIR 1/115/15/39/68. Admiralty to Captain Elder, 27 July 1916.

10. PRO, AIR 1/508/16/3/52, Report of Aviation Conference, 4 July 1916.

11. Ibid.

12. Neville Jones, *The Origins of Strategic Bombing: A Study of the Development of British Air Strategic Thought and Practice up to 1918* (London: Eimber 1973), 107.

13. PRO, AIR 1/1976/204/273/39, "Account of the Aviation Plan of Bombardment by Airplanes," French General Staff, 18 November 1917, trans. by Technical Division, US Air Service, 3 December 1917.

14. Ibid.

15. AIR 1/1976/204/273/39.

16. Sir Walter Alexander Raleigh, *War in the Air*, vol. 1, 451; Cooper, 13.

17. H. A. Jones, *War in the Air*, vol. 2, 452.

18. AIR 1/515/16/2/84, memorandum to Air Board, 26 October 1916.

19. ADM 1/8844/39A, "Defence Against Zeppelin Raids," 4 April 1916.

20. PRO, AIR 1/978/204/5/1139, Chief General Staff (CGS) to Air Board, 3 June 1916.

21. ADM 1/8844/39A, Haig to Army Council, 1 November 1916, 405–7.

22. H. A. Jones, *War in the Air*, vol. 2, 452.

23. AIR 1/2266/209/70/18, Captain Elder.

24. Ibid.; and Webster and Frankland, vol. 1, 34.

25. H. A. Jones, *War in the Air*, vol. 2, 452.

26. Ibid., Appendix 17, Table A.

27. US Army Air Forces Air Service Command, Technical Order 30-1-5, *Medical Officer's Guide*, 258–63.

28. AIR 1/2266/209/70/18, Captain Elder.

29. Ibid.; and H. A. Jones, *War in the Air*, vol. 2, 452.

30. For this raid, Jones lists five more aeroplanes (four bombers, one escort) than Elder, who, being on the spot, probably gave the more accurate total.

31. PRO, AIR 1/2104/207/36, "Results of Air Raids on Germany Carried Out by the 8th Brigade and the Independent Force, R.A.F., January 1st–November 11th, 1918," Air Ministry publication Directorate of Air Intelligence (DAI) no. 5, 1 January 1920.

32. PRO, AIR 1/1999/204/273/269, "Report on the Effects of Bombing German Blast Furnaces," Maj H. W. M. Paul to Air Ministry, 26 February 1919.

33. Neither Elder (AIR 1/2266/209/70/18) nor H. A. Jones (*War in the Air*, vol. 6, 120–21) specifies the payload; a typical Handley Page O100 bomb load is assumed.

34. H. A. Jones, *War in the Air*, vol. 6., fn. 121.

35. Ibid.

36. ADM 1/8844/39A, "Defence Against Zeppelin Raids," 4 April 1916.

37. H. A. Jones, *War in the Air*, vol. 6, 121–22.

38. PRO, AIR 2/123, Haig to War Office, letter, subject: Sir Douglas Haig's Criticism of Aerial Policy in France, 1 November 1916.

39. H. A. Jones, *War in the Air*, vol. 6, 122.

40. AIR 2/123, Lord George Nathaniel Curzon, memorandum to War Committee, 9 November 1916.

41. AIR 2/123, Haig to War Office, letter, 1 November 1916.

42. Neville Jones, *The Origins of Strategic Bombing*, 114.

43. PRO, AIR 1/111/15/39/1, Official Raid Report, Officer Commanding No. 3 Wing to Admiralty, 4 March 1917; see also Official Raid Report, "No. 3 Wing, R.N.A.S. Operations from Luxeuil and Ochey-Details of Air Raids over Enemy Territory," 26 February 1917.

44. AIR 1/111/15/39/1 Official Raid Report, 11 November 1916; and Admiralty Communiqué no. 330, 7 February 1917.

45. A "sortie" is one takeoff and one landing by one aircraft.

46. AIR 1/2266/209/70/18, Captain Elder; and AIR 1/111/15/39/1, Official Raid Report, 16 March 1917. Bombers diverted from Burbach works in Saarbrücken to Morhange (16 March 1917) and from Hagendingen to Moulin-les-Metz (16/17 March 1917).

47. AIR 1/2266/209/70/22. Lieutenant Colonel Spiers, Paris, to CIGS, cipher telegram, subject: Reprisals for Bombing Raids by the French, 9 July 1917.

48. James Clay Thompson, *Rolling Thunder, Understanding Policy and Program Failures* (Chapel Hill, N.C.: University of North Carolina, 1980), 87–91.

49. AIR 1/111/1539/1, Official Raid Reports.

50. Thompson, 92.

51. AIR 1/2266/209/70/18, Captain Elder, Appendix I.

52. AIR 1/111/15/29/1, Official Raid Report, 27 January 1917.

53. Ibid., Admiralty Communiqué no. 317, 25 January 1917.

54. Ibid., Admiralty Communiqué no. 375, 24 March 1917.

55. PRO, AIR 1/1998/204/273/262, Maj H. W. M. Paul, RAF in the field, to Air Ministry, letter of transmittal, subject: Reports of British Bombing Raids on German Railways, Railway Stations and Railway Objectives, 1918, 26 February 1919.

56. Ibid.

57. Maurer Maurer, ed., *The US Air Service in World War I:* vol. 4, *Postwar Review* (Maxwell Air Force Base, Ala.: Air Force Historical Research Agency, 1979), 364–66.

58. Ibid., 561, note 6.

59. AIR 1/1998/204/273/262, Major Paul to Air Ministry, 26 February 1919.

60. AIR 1/111/15/39/1, Official Raid Report, 27 January 1917.

61. AIR 1/1999/204/273/269, Major Paul, RAF in the field, to Air Ministry, letter of transmittal, subject: Effects of Bombing German Blast Furnaces, 26 February 1919.

62. Maurer, vol. 4, 439.

63. AIR 1/111/15/39/1, Official Raid Report, 22 March 1917.

64. Maurer, vol. 4, 439.

65. Ibid., 440–41; and Neville Jones does not distinguish between Burbach and Brebach in *The Origins of Strategic Bombing*, 122.

66. Maurer, vol. 4, 452.

67. AIR 1/111/15/39/1, Official Raid Report, 25 November 1916.

68. Ibid., Official Raid Report, 28 December 1916.

69. Ibid., Admiralty Communiqué no. 318, 28 January 1917.

70. Maurer, vol. 4, 558, note 31a.

71. AIR 1/1999/204/273/269, Major Paul to Air Ministry, 26 February 1919.

72. Neville Jones, *The Origins of Strategic Bombing*, 116; and H. A. Jones, *War in the Air*, vol. 2, 452.

73. AIR 1/111/15/39/1, Official Raid Report, 23 October 1916.

74. R. B. Davies, *Sailor in the Air* (London: 1967), 154.

75. AIR 1/111/15/39/1, Official Raid Report, 30 October 1916.

76. Ibid., Admiralty Communiqué no. 269, 6 December 1916.

77. Maurer, 386–87.

78. Ibid., 387.

79. Neville Jones, *The Origins of Strategic Bombing*, 112–13; and AIR 1/111/15/39/1, Official Raid Reports.

80. PRO, 1/1998/204/273/266, Major Paul, RAF in the field, to Air Ministry, letter of transmittal, subject: Reports as to the Effect of Various Types of Bombs on Buildings, Streets, etc., and General Conclusions, 26 February 1919.

81. Ibid.

82. Ibid.

83. Ibid.

84. Ibid.

85. Maj Gen Hugh M. Trenchard, Dispatch of 1 January 1919, Reprinted in *Aeroplane*, 8 January 1919, 129–31.

86. AIR 1/111/15/39/1, Admiralty Communiqué.

87. Ibid., Admiralty Communiqué no. 318, 28 January 1917.

88. Ibid., Admiralty Communiqué no. 330, 7 February 1917.

89. Ibid., Admiralty Communiqué no. 375, 24 March 1917.

90. Ibid., Admiralty Communiqué no. 388, 10 April 1917.

91. Ibid., Admiralty Communiqué no. 379, 28 March 1917.

92. Maurer, 444.

93. Ibid., 440

94. Ibid., 441.

95. H. A. Jones, *War in the Air*, vol. 6, 122.

96. Neville Jones, *The Origins of Strategic Bombing*, 123–24.

97. Ibid., 123–28.

98. Ibid., 129.

99. PRO, AIR 1/477/15/312/229, Lieutenant Colonel Davidson, DDAI, to Director of Flying Operations, subject: The Increase of (1) German Home Defence Flights and (2) Anti-Aircraft Defences of Germany, 24 September 1918. See also AIR 1/682/21/13/2217-8 and AIR 1/7/11/27/13/2214.

100. Nebel Papers, Deutsches Museum, Munich, Germany, Kampfeinsitzerstaffel 1a, squadron records. Quoted in Malcolm Cooper, note 5 above, 40.

101. Cooper, "The British Experience," 17.

Chapter 2

British Bombing Begins

Following the demise of No. 3 Naval Wing, the British government's concern with strategic bombing dwindled. Official interest in aviation detachments committed to independent bombardment almost disappeared. The exception was No. 5 Wing, Royal Naval Air Service at Dunkirk. The Admiralty continued to underwrite No. 5 Wing, which raided German naval bases along the Belgian coast with DeHavillands and Handley Pages.

However, No. 5 Wing eventually found itself saddled with diverse tasks unrelated to long-range bombing. This dissipation of effort, and the willingness of Vice Adm Sir Reginald Bacon, commander of the Dover Patrol, to subordinate squadrons to Field Marshal Haig, kept the wing from its primary mission. It never waged a systematic bombing campaign of sufficient intensity to substantiate the worth of its independent activities, defaulting to Germany the strategic initiative for conducting long-range aerial operations. No. 5 Wing, RNAS became No. 5 Group, Royal Air Force in April 1918.[1]

The forced retirement of RNAS brought a de facto acceptance of the RFC attitude about the division of responsibilities.[2] Sir David Henderson, Director-General of Military Aeronautics (DGMA), sent this memorandum to the Admiralty in late 1916:

> It is, to my mind, absolutely essential that during this winter, the duties and requirements of the different air forces should be definitely laid down. The French ought to be able to look after their own front, and I have no ground for believing that they are unable to do so. The Navy have our own, and hostile coasts to look after, and their duties with the fleets. For the performance of these latter, not much material appears to be at present necessary. . . . All air duties . . . with the Field Armies should be carried out by the Royal Flying Corps, and it is for the military authorities to decide the relative numbers of the different types of aeroplanes to be used for these purposes.[3]

The DGMA left no doubt that satisfying the aviation requirements of Field Marshal Haig should have first call on British

35

aircraft production. The navy, with strictly maritime responsibilities (as defined by the War Office) would need far fewer machines. The French aviation service, now that the Sopwith 1½ Strutters at Luxeuil had been transferred to the RFC, was to be left to its own resources. This army position, which reduced air force roles to cooperative support of their respective parent services, represented a return to the uneasy status quo ante for No. 3 Wing. The proposal required no extensive rearrangement of the British command structure.

The opposite perspective, that strategic bombardment embodied a potential independent of land and sea campaigns, contained major doctrinal and organizational perturbations for the conduct of modern warfare. At the time, British command authorities preferred to acquiesce in the War Office's evaluation. However, this expedient solution survived only until the Germans resumed daylight raids on Britain in summer 1917. Gothas forced a reappraisal of the air issue.

The new German offensive had an impact upon British public and political consciousness out of all proportion to the force that the enemy dedicated to their bombing attacks. Initially intended as an experiment to try British morale and produce propaganda, these raids from Belgian aerodromes employed approximately one-fourth of the German heavy bomber strength.[4]

The German bombing offensive was halted in May 1918 so that the Gotha squadrons could be committed elsewhere. The shift was not due to the relatively high wastage rate (15 percent), which was caused more by accidents than by British defenses.[5] Between May and August 1917, two daylight attacks (of eight for the period) reached London. Between August 1917 and May 1918, 15 night raids (of 19) penetrated to the capital. Casualties included three thousand killed or injured and 1.5 million pounds in property damages; the Germans had dropped 120 tons of bombs.[6] These raids, particularly two daylight raids on London (13 June and 7 July), accelerated review of the British air program, transforming it from an interservice issue into a political question of considerable public interest.

After more than a year of procrastination, the Lloyd George government reacted with all possible speed to resolve its chronic difficulties with the military and naval air services. Enemy bombs on London had highlighted inadequacies in the present organization. In a matter of weeks, decisions were taken that eventually unified the two fractious components as the Royal Air Force. The issue of strategic bombardment was from the outset inextricably conjoined with the creation of the third service.

Even with this crisis, politicians might have been deterred from such a merger during wartime. Their impulse wavered momentarily "in the hiatus between the summer daylight raids and the start of the fall nighttime series."[7] The German "Harvest Moon" attacks, which commenced in September 1917, remotivated the British decision makers. The Cabinet hoped to quell not only the public outcry for a workable home defense system but also for prompt reprisals in kind against German cities, since civilians at home now seemed to share the same risks as their uniformed colleagues in France. Besides satisfying these popular demands, the government also sought to solve the recurrent problems of duplication, shortages, and waste caused by RFC-RNAS rivalries. Unification also seemed likely to provide the means to exploit the potential of an aerial offensive, an attractive alternative to the campaigns on the Western Front. "The great motive force of the Royal Air Force was the offensive one enshrined in the idea of strategic bombing."[8] The locus of this force lay within the War Cabinet.

Faced with these difficulties, the government summoned Trenchard to London for discussions on strategy. But his first appearance before the Cabinet (20 June 1917) provided little encouragement; he dismissed the politicians' scheme to mount an airborne patrol belt across southern England as purely defensive and doomed to fail. To halt the Gothas, he advocated seizure of the Belgian coast, where they were based, as "the most effective step of all."[9] This overland offensive would dovetail nicely with the plans of Trenchard's superior, Sir Douglas Haig, who presented his plan for the forthcoming Flanders campaign to the War Cabinet.

As the next best solution, Trenchard proposed an aerial counteroffensive on the Western Front to destroy the enemy's "aeroplanes and bases," thus "reducing his power to send expeditions to England."[10] Attrition, said Trenchard, would eventually force the German aviation service to redeploy squadrons in order to minimize high tactical losses. There would then be no surplus of suitable machines to undertake long-range bombing.

Both suggestions reflect Trenchard's faith in maintaining constant offensive pressure and keeping aviation tied to the ground plan. They also echo his 1916 objections to the Admiralty's creation of No. 3 Naval Wing at a time when aerial assets were in scant supply. Trenchard then had convincingly argued that no surplus of machines could be combed out to equip independent detachments such as the Luxeuil long-range bombing force. His assertions that all available planes should be sent to understrength RFC squadrons had ultimately prevailed.

Trenchard's logic also reveals that he projected upon his German antagonists his own assessment of strategic bombing. The head of the RFC assumed that the Germans would consider strategic bombing only if they possessed air forces surplus to the requirements of tactical support of their armies. Any need to recoup losses would deplete their aerial surplus; tactical attrition in France could therefore hinder strategic bombardment of London. An unrelenting RFC offensive on the Western Front would theoretically place German aviation in just such an irksome circumstance. Trenchard's reasoning demonstrated that he had not significantly altered his view; that is, long-range bombardment should be low on the list of aerial priorities.

Trenchard objected on pragmatic grounds the reprisal bombing of German cities, the course of action espoused by Lloyd George and buttressed by public opinion.

Reprisals on open towns are repugnant to British ideas but we may be forced to adopt them. . . . The enemy would almost certainly reply in kind. Unless we are resolute, it will be infinitely better not to attempt reprisals at all. At present we are not prepared to carry out reprisals effectively, being unprovided with suitable machines.[11]

For Trenchard, the prime minister's proposal for reprisals against the poison gas works at Mannheim exhumed the same questions of means and priorities that No. 3 Wing's activities had done. Trenchard again argued that no aerial force for independent operations, retaliatory or otherwise, could be created until the requirements for squadrons to support Haig had been met. Like his chief, he kept his attention fixed on the Western Front. These assessments, however, seemed unduly restrictive and somber to the War Cabinet. They subsequently discounted Trenchard's hardheaded analysis in favor of a more pliable approach.

On 7 July 1917, the War Cabinet decided to reinforce home air defenses by withdrawing operational squadrons from the front and by diverting new fighting machines scheduled to go overseas. They also decided to launch at least one retaliatory raid on Mannheim as soon as possible.[12] Four days later, the prime minister appointed a committee of two (himself and Jan Christiaan Smuts, the highly regarded South African general and statesman) to reevaluate British air policy. In particular, they would examine home defense and the air organization:

1. The defence arrangements for home defence against air raids.
2. The air organisation generally and the direction of aerial operations.[13]

These initiatives must now be examined insofar as they affected the program to resume the long-range bombardment of Germany.

To this end, Smuts's "Second Report of the Prime Minister's Committee on Air Organisation and Home Defence against Air Raids," submitted on 17 August 1917, provided considerable impetus. (His first report, 19 July 1917—completed within eight days of its War Cabinet mandate—analyzed the organization and forces necessary for defending London.)[14] An outsider, Smuts naturally sought expert advice—first from Weetman Dickinson Pearson (Lord Cowdray), president of the Air Board, and then from Sir David Henderson, director-general of Military Aeronautics—in drafting his second report. His evaluation, however, neither tapped the empirical wisdom of the air establishment in the field nor acknowledged the immense difficulties attendant upon implementing its precepts.

39

Smuts's Second Report was unduly influenced by a minority view. In effect, he was "exposed almost exclusively to reports advocating the formation of some sort of independent air ministry and the prosecution of a strategic bombing campaign."[15] General Trenchard, the apotheosis of dissenting opinion, had been unavailable for consultation because RFC was supporting Haig's Ypres offensive. Both Haig and Trenchard were justifiably concerned that London's preoccupation with home defense and retaliatory raids would interfere with their own plans and with the flow of reinforcements at a critical time.[16] The entire affair bore a disturbing resemblance to the situation regarding No. 3 Wing and the French Air Service less than a year earlier.

Not surprisingly, Smuts's final paper incorporated the biases of his advisors. Henderson's "Memorandum on the Organisation of the Air Services," submitted to Smuts on 19 July, had argued for prompt creation of an Air Ministry, fully staffed and endowed with executive responsibility for the air war, coequal in ministerial authority to the Admiralty and the War Office.[17] Lord Cowdray's report of 28 July, "The Duties and Functions of the Air Board," predicted a "Surplus Air Fleet" of some four hundred to five hundred bombers by the year's end, with ranges of over four hundred miles carrying payloads of three hundred to five hundred pounds. By 1918, said Lord Cowdray, more machines would swell this superabundance. He urged that this fleet be earmarked exclusively for War Cabinet employment, distinct from the cooperative duties of RFC and RNAS units in the field.[18] This glowing estimate perpetuated the on-paper protections of aerial might that the Air Board had been producing since spring 1917;[19] the machines had yet to materialize in France.

Six weeks after the War Cabinet injunction, Smuts submitted his second report. Its scope and vision offered an attractive panacea to the vexed politicians.

[Air forces] can be used as an independent means of war operations. Nobody that witnessed the attack on London on 11th July could have any doubt on that point. Unlike artillery, an air fleet can conduct extensive operations far from, and independently of, both Army and Navy. As far as can at present be foreseen, there is absolutely no limit to the scale of its future independent war use. [Germany] is no doubt

40

making vast plans to deal with us in London if we do not succeed in beating him in the air and carrying the war into the heart of his country.

The program of aircraft production which the War Cabinet has sanctioned for the following twelve months is far in excess of Navy and Army requirements. Next spring and summer the position will be that the Army and Navy will have all the Air Service required in connexion with their operations; and over and above that there will be a great surplus available for independent operations.

This means that the Air Board has already reached the stage where the settlement of future war policy has become necessary. Otherwise engines and machines useless for independent strategical operations may be built. The necessity for an Air Ministry and Air Staff has therefore become urgent.[20]

Smuts insisted that neither Admiralty nor War Office was especially competent to supervise this imminent armada; the creation of an Air Staff for planning and directing independent air operations would soon be pressing. The political consequences of ignoring Smuts's logic seemed perilous indeed.

On 24 August 1917, the War Cabinet endorsed Smuts's second report and charged him with its supervision.[21] Thus was conceived the Royal Air Force as an independent flying service. Its subsequent vitality depended upon a largely unseated offensive capability—the strategic potential of bombs it hoped to drop on Germany from its as yet nonexistent surplus of aircraft. "Smuts was an advocate of strategic bombing even before much possibility of carrying it out existed."[22] Britain's retaliatory will was, furthermore, distressingly short of means. This shortage was most evident to the field commanders, who would have to implement the War Cabinet's decision.

In general, the British public welcomed these developments, hoping the new organization would expedite punishing Germany from the air. As one observer noted, the 7 July Gotha raid on the capital had heightened popular susceptibility to drastic remedies for the "humiliating and intolerable situation."[23] The proposed counteroffensive mirrored the hope of British citizens that their recent disquiet under aerial attack could be visited upon the Germans. "The raids were a method of exerting psychological pressure upon Germany as a whole and the creating there of the mental complexes which were an essential condition of a readiness to accept reasonable peace

41

terms."[24] The RAF bomb that disrupted munitions output and diverted enemy fighters to defend their homeland would also convince the Hun that "two could play the same game," and would create a demand for the cessation of raids on Britain.[25] In the popular view, moral effect and material destruction seemed equal. The experience of London under the Gothas legitimized the demand for retaliation in kind.

Strategy became a topic for public speculation. In a typical instance, an illustrated weekly developed its own scheme for exacting retribution, confusing reprisals and military strategy in the process. The editor hypothesized that aerial destruction of key junctions would hasten the German collapse. To sever "such nodal points behind the German lines in France" as "Conflans . . . Mezieres on the Meuse; and Aix-la-Chapelle" would mean that German frontline troops "would be beggared for supplies."[26] The Fleet Street strategist solemnly warned of the "poetic justice" that would soon overtake enemy practitioners of the "backdoor assassination business," whose outrages included "bombing . . . open towns with the object of killing as many civilians as possible."[27] Whitehall satisfied this widespread sentiment by incorporating it into a plan of campaign aimed at the enemy's industrial and munitions centers. This shotgun approach satisfied the citizenry but frustrated the military authorities.

Political confusion over specific goals of the counteroffensive muddied the government's guidance to the field. Bombing as a practical undertaking received little more coherent direction than it had in the past. On the day following Smuts's second report, the War Office notified Haig (in reply to his query) that the War Cabinet had yet to develop a definite plan or clarify their intentions for bombing Germany. From the War Office perspective, the Air Ministry question had contributed to the delay.

The War Cabinet are now considering the establishment of a separate Department of State to control and administer the Air Services, and in the event of such a Department being formed, the strategical disposition, and the employment of such surplus force may be among its functions.[28]

The second wave of German aerial attacks on London, five of which reached the capital between 24 September and 2 October 1917, motivated the War Cabinet to accelerate its deliberations. Amidst this enemy night offensive, the Cabinet met frequently to formulate new air policies. At the morning session of 2 October, the diversion of antiaircraft artillery from France to home defense duties was authorized and the First Lord of the Admiralty reported that eight Handley Page bombers were en route to Ochey to join 41st Wing.[29] On the matter of East London's susceptibility "to give way to panic during Gotha raids," the Prime Minister decided to ask editors not to publish photographs or descriptions of air raid damage and casualties.[30] In closing, General Smuts announced that the RFC head had been recalled from the field.

At the afternoon meeting, with Trenchard present, the War Cabinet continued its discussions. These centered on the immediate deployment of a small force to begin active operations, with expansion to a large-scale offensive to occur later.[31] The CIGS promised that 20 DeHavilland 4s (DH4) in crates would be sent to Ochey, with a like quantity to follow within six weeks.[32] This "Russian Windfall" had been gleaned from the Russian government, which agreed to forego delivery on condition that 75 DeHavillands be supplied in spring 1918.[33] Thus did the government marshal the machines to initiate the British aerial offensive against Germany; urgency over-

This DeHavilland 4 was faster and more maneuverable than its successors DH9 and DH9A.

Source: USAF Photo

whelmed detailed planning. Much would depend upon the "Surplus Air Fleet" that Lord Cowdray had promised to Smuts.

Trenchard then received his orders. The prime minister, noting "the great and growing demand on the part of the British public for retaliation," emphasized the immense popular interest in 41st Wing. Very likely, the situation in the east end was still fresh in Lloyd George's mind for he impressed upon Trenchard the importance of making the forthcoming air offensive a success. He believed that success would have a moral effect on the people at home.[34]

The prime minister left his air chief in no doubt that he was expected to make a success of this endeavor. Trenchard assured the prime minister that the promised planes would begin to bomb Germany within six days of their arrival at Ochey.[35] He was never asked to evaluate the military feasibility of the scheme.

On 15 October 1917, the War Cabinet made two further decisions with regard to strategic bombardment. A new Air Policy Committee was established to "advise the War Cabinet on all questions relating to air policy." The military authorities in France were at last told that "immediate arrangements should be made for the conduct of long-range offensive operations against German towns where factories existed for the production of munitions of all kinds."[36] Two days later, eight DH4 bombing machines—of 11 launched—from No. 55 Squadron dropped 1,792 pounds of bombs on the Burbach works at Saarbrücken, a target often visited by No. 55's naval predecessors in No. 3 Wing.[37]

The War Cabinet had finally developed an aerial policy. Disregarding the views of their generals, they had favored the visionary concepts embodied in Smuts's Report of 17 August. Lord Cowdray's projected aerial surplus and Henderson's argument for an independent service had made the South African's proposals appear deceptively realizable. They had endorsed a policy of retaliation, partially as a response to public indignation and partially in the vague hope that enemy morale would crumble under every RAF bomb that fell on Germany. A second wave of Gotha attacks had underlined the urgency of this plan. A small British force was hastily assembled to undertake immediate bombing, even as schemes for expanding the strategic fleet were being debated. Preparations at Ochey continued, under the fitful scrutiny of the War Cabinet in London. The commencement of active air operations did not, however, signify that the points of contention between White-hall and the field had been resolved.

As head of the Royal Flying Corps in France, and responsible for the fortunes of this new Cabinet bombing scheme, Trenchard was particularly disturbed at the government's recent decisions. The politicians had ignored his pleas for Western Front offensives. Instead, they had adopted a policy of defense and long-range bombing of Germany; much of their rationale seemed to reflect an acute consciousness of the public mood. After the Smuts Report, Trenchard fretted that Whitehall would interfere with the RFC's primary mission: obtain army cooperation.

> Tuesday August 28. The War Cabinet has evidently decided on creating a new Department to deal with Air operations, on the lines of the War Office and the Admiralty. Trenchard is much perturbed as to the result of this new department just at a time when the Flying Corps was beginning to feel that it had become an important part of the army.[38]

The 2 October session with the War Cabinet had only increased Trenchard's misgivings. He was saddled with responsibility for a bombing scheme that he had continually opposed, in person and in principle. It seemed apparent that his political prestige had perceptibly diminished, from strategic authority to military technician. Under the circumstances, his supervision of 41st Wing, despite its prominence, was more likely to be subversive than conscientious. Once official interest in the Ochey force waned, it seemed likely that he would attempt to redirect 41st Wing from independent operations back to army cooperation missions.

The War Cabinet had also considered that, if given an opportunity, Trenchard might preempt their supervision of the independent bombing force. This matter of command and control would not be settled until after the Ochey force had begun to bomb. The 41st Wing, an organization within the RFC, was accountable to Trenchard, the wing commander. Lt Col C. L.

N. Newall had previously headed Trenchard's headquarters. Newall was unlikely to antagonize his superior, whom he admired and respected. The operational effectiveness of the long-range bombing wing depended in the main upon its links to London.

Consequently, the War Cabinet intended to supervise the activities of 41st Wing as closely as possible. Such direction would require frequent and detailed communications with the Ochey force. Detailed information would be critical in managing the long-range bombing force. Initially, however, 41st Wing reports were not promptly forwarded to London, due largely to Trenchard's intervention. To ensure that Colonel Newall had no doubt as to his ultimate superiors, the War Cabinet sent a message to Sir Douglas Haig.

> In order to enable them to decide as to the future policy as regards bombing, the War Cabinet will be glad of fullest information as to the difficulties which have hitherto been encountered by the special bombing squadrons, and the extent to which these difficulties are likely to increase in proportion as distances are extended into enemy country. In particular they require information as to the efficiency of the enemy anti-aircraft defences, difficulties experienced from climatic conditions, in finding objectives, and the losses experienced.
>
> Please, therefore, forward a detailed report from the Officer Commanding the Bombing Squadron in regard to operations which have already been carried out, and arrange that a similar report be furnished in the case of all future bombing raids. In reporting losses of aeroplanes, those experienced by the special bombing squadrons should be shown separately to those caused in normal flying.[39]

Haig's staff duly transmitted the CIGS directive to Headquarters (HQ) RFC for information and for transmission to Newall. Trenchard, however, added his own instruction in his forwarding letter.

> In future, in addition to your daily summary of work, a short report in narrative form will be sent on each raid that takes place by the first orderly subsequent to the raid. It should give a short story of the raid, machines taking part, results, etc., and should include the particulars asked for in the C.I.G.S.'s letter.[40]

One must note that the War Cabinet was mainly concerned with factors that constrained the bombing campaign; Trenchard, on the other hand, desired information on the positive aspects of the missions that 41st Wing had actually flown. He was interested in data corroborating the success of the Ochey force, in accordance with Lloyd George's admonition on the afternoon of 2 October.

On 29 October, even as the CIGS letter was filtering down to Newall, the War Cabinet again asserted its desire to control the strategic bombing campaign. In this instance, they required 41st Wing to submit justifications for inactivity.

> War Cabinet desire to have a daily report on working of bombing squadrons on NANCY front stating weather conditions or other causes which prevent operations when none have taken place.[41]

This report was to include such meteorological data as cloud height, wind direction, and wind strength. The message was clear: the War Cabinet expected 41st Wing to mount operations against Germany unless prevented by circumstances beyond their control. Such messages lucidly and repeatedly reminded field commanders of the War Cabinet's desires for timely information from Ochey. However, the politicians were still uneasy about their direction of the strategic bombing force; they worried about the influence that Haig or Trenchard could potentially exert by virtue of their positions.

The issue surfaced in Whitehall at least twice more, the first time at the 31 October 1917 meeting of the new Air Policy Committee.[42] At the War Cabinet session two days later, command and control of 41st Wing received further consideration. The discussions at that meeting also disclose the degree to which the British independent bombing force was an ad hoc aggregation of personnel and machines, building aerodromes and billets even as they undertook to fly missions.

> As regards independent aerial offensive operations in France, all the necessary preparations were being made. Aerodromes were being constructed, and depots for the Air Service were being established in France, to be ready for the large independent operations it was intended should be carried out during the following summer. There was, however, a slight difficulty to be overcome in regard to the Command and Second–in–Command of these independent offensive operations. Sir Douglas Haig desired that they should be under General Trenchard, commanding the Royal Flying Corps in France. The idea of the Air Policy Committee was that they should be under the direct orders of the Field–Marshal Command–in–Chief in France for the present, as if they were placed under General Trenchard, there was a possibility that they might be subordinated to the ordinary

operation of the Royal Flying Corps in Flanders. The question was one of many.[43]

To "discuss command of independent aerial operations," the War Cabinet delegated the indefatigable Smuts to see the CIGS and Haig in Paris the next day.[44] However, the Royal Flying Corps had already settled the matter.

After the 41st Wing had begun to fly and in the absence of any timely directives from London, HQ RFC had quietly drawn the Ochey force firmly into its orbit. The need to establish channels to transmit administrative data and operational results made a workable hierarchy imperative. The RFC units arranged their information conduits to conform with military practice. As the War Cabinet had feared, such initiative placed Trenchard at the keystone of the command arch.

Routing of correspondence such as detailed raid reports, submitted immediately after each mission, illustrates the de facto command arrangement between 41st Wing and London. Initially, paperwork passed from Newall at Ochey to Trenchard at HQ RFC and stopped. Trenchard did not forward documents to GHQ at Montreuil until specifically directed to do so by the CIGS. Eventually, this routing included Sir Douglas Haig, who in turn communicated with the CIGS. Only then was the War Cabinet able to enjoy access to materials that 41st Wing had originated. As the ranking authority on military aviation, and as one who enjoyed the confidence of Haig, Trenchard was ideally situated in the hierarchy that supervised long-range bombing.

On 1 November 1917, DH4s from No. 55 Squadron dropped 1,362 pounds of bombs on a munitions factory south of Kaiserslautern.[45] The detailed raid report for this mission was sent from Newall at 41st Wing to Trenchard at HQ RFC in the field on the following day. Upon request from CIGS for raid results, Trenchard's headquarters staff retyped the 41st Wing detailed raid report, appended their own comments, and forwarded the information to GHQ on 4 November. On that same day, the report and Trenchard's letter, plus GHQ's own comments, were sent to the CIGS. Forty-first Wing's detailed raid report on Kaiserslautern, with accretions from intermediate staffs, circulated among the War Cabinet on 6 November, five days after the mission.[46]

All subsequent detailed raid reports followed the same channel to the War Cabinet. HQ RFC customarily transcribed Newall's reports into more presentable formats and occasionally appended its own narratives—and typographical errors.[47] The flow eventually became a routine that kept everyone informed of 41st Wing activities. The chain of command directing strategic bombardment included those who had vigorously opposed its inception and prosecution. They were well placed to influence its objectives.

Trenchard exhibited the disconcerting habit of monopolizing information pertinent to long-range bombing operations. In instances in which he was directed to forward materials, he managed to interpose his command presence through letters and summaries accompanying 41st Wing reports. When Trenchard became responsible for strategic bombardment (as general officer commanding [GOC] of the expanded and renamed Independent Force) in early June 1918, submission of detailed raid reports to the War Cabinet ceased.[48] Thereafter, his staff at IF headquarters collected after-action data from subordinate squadrons and compiled all intelligence returns that reached Whitehall. Personally charged with responsibility for the success of the campaign, he insisted upon retaining a monopoly over its documentation.

Trenchard's refractory attitude toward independent bombing did not change appreciably during the final months of 1917. His philosophy was explicated at length in his view of the probable contributions of American aviation to the war. In his evaluation, he took the opportunity to present a compendium of his canon on airpower. He noted that the bombing of Germany had been projected to begin "as soon as resources permitted, and every preparation has been made to carry out the policy with the greatest vigour."[49] He cautioned, however, that one must not lose sight of priorities in the meantime.

It is essential to remember however that long distance bombing can only be carried out on a sufficient scale if we are able, by pursuing our offensive policy elsewhere, to prevent undue interference with our bombing machines. . . . The completion of the programme of fighting squadrons is therefore of primary importance and nothing should be allowed to interfere with the output of these machines.[50]

Trenchard again stressed that strategic bombing was an aerial luxury to be indulged only after the needs of army cooperation squadrons had been met. Likewise, insofar as American aviation units could be expected to assist, they could do so only after the requirements of Gen John J. Pershing's infantry had been satisfied. Trenchard expected their first priorities to be for "the necessary local work with their own Army."

[However,] as their production increases and in view of the enormous resources they should eventually possess, [they] will be of especial value for bombing operations in GERMANY.[51]

The RFC chief postulated that the American Air Service could eventually take over responsibility for long-range bombing from 41st Wing at Ochey, thus permitting his machines to return to the British sector to operate from bases close to Sir Douglas Haig's forces.

Assuming that the American Army will occupy its present situation in the line, the American aviation will be very favourably placed to bomb German industrial centres in the Upper RHINE Valley and should gradually allow us to withdraw our squadrons from the NANCY neighbourhood to our own Army area whence they should be able to bomb targets in the Lower RHINE Valley and beyond with the machines which should then be available. The advantages of operating from our own Army area are obvious.[52]

Geographical collocation of the strategic bombing force with the British armies would have placed Newall's wing firmly under military control, as opposed to War Cabinet control. Under such an arrangement, Haig's and Trenchard's priorities might well have prevailed. Bombing machines might have been diverted to tactical contingency missions even more often than they in fact were. Trenchard's implicit intentions corroborated the doubts that the War Cabinet had aired at their 2 November meeting.

The RFC chief closed his memorandum with an oblique thrust at Lord Cowdray's "Surplus Air Fleet," and at Smuts.

I would repeat that it is essential to get into touch with the Americans at once and decide upon our future joint production. Policy must in fact guide production instead of production dictating policy.[53]

50

Trenchard continued to protest against what he considered to be a mistaken critical decision, even as he took steps to translate War Cabinet policies into "aeroplanes, aircrew, and aerodromes." Before the end of 1917, he would alter his tactics if not his position, owing to his forced participation in the other organ of the War Cabinet's scheme: the new Air Ministry.

Concurrent with the government's bombing initiative had been the amalgamation of the RFC and the RNAS into a unified fighting service. Trenchard was of course the unanimous choice to become the first-ever Chief of the Air Staff (CAS). He did not want the job, preferring his field command. Sir Douglas Haig argued that he would release his aviation chief only on condition that he also retain his position as GOC of British aviation in France. Whitehall overruled this peculiar proposal and in December ordered Trenchard home to a desk.

Trenchard reluctantly left France to assume his new post. Haig noted that Trenchard confided "the Air Board are quite off their heads as to the future possibilities of Aeronautics for ending the war."[54] Even after he occupied the position of CAS, Trenchard continued to doubt the viability of the new service. He was especially perturbed by the policies of the Secretary of State for the Air Force, Harold Sidney Harmsworth (Lord Rothermere), one of Lloyd George's less enlightened political appointments.

> All this is very sad at a time when officers and men are so badly needed. Trenchard thinks that the Air Service cannot last as an independent Ministry, and that Air Units must again return to the Army and Navy.[55]

Now chief of the Air Staff, Trenchard could hardly criticize policy as Britain's preeminent field authority on airpower. His selection as first CAS trammeled his prestige and integrity to the very organization he now supervised. Despite his views, he had to operate within the bureaucratic confines of the Air Ministry. Trenchard would have to modify his tactics in order to influence the system from within.

Once it became apparent that the War Cabinet intended to persevere in a large-scale aerial offensive, the CAS's strategy was altered. When head of the RFC, so long as his objections could siphon aircraft from independent bombing schemes and into his own units, he had protested to London. To continue on that tack would be futile, in the face of the government's commitment. Further, such obstinacy with regard to policy would diminish his influence. He would need a different dialectical approach to Whitehall; henceforth, he endeavored to make the campaign conform to his own philosophy of bombing.

Indeed, Trenchard found himself consulted by the War Cabinet for his views. In late November, his RFC headquarters in France had prepared a lengthy paper on the issue, "Strategic and Tactical Considerations involved in Long Distance Bombing," which had accompanied Trenchard to the Air Ministry.[56] The CAS-to-be enjoyed some success in impressing his airpower premises upon the government.[57] In January 1918, the Air Policy Committee incorporated parts of his study, virtually verbatim, into their policy statement, "Memorandum on Bombing Operations."[58] This widely circulated memorandum and Trenchard's RFC paper are of considerable significance in understanding the final British plan.

Together, these reports synthesized political and military positions into the broad strategy intended to guide bombing. Trenchard contributed the concepts of continual offensive action and the targeting of German morale. These two factors overshadowed any other considerations and to an extent hindered the formulation of a specific and feasible scheme of operations.

Moral effect, as the 26 November 1917 RFC paper makes clear, represented for Trenchard the foremost consequence of strategic bombing. He considered attacking the enemy's morale to be a "definite military purpose," one that could yield significant or even decisive results.[59] Like the French, he considered reprisals to be separate from this military goal. Unlike them, he linked indirect "moral" effects to the direct "damaging" effects of aerial ordnance. (His Gallic colleagues considered devastation as their sole criterion; German morale was not considered a worthwhile objective.) Trenchard's fusion of moral effects and material results was never seriously challenged by Whitehall, though a few felt he overstated his case.[60]

This union of direct and indirect results, largely attributed to British experiences under the Zeppelins and Gothas, characterized their assumptions about strategic bombing.

Since constant attack would undermine enemy morale, Trenchard's emphasis upon an unrelenting offensive becomes comprehensible. Likewise, as maximum moral effect did not depend upon actually obliterating German industrial centers, one scheme of operations was probably as good as another. These premises supported Trenchard's entire rationale.

> Long distance bombing is an integral part of the offensive aerial work on the Western Front. It is designed to serve a definite military purpose, quite independently of any question of retaliation for what the enemy may do. That purpose is to weaken the power of the enemy both directly and indirectly—directly by interrupting his production, transport and organization through infliction of damage to his industrial, railway and military centres, and by compelling him to draw back his fighting machines to deal with the menace—indirectly by producing discontent and alarm amongst the industrial population. In other words, it aims at achieving both a material and a moral effect.

> Actual experience goes to show that the moral effect of bombing industrial towns may be great, even though the material effect is, in fact, small.[61]

Trenchard asserted that every bomb dropped on German territory would be destructive, directly or indirectly. Later, the Air Ministry would likewise argue that bombing's impact upon morale in many instances compensated for the apparent lack of perceptible results. Moral effect provided a conveniently protean index for the airpower strategist.

On the importance of moral effect and actual damage, Trenchard referred dismissively to the French policy of bombing only accessible, vulnerable targets.

> It must be remembered that a very large portion of the iron ore used by Germany in the war comes from Lorraine and Luxembourg, and therefore the systematic and regular bombing of industrial towns in those areas is calculated to inflict quite a severe material damage on the enemy as reaching even more distant targets. On the other hand, it is essential to be provided with machines which can travel further into enemy territory in order to secure the all important moral results of bombing purely German towns.[62]

At this time, the British authorities were aware of their ally's bombing plan. However, they identified a more ambitious goal—erosion of enemy morale. This concept diminished any chance of cooperation between the British and French bombing wings. To a large degree, the vulnerability of the German population's will would depend upon the scale of the aerial offensive launched against it. Trenchard estimated that 15 squadrons would be available by 31 July 1918, and 31 by the end of October 1918.[63] When units failed to appear, however, British plans did not lessen proportionately.

The CAS-elect stipulated further that a continuous offensive was necessary to realize the highest returns. After naming suitable aeroplanes, competent aircrews, and suitably located aerodromes as prerequisites, he outlined the spirit needed for success. Trenchard emphasized that, "long distance bombing, which has already been carried out as far as our means admitted, ought to be vigorously developed, as part and parcel of the offensive policy of the Royal Flying Corps."[64] He did not dwell upon the high casualty rates that had accompanied this policy in the past.

The Air Policy Committee concurred in the propositions Trenchard had advanced. Their memorandum of January 1918 accepted his assessments and conclusions. However, the Air Policy Committee paper, which incorporated Trenchard's preoccupation with moral effect, ducked the question of method.

> The policy intended to be followed is to attack the important German towns systematically, having regard to weather conditions and the defensive arrangements of the enemy. It is intended to concentrate on one town for successive days and then to pass to several other towns, returning to the first town until the target is thoroughly destroyed, or at any rate until the morale of workmen is so shaken that output is seriously interfered with.[65]

The more than one hundred German cities and towns appended to the memorandum as possible targets underscores the vagueness of the authorities on this point. The committee simply noted that British squadrons should be employed "as far as possible for raids on the industrial towns on and near the Rhine, such as Mannheim and Karlsruhe."[66] When poor weather precluded such penetrations, closer targets in the Briey and Saarbrücken areas could be scheduled. The choice of objectives would be "left to the French so that the closest cooperation is secured between the Allies in this work."[67]

Significantly, civilian authorities concluded their memorandum with a passage lifted in its entirety from the CAS-elect's own study. Their summary consolidated the dual bases of constant offensive and moral effect.

> Long-distance bombing will produce its maximum moral effect only if the visits are constantly repeated at short intervals, so as to produce in each area a sustained anxiety. It is this recurrent bombing, as opposed to isolate and spasmodic attacks, which interrupts industrial production and undermines public confidence.
>
> On the other hand, if the enemy were to succeed in interrupting the continuity of the British bombing operations, their achievements (as the Allies success against Zeppelins show) would be an immense encouragement to them which would operate like a military victory.
>
> The Allies must therefore adopt a programme of bombing operations which, whenever the weather permits, must be constantly kept up and under which it can be assured that the heavy losses, which are bound to occur, can be instantly made good.[68]

With these broadly conceived goals, the British government set requirements above the capabilities of Newall's three squadrons billeted in the autumn mud of eastern France. By formulating grandiose schemes, contingent upon large quantities of suitable machines and crews, the Air Policy Committee quite overlooked the needs of their existing small bombing force. No one ever thought it necessary to determine, in order of priority, the targets to be bombed.

Ironically, British authorities, including Haig and Trenchard, could have enjoyed substantial assistance from the French in this matter. Despite the disbanding of No. 3 Naval Wing in spring 1917, the enthusiasm of the French Air Service for long-range bombing had persisted. With field experience dating from late 1915, the French periodically refined their goals and procedures. Their commanders, doubtless recalling the Admiralty's largesse in supplying Sopwiths and accepting French operational control, seemed eager to aid this latest British scheme.

Since July 1917, two days after the second Gotha daylight raid, British liaison with the French War Ministry had kept Whitehall informed of French bombing policy.[69] Examining the

French program reveals several significant points and insights useful to the British had they but seized upon them.

General De Castelnau, general officer commanding (GOC), GAE (eastern army group), signed the comprehensive "Plan of Bombardment Operations during winter of 1917–1918" on 18 October 1917. Two days later, the British received their copy, complete with map.[70] This document augmented the French statement of 9 July but did not radically depart from earlier plans.

The French air staff still defined objectives and targets on the basis of feasibility, the same criterion that had characterized their direction of the Anglo-French bombing force at Luxeuil from July 1917 to April 1917. Unless targets were both accessible and vulnerable, the French reasoned, attempting to bomb them represented an exercise in futility. French planners accepted that "prevailing weather conditions" and "types of machines actually alloted to all the bombing groups" heavily influenced selection of the overall strategic goal. Such considerations reduced their aerial offensive from the ideal to the attainable: "being the blockading of the Ore Mines and Works of Lorraine and Luxembourg."[71] The French program of October 1917 thus narrowed their earlier strategic assessment, prepared when No. 3 Wing and 4me Groupe de Bombardment had been active. The previous goal of "annihilating" those regions had been downgraded to a "blockading effort."[72] This new aim reflected their straitened circumstances; disbanding No. 3 Wing undoubtedly contributed to the French retrenchment. To isolate these regions and to curtail shipment of raw materials to German industrial centers, French analysts decided to sever key rail links, namely the "large stations and communications in the area METZ-LUXEMBOURG."

This approach also considered the capabilities of machines comprising the French bombing wings. The majority of airplanes in service were Breguets—markedly inferior in speed, range, and payload to the Sopwith 1½ Strutters, as combined operations with No. 3 Wing had demonstrated.[73] British naval aviators had considered the Breguets unsuitable for daylight missions across enemy lines; after their losses on the 12 October 1916 day attack on Oberndorf, the French agreed. They subsequently restricted the Breguets to night operations.[74] At the other performance extreme stood Escadrilles F29 and F123 of the 4me Groupe de Bombardment at Luxeuil. They had inherited from the Admiralty a number of agile Sopwith 1½ Strutter scouts (two-seaters) and bombers (single-seaters) which had escaped the depredations of the RFC.[75] Consequently, these units were employed exclusively on long-range daylight operations.

The French air staff determined target priorities based on their analysis of the most feasible mission and the weather and forces available. Two-thirds of all missions, day or night, were to be directed against the primary objectives of "THIONVILLE and BETTEMBOURG," and the junctions of "LUXEMBOURG and MAIZIERES-les-METZ" comprised the remaining one-third.[76] Cutting the German rail network at those points would virtually isolate the Longwy (northern) and Briey (southern) coal basins. Alternate targets for both day and night units were blast furnaces in the vicinity of each of the primary objectives, highly visible and readily identifiable in marginal weather conditions. These alternate targets correlated very closely with objectives the French had previously assigned No. 3 Wing aircraft. Short-range machines and those unable to reach higher priority objectives could attack rail junctions at Longeville, Courcelles-sur-Neid, Arnaville, and Wavreille as last-chance targets.

Aircrews of 4me Groupe, in Sopwiths with greater range and defensive capabilities, were assigned more challenging duties. Their bombers were to attack iron and steel works in the Briey and Ruhr districts, in addition to those in the Saar region, whenever possible. Their fighting machines were to launch mass raids on enemy aerodromes and railway stations in Alsace, "carefully avoiding the Alsatian towns and villages."[77] In this fashion, the French air staff hoped to take maximum advantage of their high-performance aircraft.

In short, the French tasked their squadrons according to their capabilities. Cutting rail links between the Luxembourg-Lorraine basins and Germany appeared to offer the best chance for success. This operationally feasible goal typified the pragmatic French approach to strategic bombing. Their rationale and detailed plan were shared with the British policy makers in fall 1917.

British response to the French plan of attack against strategic railways was understandably cautious. Because of targeting and range considerations, the newly assembled RFC bombing wing had to be based in the Nancy-Ochey vicinity. This area, miles from the British sector, included No. 3 Wing's forward aerodrome in the French GAE zone. As an isolated detachment, largely dependent upon Allied logistical support, the activities of 41st Wing, RFC, would be vulnerable to French coercion. Two squadrons of 4me Groupe, the bombing unit which had flown alongside No. 3 Wing, already occupied part of the Ochey airfield.[78] To British commanders, who had previously castigated the Admiralty's Luxeuil force as a dissipation of effort, De Castelnau's latest scheme seemed likely to reopen old questions of control and priorities. Neither the government nor Haig was inclined to cooperate with their Gallic ally to the extent which the Admiralty had in July 1916.

As squadrons of the 41st Wing began to arrive at Ochey in October 1917, De Castelnau asked whether the RFC machines could be expected to cooperate in the French plan as opportunities offered. Haig replied that few such occasions were likely to arise. He would, however, direct Colonel Newall, the officer commanding 41st Wing, to contact the French Army Group commander and "to carry out the latter's instructions as regards cooperation within the limits stated above."[79] Haig emphasized to De Castelnau that the mission assigned to the British force diverged considerably from the French concept of operations.

> While the British pilots are learning the country, they will be able to carry out attacks on targets in the Saarbrucken area, but not in the Briey-Longwy area which lies outside the line of approach to their main objectives. As soon as the British pilots have learned the country sufficiently to find their way to the Rhine by night, they will be able to cooperate in attacks on targets in the Briey-Longwy area as well, whenever the weather is not settled enough for long-distance raids into Germany.[80]

En route to their Rhine targets between Cologne and Mannheim, 41st Wing machines from Ochey would overfly the Saarbrücken area. Since no German cities lay within range beyond Briey-Longwy, British bombers at first would have no occasion to hit French-designated rail targets in that region.

The commander in chief of the British Army, in accordance with War Cabinet guidance, reminded his French colleague that the primary mission of 41st Wing was "long-range attacks on German commercial towns as reprisals for enemy air raids on Allied towns."[81] In contrast to France's dedication to a limited aerial blockade, British bombing had been committed to a more ambitious but less clear-cut goal. His reply to De Castelnau leaves little doubt that Haig considered retaliation to be a significant component of the British bombardment plan in October 1917.[82] The Air Policy Committee memorandum of January 1918, which amalgamated War Cabinet and Air Ministry positions, would do little to alter his judgment. As a soldier, Field Marshal Haig was bound by the policies of his civilian superiors. Like Trenchard, he personally did not favor strategic bombing.

The French authorities were concerned that any reprisals be strictly supervised so that they did not generate a vicious cycle of atrocities upon French and Belgian civilians. To preclude this situation, Gen Henri Phillipe Petain suggested three guidelines:

1. to limit our activity exclusively to attacks against hostile aerodromes;
2. to concentrate our efforts against territory which is entirely German (a sensitive issue, owing to enemy occupation of Alsace-Lorraine); and
3. to make it clear that these operations are conducted as reprisals.[83]

Petain did not consider German morale per se to be susceptible in this retaliatory tit-for-tat. He pointed out only that the enemy population must be aware that "Rhenish Bavaria or the Duchy of Baden" would be bombed whenever Dunkirk, Calais, or Boulogne were attacked.[84] This French policy, consistent with earlier directives to No. 3 Wing, emphasized that reprisals represented a special application of airpower.

In his reply to Petain, Haig made it clear that he did not advocate long-range bombing for reprisals or any other purpose. His views duplicated Trenchard's: Offensive support of the land campaign must constitute the sole concern of air forces; diversions such as reprisals diminished their effective-ness in this role. "Success in the air can only be attained by the prosecution of a vigorous offensive at all times."[85] The field marshal remained skeptical of the value of reprisals, even if his government did not.

> The effect which reprisals on German towns in South Germany would have on the German army on the Western Front, and especially on the German army in Flanders, is a factor the value of which has not yet been fully tested. As you know, the principle has been accepted by my Government and British air forces have been detailed for this special purpose.[86]

Even as 41st Wing mustered at Ochey, Haig communicated to Petain that he personally opposed War Cabinet policy. Petain wrote again to Haig on 21 October 1917, still concerned that the campaign, given its retaliatory genesis, might degen-erate into indiscriminate bombing of Germany. French citizens would conceivably suffer, with no compensatory military ad-vantage.

> In order to avoid comparatively slight, and in consequence somewhat ineffective, bombardments of German towns, bombardments which can have no other results than to provoke reprisals on French towns, or at least to furnish a pretext for them, I have given orders to the French bombing Squadrons not to carry out any reprisal bombardment which does not include dropping at least two hundred kilogrammes of projectiles on each objective. Scattered bombing by individual machines is forbidden.

> If you agree with these views, I shall be obliged if you will kindly give similar orders to the British squadrons which have been detached in the Nancy region. [87]

Petain quite naturally attempted to make his British Allies aware of the predicament that their undertaking might cause.

Haig's prompt response reassured the French commander. He promised that he would direct 41st Wing to conduct their missions within the constraints that the French had imposed upon their own aircrews.

> I agree with you in principle that our aerial operations should be directed with the sole aim of delivering frequent and heavy attacks on aerial objectives, and that isolated and weak attacks are unsound quite apart from the questions of provoking reprisals.

60

My instructions to the British air squadrons are to avoid promiscuous bombing and to attack selected military objectives only. As regards the scope of these attacks, I have laid down that never less than 6 machines shall be detailed either by day or night to attack any given objective. Owing to technical considerations I do not consider it advisable to lay down a minimum weight of bombs to be dropped, but I am satisfied that the result of my instructions will be the correct application of the principle on which we both agreed.[88]

Haig forwarded his correspondence with Petain to the CIGS at the War Office on 26 October 1917. British policy makers and commanders on both sides of the channel enjoyed access to French plans even as they developed their own bombing program.

However, the prospects for a coordinated campaign remained dim during the winter of 1917–18. Fundamental differences of purpose divided the French plan from British perceptions about independent strategic bombardment.

In this respect, Haig's convictions were congruent with French doctrine: Both assessed bombing's effectiveness on the basis of its military results; considerations of moral effect seemed irrelevant. Reprisals, a special category, could easily backlash if not carefully managed. By contrast, the British government placed considerable faith in aerial assaults on German civilian morale, attacks to be mounted partially in response to enemy raids and partially to cripple German war industry. These ambitious aims, direct and indirect, would require a huge independent aerial fleet and a new military air ministry to supervise it. Neither existed.

Trenchard, first GOC RFC and then CAS-elect during all this, favored Haig's outlook, although he was charged with responsibility for the British bombing effort's success. His influence led to the Air Policy Committee memorandum of January 1918, which stipulated that the British Campaign would be prosecuted by rigorous offensive action. Overall, inspiration rather than deliberation characterized the British outlook. With such a stance, neither politicians nor generals evinced much enthusiasm for the French plan, even as a point of departure for their own hypothesis.

Undaunted by British demurrals, the French pursued their own bombing policies. They updated their scheme of blockade

61

on 18 November 1917 and 5 January 1918, in response to changes in the pattern of German rail traffic. (They dutifully transmitted these revisions to their British counterparts.)[89] These documents provided lists of alternate targets, a useful service during the deteriorating weather conditions of the winter of 1917–18. As such, these revisions provided a possible basis for coordinated bombing, as Haig and De Castelnau had agreed upon in 1917.

In the 18 November update, emphasizing that it was a "result of evolution during action, rather than a strategic plan," French analysts listed nine rail stations as specific targets.[90] From the Saarbrücken and Lorraine basins, Germany obtained roughly 80 percent of the iron ore for her wartime industrial output; 40 to 50 percent was smelted locally.[91] Daily, over ten thousand rail cars moved between the basins and German works on the right bank of the Moselle, on the Rhine, and in Westphalia.[92]

To curtail this traffic, the French air service designated nine targets:

Luxembourg	Athus	Woippy
Petange	Longuyon	Thionville
Rodange	Conflans-Jarny	Bettembourg[93]

All lay on the periphery of the Briey and Longwy iron areas; not one was more than 45 miles behind the lines. Three had already appeared on the October 1917 list as primary targets (Luxembourg, Thionville, and Bettembourg). As Haig had acknowledged to De Castelnau, 41st Wing could attack these objectives whenever weather precluded long-range missions to the Rhine towns. These nine rail targets, pivotal to the French plan, made ideal short-range objectives.

The British squadrons, however, despite worsening weather, persisted in efforts to reach Germany during the last quarter of 1917. Of 18 raids attempted during this period, six were canceled due to weather and a seventh had to divert to another target (No. 55 Squadron, 5 December 1917, from Kaiserslautern to Zweibrücken and Saarbrücken).[94] Just one of the 12 missions that were completed ranged as far afield as the Rhine valley. On 1 November, six DH4s (of 12 launched) managed to reach a munitions factory south of Kaiserslautern, a town that was 80 miles from their base but 30 miles short of Ludwigshafen and Karlsruhe.[95] On Christmas Eve 1917, 10 machines (of 12 launched) finally reached Ludwigshafen, dropping 2,252 pounds of bombs on the Heinrich Lanz works, the Badische Anilin und Soda Fabrik (BASF), and the railway station. Difficult weather conditions stymied British intentions during the winter of 1917–1918. Forty-first Wing did not elect to cooperate with the French in the interim.

The first 41st Wing attack on a target on the French list occurred by accident the evening of 3/4 January 1918, when 10 FE2bs of No. 100 Squadron were assigned the blast furnaces at Maizieres-les-Metz as their objective. Only two machines bombed their target. Five aircraft aborted the mission due to extreme cold. Three pilots in the five-ship formation became disoriented en route; they bombed Woippy, just north of Metz, and a rail junction south of Metz (probably Saint-Privat). Woippy, one of the French objectives, lies between Metz and No. 100's primary target, Maizieres. Postraid reports noted that the Moselle River was frozen and snowed over, depriving aircrews of a major navigational aid on a "dark and hazy night with no moon." More bombs fell on Woippy and Saint-Privat (760 pounds) than on Maizieres (430 pounds). This mission typified No. 100 Squadron's night operations. During the first four months of its work with 41st Wing, its

This FE2c was forced down after suffering battle damage over Metz. The FE2c was virtually identical in appearance to the FE2b.

machines never were able to concentrate their payloads against a single target on any mission. War Cabinet directives and Haig's reassurances to Petain proved to be operationally unrealizable.

From a tactical perspective, the 3/4 January 1918 Maizieres mission was unremarkable. From a strategic viewpoint, 41st Wing ignored a rail station (Woippy) the French had designated six weeks previously as one of their key objectives, and picked another target just five miles away. That Woippy was hit was entirely fortuitous.

On the following evening, eight FE2bs from No. 100 Squadron were again assigned Maizieres as their main target. Again, four machines overflew Woippy to reach their objective. Another aircraft claimed hits on Woippy's railway station. Altogether, the eight FE2bs scattered bombs along 25 miles of railways, from Courcelles-sur-Neid to Maizieres-les-Metz, that night.

These two incidents typify the 41st Wing's low degree of interest in the French bombing plan. Prevented by adverse weather from attacking the Rhine towns, British crews flew past targets that their ally considered important. When short-range objectives were assigned by 41st Wing, they were likewise often located adjacent to targets on the French list. Under such conditions during their first three months of operations, the British bombed targets in the Longwy and Briey basins according to no perceptible scheme of priorities. At this stage, the 41st Wing had developed no criteria to direct its activities on those frequent occasions when poor weather kept them from the Rhine valley. Unlike No. 3 Wing, they preferred to operate autonomously rather than cooperate with the French air service.

The French revision of 5 January 1918 could have been of considerable intelligence value to 41st Wing, whether or not they persisted in operating independently. This update pointed to change effected by the enemy that lent "a different aspect to the relative importance of the various centres of traffic congestion hitherto announced."[96] French analysts now considered it necessary to bomb just four rail targets "indispensable to a successful blockade of the ferriferous watershed: BETTEMBOURG—THIONVILLE, PETANGE, ATHUS."[97] (These points lie along the northern and eastern boundaries of the Longwy area.) They concluded that the Germans had altered their rail networks for two reasons:

1. to strip the area "without using and consequently without burdening the main arteries of supply to the front" and
2. to use "the shortest possible route, in view of the shortage of rolling stock (locomotives and wagons), and in order to economize pit coal."[98]

The French consequently traced "two independent traffic systems, the one economic, the other strategic," within the enemy railway complex. From a careful study of the former system, adjudged more vulnerable, they selected their four bombing targets. German logistical reorganization in fact simplified the tasks facing the French. The British force could have reaped the same benefits.

Of more immediate concern was the information about German countermeasures contained in the second part of the French paper. The French documented significant changes in the activity of smelters in occupied territory: Lorraine foundries "are in full blast"; in the hitherto productive area of Longwy and Briey, they "have been shut down" and facilities razed or shipped to Germany.[99] In Briey, to confuse Allied bombers, iron works "are brilliantly illuminated every night in order to create an impression of activity." The enemy could have spared themselves time and effort spent on these decoys, so far as 41st Wing night operations were concerned. Neither No. 100 (FE2b) nor Naval "A" (Handley Page) Squadrons bombed them before 6 June 1918, when the Independent Force took over responsibility for bombing. As the overwhelming percentage of targets for night missions was railways, 41st Wing reaction to the French intelligence may have been more accidental than deliberate.

What is clear is that the French air staff developed their bombing policies early in 1916—before the No. 3 Wing era—and thereafter adhered to them, with periodic modifications, whether British authorities chose to cooperate or not. When, with Admiralty approval in July 1916, the French took operational control of No. 3 Wing, this subordination made possible a coordinated plan of attack. Unity of command led to joint missions, with day and night raids on the same objective on several occasions. However, from the British point of view the price for this success was French direction of the Admiralty's bombing squadrons. At the time, strategic bombing detachments were the subject of an internecine Whitehall controversy between the War Office and the Admiralty staffs.

In the urgency and emotion precipitated by the Gotha raids in summer and fall of 1917, British subordination to French views, however well intentioned, seemed politically inexpedient and militarily unpalatable. The British force, just 41st Wing in 1917 but with expansive ambitions, thus tended to ignore or minimize opportunities to cooperate with the French. British command authorities in London, preoccupied with the potential of independent airpower, approved this field attitude. In distancing themselves from their ally, the British unfortunately deprived themselves of the benefits a closer relationship might have yielded. In point of fact, the rationale for the two bombing programs demonstrates that they could have been complementary.

It seems significant that most historians of British strategic bombardment in the Great War have underestimated or oversimplified French bombing policy and its potential utility to 41st Wing. The official history describes just one phase of the French plan—the 18 November 1917 plan, which enumerated nine rail targets—without summarizing its antecedents or subsequent revisions.[100] Such oversimplification creates the impression that French aerial bombing policy was shortsighted and preoccupied solely with tactical aspects. H. A. Jones fails to examine the extent to which 41st Wing could have participated effectively in a ready-made joint bombing scheme during the winter of 1917–18. He does not comment on these lost opportunities. Instead, he leaves the reader with the mistaken conclusion that 41st Wing worked closely with the French when selecting and attacking short-range targets. That British aviators were unable to comply with the provisions of Haig's reply to De Castelnau or the Air Policy Committee's directives in this regard also eludes the scope of Jones's narrative.

Neville Jones, writing in 1973, perpetuates these impressions—primarily because he relies upon H. A. Jones' *War in the Air*. In summarizing 41st Wing's activities, Neville Jones repeats the former Jones's mistaken assertions of close inter-Allied coordination.

> The raids were not based on any bombing programme, and this is hardly surprising, since the majority of the targets it was desired to attack were not at that time operationally feasible. As a result, the choice of targets during the winter of 1917–1918 was for the most part left to the French whose bombing plan concentrated on objectives which were at short range from the Nancy base.[101]

Neither Jones places French bombing policy in its proper context vis-à-vis British plans. Nor do they analyze the significance of the Haig-Petain correspondence on reprisals and concentration of force and the consequent operational directives to 41st Wing. It is now time, having examined plans, to determine how 41st Wing fared in actuality.

Notes

1. Neville Jones, *The Origins of Strategic Bombing: A Study of the Development of British Air Strategic Thought and Practice up to 1918* (London: Eimber, 1973), 124–25, 127.
2. Malcolm Cooper, "British Air Policy on the Western Front, 1914–1918" (PhD diss., Oxford University, 1982), 245.
3. Trenchard Papers, Army Council Memorandum, November 1916, Royal Air Force Museum (RAFM), Hendon, England.
4. Public Records Office (PRO), Air Ministry Records (AIR) 1/711/27/13/2214, trans. of German Accounts of Strategic Bombing; and Raymond H. Fredette, *The Sky on Fire: The First Battle of Britain 1917–1918 and the Birth of the Royal Air Force* (New York: Holt, Rinehart, and Winston, 1966), 262–65.
5. Fredette, 262–65.
6. Ibid.
7. Barry D. Powers, *Strategy without Slide-Rule: British Air Strategy, 1914–1939* (London: Groom Helm, 1976), 95.
8. A. Noble Frankland, *The Bombing Offensive Against Germany: Outlines and Perspectives* (London: Faber and Faber, 1965), 27; H. A. Jones, *War in the Air, Being the Story of the Part Played in the Great War by the Royal Air Force*, 6 vols. (Oxford: Clarendon Press, 1937), vol. 5, 88, 90–91 and vol. 6, 122–23; Powers, 99–101; Neville Jones, *The Origins of Strategic Bombing*, 138; and J. M. Spaight, *The Beginnings of Organised Air Power* (London: Longmans, Green and Co., 1927), 126–30.

9. Andrew P. Boyle, *Trenchard* (London: Collins, 1962), 222.

10. Ibid.

11. Trenchard to War Cabinet, 20 June 1917 in Boyle, *Trenchard*, 222.

12. PRO, Cabinet Office Records (CAB) 23/3, War Cabinet 178.

13. Ibid., 181–83.

14. PRO, AIR 9/69, Smuts, First Report of the Committee on Air Organisation and Home Defence against Air Raids, 19 July 1917. This PRO file also contains his Second Report of 17 August 1917, which was reprinted in H.A. Jones, *War in the Air*, Appendix ii, 8–14.

15. Cooper, 246.

16. Paul Guinn, *British Strategy and Politics, 1914–1918* (Oxford: Clarendon Press, 1965), 249–51, summarizes the War Cabinet's "an intermittent support for Haig's planned offensive."

17. H. A. Jones, *War in the Air*, Appendix i, 1–8.

18. Science Museum, A.9 (Pearson Papers), "The Duties and Functions of the Air Board," 28 July 1917 in Cooper, "British Air Policy," 248.

19. PRO, AIR 8/2, pt. II, Air Board to War Cabinet, 17 April 1917; AIR 6/6, Air Board Minutes for March 1917, lists the practical difficulties of metallurgy design and manufacture that curtailed production of aerial resources.

20. PRO, AIR 9/69, Smuts, "Second Report," 17 August 1917.

21. PRO, CAB 23/4, War Cabinet 223–12.

22. Frankland, 16.

23. Spaight, 128.

24. Ibid., 126–17. For a contemporary analysis of the effects of the Gotha raids upon the British public, see The *"Manchester Guardian" History of the War*, 9 vols. (London: John Heywood, 1914–1920), vii, 315–20; W. O. D. Pierce, *Air War: Its Technical and Social Aspects* (London: Waltz, 1937), 66, also discusses the public demand to retaliate on the Rhineland towns; and N. Jones, *The Origins of Strategic Bombing*, 133–34, details the opprobrium visited upon those who refused to condemn the German aerial offensive.

25. Spaight, 127.

26. Edmund Dane, *The War Budget: A Photographic Record of the Great War* (London: 1917), 268–69.

27. Ibid., 268.

28. PRO, AIR 1/522/16/12/5, War Office to Haig, 18 August 1917.

29. H. A. Jones, *War in the Air*, vol. 5, 89–90.

30. Ibid., 90.

31. Trenchard's cross-channel flight of three R.E.8 planes in bad weather on 2 October caused air raid alarms to be raised; business in London was delayed several hours. See Boyle, *Trenchard*, 234–35.

32. H. A. Jones, *War in the Air*, vol. 5, 90.

33. Ibid., vol. 6, 123.

34. PRO, CAB 23/4, War Cabinet, 242–44.

35. H. A. Jones, *War in the Air*, vol. 5, 90.

36. PRO, AIR 1/678/21/13/2102, War Cabinet, 15 October 1917.

37. War Diary of Eighth Brigade, Royal Flying Corps, 11 October 1917–31 January 1919, entry for 17 October 1917, Newall Papers, RAFM, Hendon, England.

38. Robert Blake, ed., *The Private Papers of Douglas Haig 1914–1919: Being Selections from the Private Diary and Correspondence of Field-Marshal the Earl Haig of Bemersyde* (London: Eyre & Spottiswoode, 1952), 252.

39. PRO, AIR 1/1649/204/95/6, Robertson, CIGS, War Office, to Haig, letter, 27 October 1917.

40. Ibid.; Trenchard, Advisor HQ, RFC, to Newall, Operations Commander, 41st Wing, letter, 30 October 1917, Trenchard Papers, RAFM, Hendon, England.

41. PRO, AIR 1/1649/204/95/6; Letter from Trenchard, 30 October 1917; and Trenchard to Newall, letter, CRFC 1721/9/30.G, 29 October 1917.

42. PRO, AIR 1/678/21/13/2102, Air Policy Committee, 30 October 1917.

43. PRO, AIR 1/2266/209/70/25, "Extract from minutes of a meeting of the War Cabinet held at 10 Downing Street, S.W., on Friday November 2, 1917, at 8 p.m."

44. Ibid.

45. War Diary of Eighth Brigade, entry for 1 November 1917.

46. PRO, AIR 1/2266/209/70/26, File, "Reports of Bombing Operations at Ochey Squadrons, Nancy area (41st Wing and 8th Brigade), November 1917 to June 1918, including Summary of Operations by RFC, Western Front, for months of October and November 1917 (for the information of the War Cabinet)"; Correspondence on Kaiserslautern raid, 1 November 1917.

47. Ibid. For typical added narrative, see Trenchard's typed comments on the 11 December 1917 Pirmasens Raid Report; for typographical errors, signature block on transcribed raid report dated 21/22 January 1918 ("C. L. N. Newall" rendered as "C. S. Alendale").

48. Final detailed raid report is dated 26 June 1918.

49. PRO, AIR 1/725/97/6, "A Short Review of the Situation in the Air on the Western Front and a Consideration of the Part to be Played by the American Aviation," Trenchard to War Cabinet (n.d., probably late 1917).

50. Ibid.

51. Ibid.

52. Ibid.

53. PRO, AIR 1/725/97/6.

54. Blake, Haig, 273; For Sir Douglas Haig's detailed objections to Smuts' proposals, see H. A. Jones, *War in the Air*, Appendix 3, "Sir Douglas Haig's Views on a Separate Air Service," 15 September 1917, 14–18.

55. Ibid., 280.

56. PRO, AIR 1/725/97/7, "Strategic and Tactical Considerations Involved in Long Distance Bombing," Trenchard to War Cabinet, 26 November 1917.

57. N. Jones, *The Origins of Strategic Bombing*, 162.

58. PRO, AIR 1/463/15/312/137, Air Policy Committee, "Memorandum on Bombing Operations," January 1918. Reprinted in H. A. Jones, *War in the Air*, Appendix 6, 24–26.

59. PRO, AIR 1/725/97/7, Trenchard to War Cabinet, 26 November 1917.

60. For Churchill's view of the effects of bombs on civilian morale, see Sir Charles Webster and Noble Frankland, *The Strategic Air Offensive against Germany 1939–1945*, 4 vols. (London: Her Majesty's Stationery Office [HMSO], 1961), vol. 1, *Preparation*, 47.

61. PRO, AIR 1/725/97/7, Trenchard to War Cabinet, 26 November 1917.

62. Ibid.

63. H. A. Jones, *War in the Air*, Appendix 5; Trenchard to Prime Minister, 13 January 1918, Trenchard Papers, RAFM, Hendon, England.

64. AIR 1/725/97/7, Trenchard to War Cabinet, 26 November 1917.

65. PRO, AIR 1/463/15/312/137, Air Policy Committee, January 1918.

66. Ibid.

67. Ibid.

68. AIR 1/463/15/312/137; Trenchard's paper to the War Cabinet, par. 8, 26 November 1917, Trenchard Papers, RAFM, Hendon, England.

69. AIR 1/2266/209/70/22, Lt Col E. L. Spiers (Paris) to CIGS, cipher telegram, subject: Reprisals for Bombing Raids by the French, July 1917.

70. PRO, AIR 1/2266/209/70/23, "Plan of Attack against Mining District of _____, October 1917," containing the French plan, was sent to Haig at Montreuil by Petain in October 1917. It was subsequently forwarded by Spiers (Paris) to Maj Gen F. Maurice, director of Military Operations (DMO), at the War Office on 20 October 1917. Maurice's reply to Spiers on 31 October states that Trenchard was explicitly tasked to study and comment upon the French program.

71. PRO, AIR 1/1976/204/273/40 (IF "I" 4/30, HQ, IAF), "Plan of Bombardment Operations during Winter of 1917–1918," signed by GOC, GAE, 18 October 1917. De Castelnau states that the concept "was fixed by the G.O.C. in C. on the 17th of July 1917." Map in same file dated 13 March 1917.

72. AIR 1/1976/204/273/39 (IF "I" 4/28), "History of the Evolution of the Plan of Bombardment by Aeroplanes," French General Staff, 18 November 1917. This file also contains a translation of the same plan by the Technical Division, US Air Service, dated 3 December 1917, "Account of the Aviation Plan of Bombardment by Airplanes."

73. Kenneth Munson, *Bombers, 1914–1919* (London, 1968), 98–99.

74. PRO, AIR 2/123 Capt W.L. Elder, RN, to Air Board, subject: Report on Raid by British and French Airmen on Oberndorf, 25 October 1916.

75. Bruce Robertson, *Sopwith—The Man and His Aircraft* (Bedford: Sidney Press, 1970), 81–82.

76. PRO, AIR 1/1976/204/273/40, French Plan of Bombardment, 18 October 1917.

77. Ibid.

78. H. A. Jones, *War in the Air*, vol. 6, 124.

79. Ibid.

80. Ibid.

81. Ibid.

82. Ibid., 125–26, the official historian's rationalization that Haig spoke of reprisals "in a popular and not a legal sense."

83. PRO, AIR 1/2266/209/70/24, Petain to Haig, letter no. 20919, subject: Bombing behind German Lines—Views of Sir D. Haig and Gen. Petain, 20 September 1917.

84. Ibid.

85. AIR 1/2266/209/70/24, Haig to Petain, letter no. OB/1837/1, 15 October 1917.

86. Ibid.

87. Ibid.; and Petain to Haig, letter no. 24068, 21 October 1917.

88. AIR 1/2266/209/70/24, Haig to Petain, letter no. OAD 644/1, 24 October 1917.

89. AIR 1/1976/203/273/39, "Account of the Aviation Plan of Bombardment by Airplanes," French General Staff, 18 November 1917 (trans. Technical Division, U.S. Air Service, 3 December 1917); and AIR 1/1976/204/273/40, "Minute on the Blockade of the Ferriferous Watershed of Luxembourg-Lorraine," 5 January 1918. Latter revision contained in HQ, IF file "I.F. 'I' 4/30," "Bomb Targets: French Bombing Policy, October 1917–January 1918."

90. AIR 1/1976/204/273/39, French Bombing Plan, 18 November 1917.

91. Ibid.

92. Ibid.

93. Ibid.

94. No reliable comprehensive operational summary exists for 41st Wing activities. Information must be compiled from a number of sources: RAF Hendon, B392 (Newall Papers); War Diary of Eighth Brigade; B393 (Newall Papers); Detailed Raid Reports submitted by Eighth Brigade RFC/RAF to Independent Force Headquarters on Bombing Operations, October 1917–June 1918. Some of the latter are also in PRO, AIR 1/2266/209/70/26, "Reportsof Bombing Operations of Ochey Squadrons." See also AIR 1/1976/204/273/111, Intelligence Reports of Raids before 15th June 1918; Maj H. W. M. Paul (41st Wing, RFC) to Air Ministry; and AIR 1/2085/207/5/3, Approximate Results, 41st Wing, RAF, 17 October 1917-11 November 1918.

95. Distances computed from tactical pilotage charts (TPC) E-2C and E-2D (1:500,000), Director of Military Survey of Ministry of Defence, United Kingdom, HMSO, 1979.

96. AIR 1/1976/204/273/40, French Bombing Plan, 5 January 1918.

97. Ibid.
98. Ibid.
99. Ibid., French Bombing Plan, 5 January 1918.
100. H. A. Jones, *War in the Air*, vol. 6, 124–25.
101. N. Jones, *The Origins of Strategic Bombing*, 150

Chapter 3

41st Wing
Royal Flying Corps
(June 1917–January 1918)

The activities of 41st Wing, RFC, between October 1917 and January 1918 were governed by the War Cabinet's double mandate: to prepare aerodromes and bomb Germany. The former mission, more prosaic than operational, deserves explication—not only because of its contemporary importance but also because it has not been examined as a proper component of the British program. In particular, as with formulation of strategic plans, the French contribution has been ignored and denigrated.

The official history has again established the standard. Subsequent studies have accepted H. A. Jones' version of airfield construction difficulties in the French sector. His narrative relied heavily upon Trenchard's final dispatch of 1 January 1919 and a retrospective interview granted by the retired Chief of Air Staff in April 1934. However, other records and accounts from the period tend to contradict Jones' conclusions. It now seems questionable that Trenchard faced an Augean task in erecting aerodromes on inhospitable terrain ceded by the French only after protracted negotiations.

In August 1917, prompt construction of airfields to house Smuts's and Cowdray's bombing fleet indeed seemed critical. Charged with building aerodromes for 10 long-range bombing squadrons by the end of August 1918, Haig opened discussions with the French in June 1917.[1] During summer and fall of 1917, Trenchard, as GOC of the Royal Flying Corps, had reconnoitered possible sites in the zone of General De Castelnau's Eastern Army Group.[2] In November 1917, after these personal surveys, he informed the Air Policy Committee that the French hesitated to provide support because they "were strongly opposed" to their Ally's plan to bomb German cities.[3] The official history notes that he later informed the Air Council in 1918 that "there were grave difficulties in the way of obtaining aerodrome accommodation."[4] In 1973, Neville Jones, echoing this verdict, agreed that securing a British base of operations at Ochey required "difficult and protracted negotiations" with the French.[5] He further observed that Trenchard confided to H. A. Jones in 1934 that "the French had put every difficulty in the way."[6] These allegations deserve further scrutiny.

Neville Jones, with Trenchard's biographer, A. P. Boyle, attributes French opposition mainly to the effects of the mutinies following the Nivelle offensive begun 16 April 1917.[7] Jones asserts that disaffection, involving over half the French army, also depressed civilian morale. French cities thus would have been susceptible to the shock of German air raids as reprisals for 41st Wing attacks. Certainly Petain, who succeeded Robert-Georges Nivelle on 15 May, realized that his nation could not sustain a prolonged offensive until confidence and discipline had been restored. As Cyril Falls recorded, although 119 cases of "collective indiscipline" were distributed among 54 French divisions, mainly between 25 May and 10 June, only 55 mutineers were ever shot.[8] Trenchard well may have encountered a few localized examples of French military disintegration during his site surveys around Nancy and Ochey.

That his testimony before the Air Policy Committee in late November should contradict the consensus reached by Haig and Petain the month before is even more puzzling. Their correspondence reveals that the two commanders reached virtually complete accord on policies, especially for reprisals, before Trenchard left France for the Air Ministry. Given Trenchard's cordial working relationship with Sir Douglas Haig, he would have been privy to this exchange. It is therefore difficult to accept his views, either by contemporary documentation or through the speculations of later historians.

Similarly, the persistent notion that French authorities contributed little toward the success of British bombing seems mistaken. Neville Jones, again taking his lead from the official history, has concluded that the French "were prepared to give no more than the minimum of assistance, and even that was given reluctantly."[9] Surviving records do not fully justify this verdict. In his final dispatch after the Armistice, Trenchard himself praised De Castelnau and his GAE staff "for the very valuable assistance" they had rendered to the British bombing force.[10] The euphoria of victory might conceivably account for such magnanimity; however, French aid to Newall's 41st Wing merited such praise.

In autumn and winter of 1917, the French had readily agreed to support the 41st Wing operation to the maximum extent possible. In October 1917, a British liaison officer inspected the sites of proposed aerodrome areas and spoke with the local French commander about the possibilities of French cooperation. In his report to HQ RFC, the officer assured Trenchard that the French commander "gave us to understand that every facility would be given and that the French would do all they possibly can to help us."[11] Specifically, the French agreed to

- a) arrange for hiring agricultural instruments and horses for airfield levelling;
- b) make available "any ground required . . . on our behalf" through appropriate administrative action;
- c) provide their own vehicles for transport, up to a maximum of thirty lorries;
- d) issue French rations to working parties; and
- e) arrange for suitable billets for working parties.[12]

Furthermore, wrote the RFC liaison, the French "had no objection to Black labour" battalions for airfield work. Given this response to British requests, French aid to 41st Wing has been belittled in retrospect. In fact, the French continued to render considerable logistical assistance throughout the British program of expansion.

On the British side, building aerodromes often absorbed more attention than monitoring 41st Wing's missions. While RFC chief, Trenchard, accompanied by Maurice Baring and a French liaison officer, visited Newall's base area between 8 and 10 November.[13] His itinerary included, besides the usual briefings with squadron commanders and officer aircrew, tours of the sites for the aircraft depot at Rambervillers and the Azelot aerodrome.[14] Three Bengal Indian labor companies, approximately twelve hundred men, had been engaged in construction at these locations since the latter part of October.[15]

75

Trenchard's subsequent report to Haig described the "stupen-
dous" work necessary in the 41st Wing area to house 12
squadrons at Xaffevillers and Azelot.[16]

With an eye to the future bombing fleet of Smuts and Cowdray, the GOC RFC asked that "formal application be made"
for three more airfield sites. Though Gen Maurice Duval, chief
of French Aviation, had tentatively allocated sites near Orton-
court, St. Reminont, and Bettoncourt to the US Air Service,
work had not yet begun. As the bulk of the American squadrons were to be emplaced west of the 41st Wing rear area,
southwest of Toul, the French promptly acceded to Trenchard's request.[17] Two weeks later, another twelve hundred
Indian laborers of the 58th, 72nd, and 75th Companies arrived; on 4 December 1917, Colonel Dixie of the Royal Engi-
neers and Colonel Harrison of the Works Directorate arrived to
supervise aerodrome construction.[18] Throughout November
and December 1917, frequent visits from observers attached
to London or Montreuil kept authorities abreast of developments.[19] By the end of the year, Colonel Newall's three operational squadrons were overshadowed and outnumbered five-
to-one by the rank-heavy labor organization dedicated to
housing the future might of British strategic bombing.

Throughout December 1917, aerodrome construction remained a matter of urgency owing to War Cabinet preoccupation with forecasts of increased aircraft production. These inflated predictions complicated the supporting plans of British
ground and air commanders in the field.

At this time, Trenchard summarized his proposals for airfield expansion for Haig, outlining his current situation and
the units scheduled to arrive throughout 1918. Already in
place were two night-bombing squadrons, No. 100 (FE2b) and
Naval "A" (Handley Page); they shared the spacious French
aerodrome at Ochey with components of De Castelnau's
bombing force.[20] The sole day unit, No. 55 (DH4) was in the
process of moving from Ochey to a new field at Tantonville,
with well-camouflaged hangars recessed into surrounding
woodland. As a member of No. 55 observed, "The aerodrome
was loaned from the French, and the work on it had all been
done by comic little stock French colonial troops from Cochin

China."[21] (In fact, the French provided all the necessary accommodations and facilities to support the British bombing campaign during 1917, including Newall's headquarters building in Bainville-sur-Madon.)

By summer 1918, Trenchard had been warned to expect a force comprising 25 line squadrons, plus support agencies that would include five Wing headquarters, one Brigade headquarters, and two aircraft replacement parks. The War Cabinet planned for seven DH4 day squadrons and two Handley Page night squadrons to be active by April 1918, with an increase thereafter of five squadrons monthly.[22] In anticipation, Trenchard requested even more Indian labor units to augment twenty-five hundred workers already employed.

Just three weeks later, on 26 December 1917, he revised this scheme in view of the latest pronouncements from the Air Council. In addition to the 25 squadrons forecast earlier, he was to expect 15 more squadrons by June 1918 and another 15-squadron increment no later than August.[23] Confronted with ever-increasing projections of aircraft, military commanders adjusted priorities accordingly. At times, construction took precedence over flying. American records provide a perspective on this climate of uncertain cooperation between British and French.

At the end of 1917, the newly arrived Americans entertained hopes of instituting their own bombardment plan for the air service accompanying the American Expeditionary Force (AEF). In early December, to expedite this program, Chief of US Air Service Brig Gen Benjamin D. Foulois delegated newly promoted Lt Col Edgar S. Gorrell to coordinate with Allied air commanders.[24] Gorrell, the energetic "Head of Strategical Aviation, Zone of Advance, A.E.F.," was eager to develop his program from the best of the Allies' plans. His summary of British and French attitudes illuminates their several points of variance.[25]

It appears that personality clashes aggravated fundamental differences in bombing philosophies. At the aviation conference held at French General Headquarters (GHQ) on 22 December 1917, Trenchard's uncompromising tone made it clear that joint cooperation was not his major goal.

> At this meeting General Trenchard told that he had been ordered by his Government to establish a force of bombardment aviation in the vicinity of Germany, that whether or not the Allies intended to join with him in this work did not affect whether or not he continued such work, and that he intended to increase the size of his force and to push this work to the maximum extent in compliance with the orders of his Government on this subject.[26]

General Duval, commanding the French Air Service in the field, replied, "it did not pay to heterogeneously bombard enemy industrial centres."[27] Duval pointed out that German bombardment of Allied towns "was a much easier task" than the converse; here he echoed the same fear of enemy reprisals that Petain had expressed to Haig two months before. The French air chief also emphasized that the British plan was not feasible. Firstly, neither ally had sufficient material to conduct an effective campaign of strategic bombing. Secondly, "the use of bombardment aviation as contemplated by the British did not agree with French tactical plans." He concluded with the warning that "the French do not expect to join this operation."

On paper, the respective bombardment programs appeared to be commensurate. As Haig had explained to De Castelnau, British bombers eventually could be expected to attack targets on the French list. However, the divergent attitudes that characterized the 22 December conference made even limited cooperation unlikely. One would even expect hitherto cordial relations between Newall's 41st Wing and the French to deteriorate, following disagreements of their chiefs.

The relationship between the British and American air chiefs on this question is also enlightening. Although the French had demurred at the Compiègne meeting, Colonel Gorrell reacted tentatively but affirmatively to the British statement.

> The American representative stated that it was the intention of the United States to also undertake this work along the lines now being commenced by the British but that he could not pledge the United States or the AEF to such a procedure for the reason that decision on that subject lay with GHQ, AEF.[28]

At that time, Trenchard hoped to incorporate American units into the force to be expanded from 41st Wing. During the Christmas holidays, 1917, General Foulois and Colonel

Gorrell visited Headquarters Royal Flying Corps (HQ RFC) in the field, to discuss this matter. Lacking both training and maintenance facilities, the Americans readily accepted Trenchard's proposal to billet their squadrons at aerodromes occupied by seasoned British units. The combination of squadrons would be commanded by a British officer, though Americans would take back control of their aviators once their force outnumbered the RFC in the area.[29] Since the American rate of growth remained disappointingly low until the Armistice, this agreement mainly affected individuals rather than squadrons. On this diminished scale, it was mutually satisfactory.[30]

Later, in June 1918, this happy state of affairs disintegrated. As Gorrell observed, Allied cooperation was a two-edged sword.

> Later, approximately the summer of 1918, the British Bombardment Forces in the vicinity of Nancy were separated from the Royal Air Force in the Field and placed under the command of General Trenchard who would honor the orders of no one except the British Air Ministry. General Trenchard received no orders and would acknowledge no superior in the Field, not even Marshal Foch, who we supposed to command the Allied forces on the Western Front.[31]

On 18 June 1918, the AEF Chief of Staff decided that the US Air Service could no longer assist the British bombing campaign. Henceforth the Americans would support the coordinated plan promulgated by Foch as commander in chief. In the case of the United States as well as of France, British intransigence did much to alienate an initially cooperative ally. These and similar incidents make Trenchard's remarks to the official historian at their 1934 interview more intelligible. In late 1917, Trenchard, the man responsible for the success of British bombing, clearly valued autonomy above cooperation. His was a myopic view of the principle of unity of effort. Also, the RFC chief was being kept busy by his superiors in London at the time.

The War Cabinet was not easily reassured, chronically fearing that airfield space would constrain the bombing program. The perspicacious Maurice Baring captured the mood perfectly in his diary entry for 19 December 1917:

> There was, at this time, a panic in London about the Aerodromes at Ochey. It was thought apparently that not enough energy was being

put into the matter. Gracious heavens, did they but know! The General thought he might have to go there, and we were ready to start. I was summoned hastily back from St. Omer, whither I had taken Mr. Grey (i.e., G. C. Grey, editor of *The Aeroplane*). However, Commodore Paine was sent out from London to see the place, and he reported that the Aerodromes would be ready long before we had one-tenth of the number of machines which they were to accommodate, which proved to be more than true.[32]

The promised bombing fleet had failed to materialize by late spring 1918, and the strategic force numbered just four squadrons.

The Aerodromes which we had seen in the autumn, and which at that time had looked like unreclaimable moorland, were now wide and smooth surfaces of grass. Thanks to Newall, the miracle, the impossible had been accomplished.[33]

Except for Trenchard's postwar allegations, none of the surviving contemporary documents attest to other than full cooperation by the French in this endeavour.

One last point on British aerodrome construction concerns the suitability of terrain allotted for building airfields. In his final dispatch, Trenchard directed the attention of his Minister, Lord Weir, Secretary of State for Air, to the difficulties encountered in carrying out the government's construction schemes.

My first work was at once to push on and arrange for the accommodation of a Force in the neighbourhood of 60 squadrons. This was a much larger task than may appear at first sight.

The country is throughout hilly and woody, and where there are any level places they consist of deep ridge and furrow, there being as much as 3 ft. 0 ins. between furrow and ridge.

The aerodromes had to carry heavy machines and heavy bomb loads; in order to enable this to be done, draining work on a large scale had to be very carefully carried out, and arrangements had to be made for a large installation of electrical power for workshops and lighting and petrol in order to save transport.

The work was practically completed by Nov. 1st, 1918.[34]

Twenty miles of drains had to be laid on Azelot aerodrome and 60 miles at Xaffevillers for the field to be leveled and sown.[35] However, similar exertions would have been necessary in almost any sort of terrain. Azelot and Xaffevillers are atypical examples in that they lie in the deeply furrowed country north of the Moselle; only two other bombing aerodromes were ever built in that inhospitable neighborhood.[36]

The 41st Wing in fact occupied relatively more favorable land than the US Air Service had been allotted; a topographical map study substantiates this observation.[37] The same study also reveals numerous military and private airfields still in use in the region, proportionately more on the sites of old British aerodromes than in the American base area. Trenchard and Newall admittedly faced an urgent task in building sufficient aerodromes to satisfy the War Cabinet. However, their concerns were neither unique nor prohibitively difficult in that regard.

With headquarters at Bainville-sur-Madon, Colonel Newall and his staff were roughly equidistant from 41st Wing's main bases at Ochey (seven miles west) and Tantonville (eight miles south). Early in November 1917, No. 55 Squadron (the daylight unit) had moved to the latter aerodrome, leaving No. 100 and "A" Naval Squadrons with the French at Ochey.[38] As the squadron represented the smallest self-contained operational unit of the bombing force, a brief overview of its organization and responsibilities is necessary at this time.

Besides its aircraft flights ("A," "B," and "C"), the squadron contained specialized sections that performed functions ancillary but essential to flying. Generally a major, the squadron commander controlled five support groups—headquarters, orderly room (administration), armament, stores, and transport—as well as his flyers.[39] Headquarters section (one captain, one technical warrant officer, one flight sergeant, 10 other ranks) managed the unit's maintenance program and supervised special tasks ranging from ensuring aerodrome readiness to incising memorial crosses.[40] Duties of the armament, stores, and transport sections were much as one would expect.

The orderly room section, responsible for discipline and administration, kept records and forwarded returns to 41st Wing headquarters. To assist the recording officer (adjutant), the section included a warrant officer in charge of disciplinary matters and a flight sergeant (chief clerk) who supervised two administrative clerks. A telephone operator and a motor-cyclist dispatch rider provided communications to and from Bainville-sur-Madon. This orderly room section typed, filed, and forwarded the raid reports and supporting documents that eventually reached the War Cabinet. From a purely administrative viewpoint, the squadron commander was adequately supported.

Because of its isolation, the squadron also had specialized officers: a chaplain, a medical officer, a meteorological officer, and a photographic technician. Since one of the unit's key tasks was to provide postraid results and assessments to wing staff as quickly as possible, a branch intelligence officer was assigned.[41] In practice, however, the squadron commander customarily debriefed returning aircrews, collected their observations, and composed, edited, and signed the squadron's raid report. This summary was en route to 41st Wing Headquarters by motorcycle within three to six hours of the mission's completion.[42] Maj W. R. Read, who commanded a Handley Page squadron during 1918, described this tedious but vital routine.

> It takes an awful time after the raid is over to collect all the pilots' and observers' reports. From all these reports I have to make a general report which takes about an hour. All this then has to be typed twice over in order to make 6 copies and this takes anything between 1 and 2 hours according to the length of the report. I have to wait up till it is all finished to read it through and sign them all. Then they go off to the Wing at Xaffevillers—50 miles distant by a dispatch rider so that Wing may have them before 7 a.m.[43]

The main sources of information used by Whitehall and others to ascertain bombing results were the reports submitted by aircrews to their squadron commanders.

The cutting edge of the squadron was the flight, consisting of six planes and generally eight or more pilots, under the RFC system of unit organization. Three such flights comprised a squadron in 41st Wing, except for "A" Naval whose Handley Pages were organized into two flights of five machines each. The flight commander, a captain and the highest-ranking officer to participate in frequent service flights over the lines, generally held his position by virtue of his tactical experience.

The success of each mission depended upon his flying skills and leadership qualities.[44]

The aircraft types in Newall's force represented the contemporary state of the art in late 1917. Whatever their other obstacles, British bombing squadrons were not hampered by unsuitable aircraft designs.

No. 55's DeHavilland 4s, first flown at Hendon in mid-1916, represented one of the more successful types of its day. Like the Sopwith 1½ Strutter of No. 3 Wing, it was an open-cockpit, two-seater biplane used for day bombardment; unlike the Sopwith, the DH4 carried its bombs on external wing racks.[45] During its mobilization at Lilbourne in spring 1917, No. 55 Squadron had been the first RFC unit to receive the DH4, then powered by the 250-horsepower Rolls Royce Eagle III. They flew DH4s throughout the war, preferring the model that became available in January 1918, with the 375-horsepower Eagle VIII, an engine originally allocated to the RNAS. With a service ceiling of 23,000 feet, the DH4 (Eagle VIII) generally bombed from 16,000 to 17,000 feet, taking approximately 45 minutes to climb to that height after takeoff.[46]

The main disadvantage of the DH4 arose from its main fuel tank, sandwiched between the cockpits for the pilot and observer. The design undoubtedly simplified Geoffrey DeHavilland's attempts to maintain a stable center of gravity. However, this arrangement made crew coordination extremely difficult, even with speaking tubes. In a crash, the tank often left its bedding and crushed the pilot against the engine, a tendency compounded by the relatively weak undercarriage of the DH4. In combat, one experienced pilot complained that the "tank is unprotected, works by pressure and explodes when shot up."[47]

Of 33 DH4s lost to enemy action by the US Air Service, eight fell in flames—"no worse than the average at the time."[48] (On 12 November 1918, the day after the Armistice, the first DH4 fitted with a self-sealing fuel tank arrived in France.)[49] Later DeHavilland designs, notably the DH9 and DH9A, relocated the fuel tank just aft of the engine and incorporated a wind-driven petrol pump. This arrangement placed the pilot and observer within arm's length of one another and minimized fire and crash dangers.

With their DH4s, No. 55 Squadron adopted tactical procedures of formation takeoff in two six-ship wedges, a configuration maintained to and from the target area. The raid leader normally fired a red Very signal to alert his companions, who released their payloads when they observed the leader's bombs falling. Similarly, the raid leader was responsible for navigating en route and selecting alternate targets if formations proved unable to bomb their assigned objective.[50] This follow-the-leader approach, besides being tactically sound, permitted newly trained and inexperienced aircrews to be used on missions. In at least one instance when the flight commander had engine trouble and had to return to base, his wingmen, either unaware of or misreading his flare signal, dutifully accompanied him all the way home.[51] Since massed fire from the observers' Lewis guns somewhat discouraged close-range attacks on the formation, the six-ship wedge also afforded protection against attacks by enemy planes. In daylight raiding, survival and accurate bombing depended upon formation flying.

By contrast, night operations used machines of relatively low performance that operated singly after takeoff. Aircrew skill and judgment determined the aggregate success of the squadron's particular mission. Navigational difficulties offset the decreased risk of enemy countermeasures during darkness; mass raids, owing to the danger of midair collisions, were seldom attempted. However, the 1,500-pound payload of the Handley Page made its offensive power roughly equal to that of an entire formation of smaller FE2bs. Bombing altitudes ranged between four thousand feet and chimney level, a tactic which substantially assisted accuracy.[52] Overall, the pilot of each night bombing machine had to exercise the same skills expected of a flight commander/raid leader in a daylight unit.

From its arrival in France on 21 March 1917, No. 100 Squadron flew lattice-tailed FE2bs until it converted to Handley Pages in August 1918. The "Fee," a type with the RFC

since the initial weeks of war, was relegated to night operations.

> The F.E.2b proved to be, by the standards of its time, effective as a
> night bomber. It gave its crew exceptionally good forward vision, could
> lift a fair load of bombs, and under cover of darkness its lack of
> performance mattered little. Thus when the first British squadrons to
> be formed as a night bombing unit came into being in February 1917
> its aircraft were to be F.E.2b's.[53]

An undercarriage modification permitted the machine to
carry both the standard 230-pound aerial bomb and the 112-
pound model. In November 1917, HQ RFC ordered that all
FE2bs issued to No. 100 have the original 24-gallon petrol
tank replaced by a 36-gallon tank. The machine's airborne
endurance increased from three hours to four and one-half
hours.[54] Since the FE2b cruised at speeds under 70 miles per
hour with bomb load, its maximum tactical range, even with
the larger tank, was roughly 110 miles, allowing 30 percent
fuel reserve for contingencies. Even with this constraint, the
aircraft could reach all the rail targets designated as critical in
the French air plans of October and November 1917. The
performance of the FE2b suited it for inter-Allied operations,
particularly the bombing program envisioned by the War Cabinet and Sir Douglas Haig's headquarters.

Conversely, the Handley Page night bomber had been designed expressly for long-range bombing missions. Spanning
exactly 100 feet, it stood 22-feet high, huge in its time. The
Handley Page 0/400, which began to replace the 0/100 in
early 1918, differed mainly in having its fuel tanks within the
fuselage rather than in the engine nacelles.[55] Although it flew
lower (7,000-foot service ceiling) and slower (under 80 miles
per hour at 6,500 feet) than its daylight counterparts, the
Handley Page typically carried sixteen 112-pound bombs,
roughly five times the payload capacity of the DH4.[56] Both
Handley Page models required one pilot and two observers.
One observer manned the front .303 Lewis gun and served as
bomb-aimer; the other attended to maps, and to the bombs,
which were carried within a small cabin called the "engine
room."[57]

With an eight-hour airborne endurance, the Handley Page possessed a combat radius of over 220 miles. Allowing for 30 percent reserve of fuel, it could carry over thirteen hundred pounds of bombs to Frankfurt or Cologne. With its FE2b companions in No. 100 Squadron, the Handley Pages of "A" Naval Squadron provided 41st Wing with a complementary pair of night-bombing aeroplanes. Newall had the potential to implement not only the British bombing scheme but also to work closely with the French program.

Aircrew opinions indicate that they were generally satisfied with their machines. Lt Leonard "L. M." Miller, author of the unofficial history of No. 55 Squadron, characterized the De-Havilland aircraft: "It can be safely said that the D.H.4 was a success."[58] A squadron song, "In Formation" extolled the virtues of the machine.[59] Of the little FE2b, Maj C. Gordon Burge, commander of No. 100 Squadron at the Armistice, declared the Fee "a most excellent machine for night bombing," and spoke of the "magnificent work it performed."[60] Burge evidently voiced his crews' collective assessment, since RFC/RAF policy did not permit his flying missions over the lines. One of his pilots, Lt A. R. Kingsford, expressed a qualified affection, noting that "these old Fees did some great showing." When No. 100 traded their "good old friends" for Handley Pages in 1918, Kingsford described the transition to be "like driving a motor lorry after a Baby Austin."[61] Soon after, he recorded that he and his colleagues were very happy with the new machines and happier still that everyone had survived the conversion training without mishap. Though the ponderous Handley Pages could be "devils" when caught in enemy searchlights, they were otherwise "great."[62] Given their own training and tactical experience, 41st Wing aircrews found little to criticize in their machines.

As had been the case with No. 3 Wing, weather largely determined the tempo of 41st Wing bombardment. Though Newall's force of one day squadron (No. 55, DH4) and two night squadrons (No. 100, FE2b; "A," Handley Page) was constituted on 11 October 1917 at Bainville-sur-Madon, poor flying conditions prevented operations for nearly a week.[63] After an inaugural mission to the Burbach works at Saarbrücken on 17 October 1917, adverse weather did not permit subsequent raids until 21 October. (No. 55 attempted to launch two missions on the nineteenth.) At four o'clock on the afternoon of the 21st, No. 55 dropped 2,464 pounds of bombs on Bous and Wadgassen, losing one DH4. "A" Naval and No. 100 Squadrons launched their first missions on the night of 24/25 October, when they bombed factory and railway targets in the vicinity of Saarbrücken.

In all, Newall's squadrons were able to fly on 20 occasions, launching 10 squadron-sized daylight missions (all by No. 55 Squadron, the sole day unit) and 14 night raids (10 by No. 100 in FE2bs and four by the Handley Pages of "A" Naval Squadron).[64]

On 24 December, more than two months after active operations had begun, 10 DH4s from No. 55 Squadron visited Mannheim (actually, Ludwigshafen) with 2,252 pounds of bombs. Three weeks later, on 14 January 1918, 12 machines from the same unit dropped 2,752 pounds of bombs on the munition works and railways around Karlsruhe in a four-hour mission (takeoff, 1015-1020; land, 1410+).[65] Only one raid had been mounted in November—to Kaiserslautern on the first of the month. More than a month elapsed before the next operation.

During the three-day period in which conditions were favorable (between 29 October and 1 November 1917), four missions were flown: two by day and two by night. However, 41st Wing planners did not attempt to achieve a concentration of effort or even minimal day-night coordination. Of the targets struck, Saarbrücken, Pirmasens, Völklingen and Kaiserslautern, the two nearest (Saarbrücken and Völklingen) are six miles apart and were bombed on the nights of 29 and 30 October. Pirmasens and Kaiserslautern lie 24 miles and 33 miles, respectively, from the center of Saarbrücken. Six DH4s (half of the force) on the Kaiserslautern mission of 1 November were turned back by enemy action; they dropped their payloads into adjacent woods.[66] Performance fell short of expectations through January 1918, largely due to poor flying weather and organizational inexperience.

The fortunes of the two night-flying squadrons indicate the impact of time. "A" Naval Squadron, a conglomeration of machines and aircrew hastily assembled and dispatched to Ochey, had relatively more difficulties than No. 100 Squadron, which had been flying FE2bs on active service with the RFC since April 1917.

The naval aviators, flying long-endurance Handley Page machines, were especially susceptible to adverse weather. After "A" Naval Squadron's maiden mission (nine machines) to Saarbrücken on the night of 24/25 October, they did not fly again till 5/6 January 1918, when a single aeroplane dropped one-half ton of bombs on railways near Courcelles. The Handley Page crew bombed Courcelles because poor visibility over Maizieres-les-Metz, their assigned objective, forced an in-flight diversion. Neither Saarbrücken nor Courcelles lay more than 38 miles over the lines, and Maizieres-les-Metz was just 18 miles behind the trenches. Only two missions flown in 10 weeks, stretching the Handley Pages to less than a quarter of their combat radius, is a pace indicative of chronic difficulties. During this period (24/25 October 1917 to 5/6 January 1918), the short-legged FE2bs of No. 100 Squadron managed to conduct six raids, including three as far afield as Saarbrücken (24/25 October and 29/30 October) and Völklingen (30/31 October).

The Admiralty squadron's inexperience also led to high initial wastage. After just two weeks and only one mission with 41st Wing, "A" Naval Squadron had five Handley Pages (of 10) out of action. By the end of October, two had been lost on the unit's first operation and three had been lost in accidents. The commander of the Admiralty's Dunkirk squadrons, following an inspection visit to "A" Naval, deplored the policy of hurriedly collecting machines, aircrews, and personnel to use immediately on active service.

> After two years experience, I feel convinced that to obtain good results with a minimum of loss it is absolutely necessary for a squadron to be thoroughly trained.[67]

"A" Naval launched four Handley Pages to attack Mannheim on the night No. 100 bombed Völklingen, but deteriorating weather forced the "A" mission to be abandoned—and one machine went missing. Thereafter, the naval aviators adopted a more conservative policy. From January to August 1918, the unit lost but two Handley Pages to enemy action. During their entire wartime service with the long-range bombing force, "A" aviators lost a total of six planes over the lines.[68]

Weather, the most significant factor affecting 41st Wing activities, prohibited the bombing force from conducting the crushing offensive desired by the War Cabinet. During the 1917–18 winter, 41st Wing canceled seven attempted raids after losing one Handley Page and one DH4. Of missions that crossed the lines, six had to be diverted, wholly or partially, to targets other than their assigned objectives because of poor flying conditions. In the absence of a feasible contingency plan, Newall's force improvised as best it could under the circumstances. Conscientious efforts, however, have never guaranteed worthwhile results.

Wastage through accident, as well as enemy action, remained an inescapable fact of life during training and operational flying. It affected the availability of experienced personnel within line squadrons; bombing effectiveness depended upon the skills of a few highly qualified and experienced officers. Because of the demand for replacements, the consequence of RFC's policy of incessant offensive action, both the home training establishment and units overseas found themselves hard pressed to keep the pipeline and mess chairs filled. Personnel turbulence required neophyte aircrews to learn fundamental skills under fire during active operations.

According to official files, more British pilots were killed during training in the United Kingdom than were killed in action: eight thousand fatalities to 6,166.[69] The US Air Service, which admittedly had the latitude to train replacements in a less urgent environment, experienced these results:

1 fatality to 90 graduates in preliminary work, 1 fatality to 9.2 graduates in pursuit training, and an average of about 1 fatality to 50 graduations in observation and bombardment. The total average appears to be one fatality for every 18 completely trained flying officers available for service.[70]

British casualties for each phase of training were proportionately higher; nor did the problem confine itself solely to the home establishment.

In late 1917 and throughout most of 1918, inexperienced pilots had to be shipped to France to fill operational billets. For example, when Lt C. E. V. Wilkins, RNAS, joined No. 16 Squadron (formerly "A" Naval Squadron) on 22 March 1918 to fly Handley Page night bombers, he had amassed nine hours, 38 minutes total solo flying time on that aircraft. His night flying experience totaled just six hours, 30 minutes.[71] Not unexpectedly, during its tenure from October 1917 to the Armistice, the British strategic bombing force lost roughly three times as many aircraft to accidents as to enemy action.[72] In the worst case, No. 100 Squadron wrecked 56 FE2bs while losing only 11 over the lines.

According to the official history, a typical DH4 squadron of 18 planes would need 56 replacement machines annually.[73] During two months of summer, 1918, the overall accident rate in the RAF per hundred flying hours for Handley Pages was 1.55; for DH4s, 1.89; and for FE2s, 1.93.[74] Generally, an adequate equipment reserve for a squadron ready to deploy overseas included six aircraft to make up "wastage during mobilization and transit to France," six machines overseas within the RFC logistical system and six planes to organizational training units in the home establishment to produce follow-on pilots and aircrews.[75]

Soon after the war, Air Commodore Brooke-Popham, newly appointed head of the Research Department of the Air Ministry, discussed the consequences of losses upon unit performance. In a lecture delivered before the Royal United Services Institute in December 1919, Air Commodore Brooke-Popham reviewed the effects of wastage.

During the last eighteen months of the war, the average wastage was 51 per cent per month, i.e., all the machines with squadrons in France had to be replaced once every two months or six times a year. In other words, each machine only lasted an average of sixty days, which would mean a little over sixty hours' flying time per machine.

As regards the causes of wastage, that known to be due directly to enemy action never reached 25 per cent. To that should be added a proportion of the missing machines, but even adding these in, it is very doubtful if the wastage due to enemy action ever amounted to more than a third of the total losses. The wastage due to errors of pilots varied. Whenever we had heavy casualties in pilots it meant that a large batch of new pilots came out from England, who were unused to the country and lacking in experience; consequently a heavy casualty list was generally followed by a large increase in the number of aeroplane casualties due to errors of pilots.[76]

As described by the air commodore, the situation would be self-perpetuating. Newly arrived pilots would likely be shot down and their replacements would also become casualties, requiring replacement in their turn. Under such conditions, squadron commanders and higher officers had to be grounded simply to guarantee a minimum of organizational continuity.

Rather than reexamine their offensive policy, the RFC adopted the expedient course of disguising the extent of their losses. RAF Routine Orders of 27 June 1918 complicated casualty reporting by eliminating the previous category of losses due to accidents: "In future strictly flying accidents resulting in death will be reported as death in action. Injury resulting from accidents will be reported as 'sick.'"[77] Such administrative obfuscation makes a subsequent classification of casualties difficult. In the case of No. 100 Squadron, the "Roll of Honour" provides sufficient detail to make this determination possible, using the squadron's unofficial history. During service with the long-range bombing force, three aircrew were killed in action, compared to 10 who died in aircraft accidents.[78] This ratio is consistent with the wastage statistics of the official history and Air Commodore Brooke-Popham. As another investigator of the subject has observed, "By this means the inexperience of pilots and the unreliability of aeroplanes was disguised."[79] Casualty return forms used by the strategic bombing force in 1918 bore the preprinted caveat, under the heading "Accidental Casualties," that this category "does not include officers killed or injured by accident who have crossed the line and are reported as battle casualties."[80] Whether combat damage or inexperience was the proximate cause, casualties in machines wrecked returning from a raid were attributed to enemy action. Some undoubtedly were, but most resulted from pilot error. To ascribe nearly all flying casualties to enemy action masked the shortcomings of RFC training even as it justified the demand for even more new pilots and inflated the effectiveness of German air defenses.

Under the same rationale, combat losses of machines were minimized in records and bulletins. Aircraft damaged or destroyed by enemy action but which crashed on the Allied side of the lines were not reported. In his postwar article in the *Journal of the Royal United Services Institute*, squadron leader B. E. Sutton characterized the situation in 1918.

> Such figures as 45 enemy destroyed, 22 driven down, 10 of our aircraft missing, are misleading, because the word "missing" is deceptive. Casualties on our side of the lines were not reported.[81]

The 41st Wing and its successors consistently omitted from their reports aircraft losses due to forced landings and crashes.[82] These official attempts to manipulate loss data, in conjunction with other statistical and narrative evidence, reveal the extent to which training and operational wastage, of aircrews as well as machines, affected the British air service.

At squadron level, personnel turbulence led to the policy of restricting participation of key officers in active operations. The senior officer with firsthand experience in flying over the lines was, with a few exceptions, the flight commander—generally a captain. This fact was not lost upon aircrews.

> Flying for inspection duties is something, but not enough; an occasional war flight does more to engender respect and raise morale of the junior pilots than the most eloquent casuistry.

> The idea that the senior officer is too valuable ever to risk his life does not find any adherents among his juniors; in fact the possibility of more rapid promotion is not unpleasing to them. The policy of confining commanders to ground duties may overlook the fact that if they did fly, they would be still more valuable; if they are only capable of conducting an Avro (i.e., Avro 504, a basic training aeroplane) round the aerodrome, they should not be placed in an executive capacity.[83]

This RFC policy ensured that no rated officer in 41st Wing above the rank of captain could reliably evaluate the validity of postraid aircrew reports. Since commanders did not accompany their flyers, they lacked the operational experience to assess raid results knowledgeably. James Clay Thompson's point about the US Air Force's Vietnam program seems applicable here: "modern organizations are characterized by a growing gap between the right to decide on the basis of hierarchical position and the ability to decide on the basis of technical competence."[84] Ministers and commanders, responsible for the success of British bombing, likewise had to rely on post-raid reports from young airmen. A tendency existed for each link in the chain of command to accept uncritically these after-action claims, since they shored up the assessments of everyone involved in the bombing effort.[85]

Evidence suggests that 41st Wing and its squadrons in the field felt themselves under considerable pressure to produce worthwhile results. The numerous occasions on which missions had to be abandoned or diverted after takeoff, and the varying ratios of unserviceable to serviceable machines indicate that Newall's force operated at full stretch.

As an RFC unit whose commander had previously been in charge of Trenchard's headquarters wing, 41st Wing exemplified the policy of carrying the air war to the enemy whenever possible. Altogether, seven squadron-sized raids had to be abandoned after takeoff while 24 missions bombed targets over the lines. The high proportion of aborted to successful raids (29 percent) suggests a command emphasis upon conducting active operations even under marginal conditions. All raids that aborted did so because of poor weather. In this regard, the conservative approach of "A" Naval Squadron provided a marked contrast to the aggressive attitude of the rest of 41st Wing. Maj W. R. Read, the RFC officer who later commanded the Handley Page unit, summarized these philosophies a few days before he took over the unit.

> I shall have to exercise a good deal of patience in working this Sqdn. at first. I can see that they have R.N.A.S. ideas deeply rooted in them.
>
> Personally (although it's against all R.A.F. principles) I think the R.N.A.S. methods of work are better than the R.A.F. The R.N.A.S. methods are slow and sure. Their motto is "fly if the weather is good but if it is doubtful *don't*." The R.A.F. methods are "Try and do the work at all costs in any weather within reason." Personally I am going to adopt a medium course in this Sqdn. I shall ginger them up a little

more than they are but I shall not go to the extreme R.A.F. methods. What now are the results of the two methods in practice.

This sqdn. has been working on this front now for 10 months and they have lost 2 machines over the lines in that time. They have perhaps (and H.Q. certainly think so) erred on the side of being too cautious about only flying in good weather.[86]

Major Read was an experienced aviator who had commanded RFC units since 1915; contrary to policy, he habitually took part in combat operations.[87] In this context, his views can be taken as an accurate reflection of the state of affairs in the bombing force.

Information extracted from aircraft status returns likewise indicates that 41st Wing geared its operations to a tempo that often proved unsustainable. Data on ratios of machines launched to those that managed to bomb support this suspicion.

The serviceability returns for 24 December 1917 seem unreliable, in light of preceding and succeeding figures. Reporting 45 aeroplanes ready for combat might have seemed a good way for 41st Wing to conclude its first calendar year of operations. Just two weeks later, on 4 January 1918, 18 machines were unserviceable; yet, only two mission attempts (five machines total) had been launched in the interim. Similarly, on the next mission after 17 January, five FE2bs were forced to abandon the raid because of engine trouble.

Nor were all "serviceable" machines necessarily so. Of 118 aeroplanes launched on day missions, 95 proceeded to fly complete missions, a success rate of 80.5 percent. By night, 90 of 125 aircraft launched, or 72 percent, flew complete raids. Mechanical difficulties accounted for virtually all aborted missions; only eight machines went missing through January 1918. As Air Commodore Brooke-Popham noted earlier, fewer than a third of those losses could be attributed to enemy action.

During those intervals in which Newall's force mounted successive missions, such as 30–31 October, 5–6 December, and 4–5 January, numbers of unserviceable aircraft rose in consequence. No aircraft was lost or missing due to enemy action during any of these three periods. The strain alone—of conducting active operations—caused unserviceable rates to rise sharply. This trend brings into question 41st Wing's ability to conduct a sustained campaign. In attacks against lightly defended targets at short range (the sort of objectives envisaged by their French counterparts), Newall's forces were unable to mount a systematic bombing offensive without significant wastage.

Finally, in mid-January 1918, after Trenchard had become Chief of Air Staff, HQ RFC notified 41st Wing that they no longer needed to forward aircraft serviceability information.[88] Command authorities preferred to read of successes, rather than problems, in reports from 41st Wing in the field.

Whitehall, for its part, provided maximum publicity to the activities of 41st Wing. For example, No. 55 Squadron flew the Wing's maiden mission on 17 October 1917—a day raid on the Burbach Works at Saarbrücken. The 41st Wing war diary summarized the attack.

> 17/10:—Weather - Misty, morning, clearing up later in the day. No. 55 Squadron carried out two bomb raids (11 De Havilland 4 machines), and dropped 16 - 112 lb. bombs = 1,792 lbs. on the Factories and Works around SAARBRUCKEN. Eight bombs were seen to burst on the BURBBACK [sic] FACTORY, causing considerable damage and several fires.[89]

Haig at GHQ received the report the same day, via Trenchard's staff at HQ RFC in the field, and transmitted it to the CIGS at the War Office, for dissemination to the War Cabinet. Within the day, the government and the public knew nearly all the details of the attacks that initiated the aerial offensive. Periodicals at home reproduced the GHQ bulletin verbatim:

> British squadrons carried out a successful bombing raid this afternoon into German territory. A factory of Saarbrucken, some 40 miles beyond the German frontier, were [sic] attacked. Many bombs were dropped with good effect, and fires were seen to break out in the factory. All of our machines returned safely.[90]

Interestingly, this heartening news was released to the public even before the 41st Wing intelligence officer, Major Paul, had compiled and submitted his final assessment of raid results on 19 October 1917.[91] In fact, GHQ's practice of publicizing information concerning the bombing campaign gained momentum throughout the winter.[92]

Date of GHQ Bulletin	Extract
21 October 1917:	In spite of very misty weather, a further attack into Germany was carried out by our aeroplanes.
30 October 1917:	On the night of 29th-30th inst. Our machines again attacked the railway; station and lines around Saarbrücken in Germany.
31 October 1917:	Following on those of the night of the 29th-30th inst., and of yesterday morning, another raid into Germany was carried out.
1 November 1917:	To-day another successful raid was carried out by our aeroplanes into Germany.
6 December 1917:	To-day another successful raid was carried out by our aeroplanes into Germany.
25 December 1917:	In daylight on the 24th inst. one of our squadrons visited Mannheirm-on-the-Rhine with excellent results.
15 January 1918:	Following on the very successful daylight raid into Germany on the 14th inst., another was carried out during the night of the 14th-15th inst.

Public releases gleaned from official channels also stressed the continuity and intensity of the bombing effort. The tone of these extracts led readers to understand that an aerial offensive against targets deep in the enemy homeland was finally underway. Details of targets, bomb poundage totals, and observed results lent to these bulletins a considerable aura of authority.

Date of GHQ Bulletin	News Release
21 October 1917:	A foundry and railway station ten miles north-west of Saarbrücken were bombed, over a ton of bombs being dropped. Very good results were obtained, and bursts were seen on the foundry and railway station. A big explosion took place.
30 October 1917:	This morning, at 11 a.m., 12 of our machines went further afield, and attacked the muni tions works and gasworks at Pirmasens, 20 miles beyond Saarbrücken. Bombs were seen to burst on the factories and on the gasworks with excellent results.
31 October 1917:	On this occasion the steel works and stations of Volklingen (northwest of Saarbrücken) were attacked with excellent results. Direct hits were observed on the furnace and power-house, and on a train.
15 January 1918:	The objective in this case was the steelworks of Thionville, midway between Luxembourg and Metz, where a ton of bombs was dropped. A further half-ton was dropped on two large railway junctions in the neighbourhood of Metz.

Comparison of dates of GHQ bulletins with their dates of public release reveals that an interval of less than a day between official release and subsequent printing was commonplace.[93] Missions of special interest, such as raids by No. 100 or No. 55's day attack on Mannheim on 24 December, often provided the basis for more than one bulletin.[94] Subsequent releases amplified successes; material covering the Mannheim mission illustrates this practice:

(GHQ Bulletin, 24 December 1917) In daylight on the 24th inst. one of our squadrons bombed Mannheim-on-the-Rhine with excellent results. A ton of bombs were dropped, and bursts were observed in the large main station, in the works, and also in the town, where fires were started. Very heavy anti-aircraft gunfire was directed against our aeroplanes when over the objective, and one of our machines was damaged and forced to land.

(War Office Bulletin, 29 December) The following further information about the bombing raid on Mannheim carried out on December 24th has now been received:—Two of our formations, totalling 10 machines, crossed the line at a height of 9,000 feet between 10 and 10.15 a.m. The two formations arrived over the objective almost simultaneously, and, in spite of heavy and accurate anti-aircraft fire, dropped their bombs from a height of over 13,000 ft. Sixteen 112-lb. bombs and two 230-lb. bombs were dropped in all, four bursts being observed in the main station, several in the Lanz works, two in Ludwigshafen, and several in the munitions factory between Mundenheim and Rheingonnheim.[95]

The same periodical listed the pilot of the forced-down aircraft as "2nd Lieut. C. F. Turner," but did not mention his observer, 2d Lt A. F. Castle.[96] From the public perspective, such timely and specific information, disseminated under official *imprimatur*, attested to the success of the strategic bombing campaign.

Newspapers cooperated, habitually reprinting in their entirety dispatches from GHQ, which had forwarded them to Fleet Street in time for inclusion in the next day's issues.[97] French editions likewise promptly received bulletins outlining British aerial successes over Germany.[98] For the initial attack on Saarbrücken, *The Times* published the GHQ dispatch under its own headlines: "BRITISH AIR RAID INTO GERMANY; BOMBS DROPPED ON SAARBRUCKEN; FACTORY SET ON FIRE."[99]

When 41st Wing machines finally reached the Rhine towns of Mannheim-Ludwigshafen and Karlsruhe, the newspaper included not only headlines, but also a sketch map of 41st Wing's operating area. A short summary explaining the military importance of these objectives accompanied each story.[100] Daily and weekly periodicals faithfully reproduced variant spellings of geographic locations ("Oberbilig"—"Operbillig") and factual errors (such as transmitting Pirmasen's tanneries into munition works) that distinguished GHQ dispatches from 41st Wing reports.[101] As Lloyd George had requested, the Royal Flying Corps, with the assistance and endorsement of Haig's staff, ensured that only optimistic reports of 41st Wing successes reached the British public.

Underpinning this favorable publicity was the network of official reports and assessments that originated with 41st Wing. For domestic audiences, one would expect information to be released selectively in order to inflate somewhat the bombing force's accomplishments. Conversely, command authorities ex officio required access to every detail of 41st Wing in order to gauge its work. As indicated by its cautionary note of 27 October 1917, transmitted through the CIGS and GHQ to Trenchard and Newall, the War Cabinet was acutely concerned with all limitations, shortcomings, and constraints that affected the strategic bombing campaign.[102]

The RFC chain of command had responsibility for keeping Whitehall informed, promptly and fully, particularly of bad news. However, 41st Wing records for October 1917 to January 1918 routinely omitted information concerning recurrent difficulties and shortcomings. Of special interest is the information that each organizational level collected and evaluated before submitting to higher echelons.

The fundamental source of information about any military unit is normally its war diary (for the RFC, Army Form C.2118), a summary of daily activities completed in accordance with Field Service regulations.[103] To reflect operational results accurately, the war diary of 41st Wing depended upon data forwarded from the line squadrons. Postmission debriefings conducted by squadron commanders of returning aircrews provided the raw material; the firsthand observations of pilots and observers would determine the reliability of the entire intelligence effort. In winter 1917–18, 41st Wing intelligence staff had little choice but to accept at face value raid summaries forwarded from the squadrons. As its name implies, the war diary condensed these raid reports for transmission further up the chain of command.

Within 41st Wing and its successor (Eighth Brigade), the flow of operational data to the authorities followed usual administrative practices. The official pipeline led from the wing to HQ RFC and on to Haig at GHQ. Reports then crossed the channel to the CIGS at the War Office and, finally, reached the War Cabinet.[104] This routing provided material for public news releases, as summarized above.

For missions of particular interest, squadron commanders submitted a comprehensive account to Wing HQ as soon as possible, usually within 24 hours. This amplifying information was used at HQ to compose the "detailed raid report," a restricted-access, detailed summary of mission results.[105] These reports, circulated to the War Cabinet, were also forwarded to Allied headquarters for De Castelnau's and John J. "Black Jack" Pershing's information.[106] Their distribution lagged a day or two behind the postmission bulletins that GHQ released to the British public.

While postmission bulletins and detailed raid reports were forwarded to Whitehall, two other evaluations prepared by 41st Wing remained within RFC and, later, Air Ministry, circles. Intelligence reports prepared by Major Paul, the Wing intelligence officer, supplemented post-mission bulletins and detailed raid reports, occasionally referring to remarks that Newall had included in the latter.[107] Paul's assessments drew upon reconnaissance data and photo interpretation of plates exposed during the raid.

> Although it is impossible to say whether the bomb holes shown on the photographs are the result of the bombs dropped by No. 55 Squadron or the French it is more than probable from the interrogation of observers that these are the results of previous raids. It can therefore be safely assumed that all bombs burst in the Town of SAARBRUCKEN or on the BURBACH WORKS. The photographs show two good bursts on Laminoir. (See sketch and photographs already forwarded.) A fire appears to have been started which is visible on the two aeroplane photographs (wide smoke of great density and spreading.) From reports it is understood that these bombs were the first two dropped.[108]

These intelligence reports also contained routes flown to and from the objective, as well as the location, intensity, and effectiveness of any enemy countermeasures encountered. Information concerning casualties, wastage, and weight of bombs dropped was not normally included, since previous bulletins had forwarded these numbers.

The Air Ministry Directorate of Air Intelligence, Section A.I.la, responsible for "compilation of Daily Air Intelligence Summaries," received five final copies of Paul's field reports.[109] Section A.I.la occasionally included 41st Wing intelligence information in the "Summary of Air Intelligence," a confidential document published daily and circulated to the King as well as to leading political and military authorities.[110] Since the raids had been public knowledge for several days, the classified conclusions that the Air Ministry distributed to key leaders would be taken as authoritative. Few of Paul's specific observations found their way into the Directorate of Air Intelligence daily summary, which tended to confine itself to statistics and general results available in other, faster field returns. However, the full report was available in Air Ministry files.

Within 41st Wing, the operational counterpart to Paul's intelligence report was the "approximate results," a mimeographed summary containing information of interest to the RFC chain of command.[111] In addition to the copy forwarded to HQ RFC, copies of approximate results were distributed to the Wing's line squadrons. Apparently this "downward" circulation provided a check on the accuracy of included statistics and narrative. Occasionally, data were corrected or amended.[112] The approximate results initially contained such useful information as aircraft serviceability ratios, numbers of machines that started the mission and whether they aborted, bombed the assigned objectives, or diverted to another target. Later, in the spring of 1918, changes to the categories and extent of the information they contained circumscribed their utility. However, for the period in which 41st Wing operated as a separate agency, approximate results and intelligence reports compiled from aerial photographs and aircrew observations provide detailed descriptions of the conduct and claims of 41st Wing operations.

However, these official reports and records, war diaries, squadron mission summaries, detailed raid reports, intelligence reports, and approximate results, all originating in the field and all summarizing 41st Wing operations, often differ on very basic items of information. Data concerning numbers of machines launched and their intended targets, adverse effects of weather, mechanical failures, enemy countermeasures, and wastage vary from document to document. It would seem that the interests of 41st Wing would best be served by making its difficulties known to those who oversaw the bombing program.

101

Instead, almost without exception, the wing chose to downplay those shortcomings.

The thread binding all of 41st Wing's official returns is the selective omission of any adverse data. For example, if information concerning operations during December 1917 are compared, a number of discrepancies emerge. War diary accounts and other records (primarily detailed raid reports) differ significantly with respect to obstacles imposed by mechanical difficulties, aircrew inexperience, and poor weather.

> About 1.40 p.m. No. 55 Squadron (11 machines) successfully carried out 2 bomb raids. 12 - 112 lb. bombs were dropped on the Railway Station and Sidings at ZWEIBRUCKEN. 8 - 112 lb. and 8 - 25 lb. bombs were dropped on the factories immediately West of SAARBRUCKEN. A-A fire was accurate. All machines returned safely. Total explosive dropped 2.400 lbs.[113]

This entry, by virtue of specific figures connoting a high degree of precision, coupled with its concise, matter-of-fact narrative, conveys a definite, unambiguous impression of the day's events. By contrast, extracts from the Detail Raid Report reveal considerable improvisation underlying this 5 December mission.

> Two formations of six De Havilland 4s. each started at 1.35 and 10.40 a.m. respectively to bomb the Chemical Works at LUDWIGSHAFEN (MANNHEIM). One machine was forced to return to its Aerodrome owing to petrol stoppage.
>
> Owing to a very strong wind high up the two formations took three hours to reach a point approximately 5 miles south of KAISERSLAUTERN. The leader then decided that it was not possible to reach the ordered objective, as, in addition to the strength of the wind, weather conditions became very cloudy and the Rhine Valley was seen to be obscured by a thick mist. The two formations then turned South West.
>
> One formation attacked the Railway Station and Sidings at ZWEIBRUCKEN, dropping 12-112 lb. bombs from a height of 13,500 feet. Four bursts were observed in the Town and a fifth on the outskirts.
>
> The Second formation attacked the Factories immediately West of SAARBRUCKEN, dropping 8-112 lb. and 8-25 lb. bombs from a height of 12,000 feet. Four bursts were observed in the Town and one amongst the Railway Sidings. Two fires were also observed immediately South of the River.[114]

This excerpt from the detailed raid report differs considerably from the condensed narrative of the war diary. The latter's selective omissions and objective tone seriously mislead the reader.

While the war diary implied that superior aerial coordination enabled No. 55 Squadron to successfully carry out two bomb raids, the detailed raid report stated that bombs from two scattered flights of homeward-bound machines fell somewhere within the city limits of two German towns. Of two formations of DH4s, one had to abandon the mission due to engine trouble. Strong winds and deteriorating visibility forced the remaining aircraft to attack unbriefed targets. The formation became separated and one gaggle hit Zweibrücken from 13,500 feet while the lead flight of DH4s bombed Saarbrücken—15 miles away—from 12,000 feet. Except for one bomb "amongst the Railway Sidings" in Saarbrücken, all observed explosions occurred in the towns themselves. The detailed raid report, unlike the war diary, identified and assessed the impact of factors such as mechanical shortcomings and adverse weather—information that would have been of considerable interest to those directing the bombing campaign.

Not unexpectedly, the GHQ dispatch which appeared in London papers the next day inflated even the war diary account.

> On the afternoon of the 5th inst. two raids were carried out by our aeroplanes into Germany. These are the first that have been possible for over a month owing to incessant bad weather. One raid was carried out on the large railway junction and sidings at Zweibrucken (17 miles east of Saarbrucken) and the other on the works at Saarbrucken. Many direct hits were observed in both cases, and two large fires were started.[115]

According to German records available after the Armistice, however, no bombs fell into the Burbach Works at Saarbrücken, though six townspeople were killed and nine wounded on 5 December 1917.[116]

Authorities in the town of Zweibrücken also recorded the raid.

> Dec. 5, 1917. Raid announced at 2.05 P.M. All clear signal given at 2.43 P.M. Time, 38 minutes. Total number of bombs dropped, 9; Cost

of damages, 13,743 marks The railroads were not bombed in this town.[117]

While one accepts that news releases composed for the home front should boost morale and that during wartime the RFC did not enjoy access to enemy reports, these two excerpts nevertheless highlight the disparity between public expectation and actuality.

On 6 December 1917, No. 55 Squadron again visited Saarbrücken. As on the previous day, poor weather conditions hampered the operation and one machine returned home with mechanical difficulties. These points were included in the detailed raid report but not in the war diary.[118] The latter reported that two formations "bombed the factories and Railways in and around SAARBRUCKEN," but postwar German records showed bursts only in the town, killing one person and injuring four others.[119]

After five days of stand-down for poor weather, No. 55 flew again on 11 December 1917. That day's entry in the war diary included these two paragraphs:

> Bomb Raid by 55 Squadron. At 1.20 p.m. on the 11th inst. machines bombed the Railway Junction N.E of PIRMASENS. 12 - 112 lb. and 10 - 25 lb. bombs were dropped from a height of 13,500 feet.
>
> At first weather conditions were good, but became very bad later and prevented Observers from seeing the effect of their bombs. Anti-aircraft fire was light. E.A. seen—Nil. All our machines returned safely.[120]

The detailed raid report narrative, given in full here, impeaches the impressions fostered by the War Diary.

> At 11 a.m. 12 De Havilland 4s. left in two formations of 6 to bomb the Railway Station and Factories at PIRMASENS.
>
> The leader of No. 2 raid experienced engine trouble, and owing to his signal not having been clearly seen, 4 other machines continued to follow him, and returned to the Aerodrome at 12.40 p.m.
>
> The remaining machines joined up with No. 1 raid.
>
> The formation of 7 then proceeded to its objective, but on approaching BITCHE, a thick bank of clouds was encountered, and the formation proceeded along the VOSGES by compass course to the objective, but on reaching this, it was found to be covered with clouds. There was a gap about 3 miles to the North, through which the important railway junction in the ERB valley could be seen, and the following bombs

were dropped from a height of 13,500 feet:-
10 112 lb. bombs
10 25 lb. bombs

It was impossible to take any photographs owing to the clouds, and the gap was covered before the Observers could see the effect of their bombs.

The weather conditions, which were exceptionally good at the start, had been becoming rapidly worse, and the whole country was under clouds when the formation returned.

All our machines returned safely. Owing to the clouds extending from 6,000 feet to 600, the formation became dispersed in descending. Then the leader landed safely at the Aerodrome at 3 p.m.

5 machines landed in a field near MARTIGNY to await improvement in the weather conditions.[121]

This mission was considerably more hectic than the War Diary admitted. Mechanical difficulties and aircrew inexperience conspired to cause the loss of nearly half the effective bombing force at the onset. The formation's navigation above the cloud layer also seems questionable, since German records indicate that no bombs fell in the vicinity of Pirmasens on 11 December 1917.[122] On their return trip, five machines descended through fog—luckily, without any midair collisions—to force-land in open country. Only the flight commander was able to locate the home aerodrome and land safely—after having been airborne four hours, a quarter-hour longer than his machine's normal flight endurance.[123]

Unfortunately, even the detailed raid reports exhibit the same biases as their more widely distributed companion. This distortion emerges when they are compared with the mission summaries that squadrons submitted to 41st Wing. For example, the final paragraphs of the detailed raid report for 11 December (the Pirmasens raid) candidly state that all machines eventually returned safely, though five DH4s landed elsewhere momentarily. The mission summary forwarded by No. 55 Squadron presented a less organized chronology:

At the time of writing five machines have been located, these have all landed near MARTIGNEY. One machine broke a vee piece of the undercarriage on landing, the remaining machine, one of No. 2 raid which joined No.1 raid, force landed and crashed at GIRONCOURT.

105

The pilot and observer were unhurt, but the machine is probably a "write off."

Twelve 112 lb and ten 25 lb bombs were dropped. It was impossible to take any photographs.[124]

Five bombers on this raid, landing "in a field near MAR-TIGNEY to await improvement in the weather conditions," (detailed raid report) actually seem to have been missing for a considerable period. Also, only three of the five were able to take off safely for return to base, according to the commanding officer of 55 Squadron.

In contrast to the war diary account, the 11 December mission to Pirmasens in reality turned into a salvage operation. Five machines abandoned the raid, four unnecessarily, within an hour of launch. The remainder of the force proceeded by dead reckoning to a rail junction, which they bombed without perceptible results. On the return journey, five DH4s force-landed, unable to locate their home aerodrome in friendly, relatively familiar territory; two of them sustained damage.

Unidentified further in Maj J. E. A. Baldwin's detailed raid report or the squadron summary, "Martiguy" is either Martigny-les-Gerbonvaux, 25 miles southwest of Nancy, or Martigny-les-Bains, 44 miles south-southwest. This level of navigational proficiency cast doubt on their claim to have located and bombed their assigned objective in Germany, some 65 miles from No. 55 Squadron's base area. While the detailed raid report asserted that "All our machines returned safely," the squadron summary indicates that their whereabouts and circumstances were unknown. This information concerning 41st Wing's sole daylight bombing unit warranted inclusion in at least the detailed raid report. Luckily, the next day proved unsuitable for service flying, which allowed the DH4 squadron time to regroup and refit. The chain of command above wing level remained ignorant of the extent to which weather conditions had influenced the course of the mission. The operation held considerably less drama on official returns than it actually had.

Nor were the interests of RFC officials above wing level furthered by rigorous analyses of 41st Wing activities. They, too, were interested in publicizing bombing successes. The classified "Summary of Work carried out by the Royal Flying Corps in the field during the month of October, 1917," prepared by Headquarters RFC for the War Cabinet, illustrates this attitude.

Besides this, raids were carried out in Germany. It is these raids which perhaps constitute the most notable feature of the month.

The raids were carried out by three squadrons which were sent down for this purpose to an aerodrome not far from Nancy.

The squadrons were at their new base ready for operations on the 16th October and from that date until the end of the month there was only one really fine day in that part of the country, when it was clear throughout the day, and besides this only one other day reported as "favourable for operations." On the remaining days, rain, snow, haze, mist, fog, heavy winds and banks of clouds were all experienced.

In spite of these circumstances, which could scarcely have been more adverse, raids were carried out against the factories of Burbach (3), those of Boos (2), on Saarbrucken Furnaces and station (2), on Marlenbach junction, Falkenbert Station, St. Avold Station, on the Pirmasens Boot Factory and Gas Works, and on the Volklingen Steel Factories.

In all 11 raids were attempted, 10 were carried out successfully and 12 tons of explosives were dropped.[125]

Without recourse to other documentation, one would accept this narrative and its statistics as an authoritative account of 41st Wing's work.

Examining the 41st Wing War Diary, itself a demonstrably incomplete record, reveals several significant points of variation with the staff summary prepared for the War Cabinet. Forty-first Wing was officially formed on 11 October, not "16th October," as claimed in the HQ RFC account. Instead of commencing active operations the next day, the impression fostered by the Headquarters summary, nearly a week intervened before the first mission.

HQ RFC also asserted that "there was only one really fine day in that part of the country" and "only one other day reported as 'favourable for operations.'" The war diary by contrast noted that on 29 October the weather was "bright and fine all day," and 30 October was likewise a "bright and fine day." At least four other days in this two-week period also seem to have been more promising than Headquarters admitted: the 17th and 21st each had "misty morning, clearing up later in the day," the 19th had "fine but low clouds," and the 24th had "low clouds and rain during the day, but clearing up towards the evening." Considering these meteorological "windows" later in the month, it seems unlikely that weather per se during the period 11–16 October precluded active operations. The war diary merely noted that "no Service Flying" occurred, without stating particular reasons.[126] Headquarters seemed to consider poor weather, a condition beyond human control, a major contributory factor in limiting 41st Wing operations. However, its cumulative effects upon missions already underway were never analyzed and seldom mentioned.

Also of interest in the HQ RFC summary is the method of determining the total number of raids flown or attempted during October 1917. For daylight missions, in which the machines of No. 55 Squadron sallied forth in formation to bomb a particular target such as the Burbach Works at Saarbrücken (17 October) or Pirmasens (30 October), each unit-sized effort can be counted as one raid. This criterion should also apply to night operations by the "Fees" of No. 100 Squadron or the Handley Pages of "A" Naval Squadron, even if individual aircrews became disoriented and struck targets in the general neighborhood of their assigned objective.

Railway attacks by No. 100 offer a case in point. On the evening of 29/30 October, nine FE2bs were launched to bomb the railways and buildings of Saarbrücken. "Owing to mist six pilots lost their bearing and returned without dropping their bombs"; the remainder dropped 865 pounds of bombs on Saarbrücken and 25 pounds each on St. Avold and Falkenberg, stations along the Metz-Saarbrücken rail link.[127] This operation should count as one raid, despite the enumeration of three targets in official reports. Likewise, on an earlier mission by No. 100 to the same vicinity, on 24/25 October, three aircraft bombed the Saarbrücken railway junction; five machines hit Merlenbach junction, on the line between Saarbrücken and St. Avold; and four other crews struck trains or stations near Willesburg, Falkenberg, St. Avold, and Homburg. Two aircraft went missing.[128] Despite the number of targets, this activity seems logically to constitute just one raid, especially when the relatively small (approximately 300 pounds) payload of the FE2b is considered. These two efforts, on 24/25 and 29/30 October, were No. 100 Squadron's only visits to Saarbrücken during the month. Yet the HQ RFC summary credits 41st Wing with one raid "on Merlenbach junction, Falkenberg station, St. Avold station," a tabulation that inflated the monthly mission total even as it disguised operational difficulties.

Similarly, the war diary recorded only four visits to objectives near Saarbrücken by elements of 41st Wing. The Headquarters summary claims five attacks, three against "the factories of Burback" and two on "Saarbrucken Furnaces and station," a generous total that also obscures the fact that the Burbach Works and the Saarbrücken Furnaces are identical. Such errors seem out of place in a summary prepared for the War Cabinet.

Counting one unit-sized effort to targets in a particular area as one raid, 41st Wing launched a total of seven completed raids during October 1917. In the same period, Newall's force attempted three unsuccessful missions, two by No. 55 Squadron on 19 October and one by "A" Naval to Mannheim the night of 30/31 October, when one Handley Page went missing in action. HQ RFC nevertheless reported to the War Cabinet that "In all 11 raids were attempted, 10 were carried out successfully." As controlling headquarters, Trenchard and his RFC staff had access to other 41st Wing operational returns in addition to the war diary. However, the diary's abbreviated, incomplete entries by themselves contradict the October "Summary of Work" report and undercut its credibility.

Similar instances of inexact terminology are also apparent in the "Summary of Work" for November 1917, during which a daylight raid on the first of the month to Kaiserslautern constituted the sole operation of 41st Wing.

At Ochey, in the southern area, the weather was still worse than in the west, and during the month only one bomb raid was carried out by 12 machines of No. 55 Squadron against the works at KAISERSLAUTERN, a distance of 100 miles from the aerodrome. Three 230 lb. bombs and six 112 lb. bombs were dropped from a height of 15,000 feet. The results were not observed owing to the clouds in

109

which there were only a few gaps. One hostile machine was shot to pieces during the operation. All our machines returned safely.[129]

Kaiserslautern, located some 75 miles behind the lines, contained several large iron and steel works, including four factories producing ammunition and weapon components.[130] Newall's detailed raid report, however, indicates a less tangible objective that day.

KAISERSLAUTERN was only seen through a small hole in the clouds, and 3 - 230 lb. and 6 - 112 lb. bombs were dropped. Owing to the clouds no actual bursts were observed, but the bombs undoubtedly fell well into the Town. The moral effect should be good as the 1st November was a Fete Day and a general holiday.[131]

Despite the optimism of the 41st Wing's commanding officer, the raid inflicted very little damage of any sort. German records reveal that only three aerial bombs fell within the city limits that day, causing no casualties and damage totaling no more than 100 marks.[132] The "Summary of Work" omitted Newall's hope that poorly aimed ordnance had moral effect, even if results were unobserved.

HQ RFC also deleted from its report any information showing the strength and effect of German countermeasures upon the Kaiserslautern mission, data of potential interest to Whitehall. The 41st Wing war diary had admitted that, of 12 DH4s launched on 1 November, "The second Raid of 6 machines did not reach its objective owing to heavy engagement with 7 E.A. [enemy aircraft] Scouts."[133] The detailed raid report illuminated the full extent of this misadventure. "Five pilots released their bombs in the open country in order that they might be better able to maneuver. The majority of these bombs fell in the Lakes and woods near DIEUZE."[134] Dieuze, over 55 miles southwest of Kaiserslautern, was less than 10 miles over the lines. No. 55 Squadron was turned back by enemy action within sight of their home aerodrome.

In its November summary, HQ RFC also failed to mention the attempted mission on the 14th, by 16 aircraft of No. 55 Squadron. After the mission had been abandoned due to poor weather, a pilot was killed and one observer "in a flying accident over Aerodrome."[135] To withhold such unpalatable information as this and the Kaiserslautern operation meant that the War Cabinet received a seriously flawed impression of 41st Wing and its potential, much as news releases fostered the same views among the public.

As had been the case with No. 3 Wing and the Admiralty, all levels in the command eventually assumed a direct, inevitable correlation between intensity of operational effort and desired results. Wishful thinking and selectively interpreting some of the few available indicators while ignoring others compounded the problem of determining progress. The absence of required information for judging relative success encouraged this approach.

The authorities instead tended to focus upon standards of unit performance they could influence and measure. Although official records and summaries differ with respect to wastage, numbers of machines, numbers of raids, and even weather conditions, they invariably agree on the total weight of bombs dropped on a given operation. Forty-first Wing staff recorded total time flown daily, sometimes less than five minutes, in the war diary.[136] Such statistics documenting activity implied concomitant results.

Also symptomatic of this organizational confusion of means and ends is the questionable method by which HQ RFC manipulated data in order to amass the highest possible raid total, discussed above. Nor would any link in the chain gain by a skeptical approach to the data it forwarded. The network responsible for British bombing of Germany also originated the reports, bulletins, and press releases by which the success of the campaign would be officially and publicly ascertained. No institutional incentive to strive for objectivity existed; the quest would be counterproductive. The prime minister's admonition to Trenchard on 2 October 1917, subsequently underlined by the publicity afforded GHQ raid dispatches, established the necessity of reporting a successful campaign.

Following the Armistice, intelligence teams of the British and American air services were able to determine the extent of the material and moral injuries inflicted upon Germany by 41st Wing ordnance. Using German records, it became possible to determine the general effects of the British offensive. Earlier, missions, machines, and bomb poundage against five categories of strategic objectives were enumerated. These categories can now be analyzed separately to ascertain the actual, direct damages caused by 41st Wing raids. The moral effects of the campaign will be assessed in a subsequent chapter. Tangible results are easier to determine, given the extent of German documentation.

The weight of British effort was directed against iron and steel works. At Saarbrücken, blast furnaces were mainly concentrated in the western suburb of Burbach.[137] Of four attacks (three day, one night) on these factories and foundries, only 41st Wing's initial mission, by day on 17 October 1917, caused sufficient damage to be logged by German industrial managers.

Raid No.	Date	No. of Bombs	Place and Kind of Damage
7	17/10/17	3	Fell on a siding in rear of coke grounds-West, near a cooling tower, and in front of the Foundry clubhouse, thus destroying some rails which were torn up from the tracks just behind the cooling tower and damaging badly the clubhouse building and the neighboring foundry officials residences. 17,500.00 Marks[138]

The equivalent contemporary cost of industrial damages in pounds sterling would have been approximately £ 875.[139] Of sixteen 112-pound aerial bombs that No. 55 Squadron aimed at Burbach, only three landed within the works, despite aircrew reports that "eight bombs were seen to burst on the BURBACK FACTORY."[140] However, this raid caused other damage totaling 53,000 marks (£ 2,650), though no civilians were killed or injured.[141] This mission, the only one to hit objectives within the Burbach Works, caused roughly three times more damage to nonindustrial sections of Saarbrücken.

Returning aircrews from three subsequent raids on the city also claimed to have inflicted substantial damage. Observers in seven Handley Pages that attacked the Burbach works the night of 24/25 October, bombing from altitudes between 400 and 1,500 feet, reported direct hits. "84 - 112 lb. bombs on BURBACK WORKS on the Western side of SAARBRUCKEN. All direct hits."[142]

Similar claims resulted from No. 55 Squadron's daylight attacks on 5 and 6 December 1917.

> 5 December 8 - 112 lb. and 8 - 25 lb. bombs were dropped in the Factories immediately West of SAARBRUCKEN.
>
> 6 December About 1.30 p.m. No. 55 Squadron (11 machines) bombed the Factories and Railways in and around SAARBRUCKEN. Bombs as under were dropped from 13,000 feet:-
>
> _ 1 - 230 lb.
> _ 18 - 112 lb.
> _ 8 - 20 lb. Total 2,406 lbs.
>
> Many direct hits were obtained. Fires were started in BURBACH and ST. JOHANN Factories and also in the Railway Station.[143]

Detailed raid report narratives corroborated war diary descriptions of these raids.[144] By contrast, German industrial records from the Burbach complex indicate that none of these attacks hit the intended target. Instead, ordnance within Saarbrücken itself killed 13 citizens, wounded 20, and caused 279,000 marks (£ 13,950) worth of property damage.[145] In a situation that invites comparison with No. 3 Wing efforts in the same vicinity, only the first of four attacks by 41st Wing against the Burbach works managed to place bombs within the industrial perimeter.

Results at other blast furnace targets on the 41st Wing mission list were similarly disappointing. American intelligence teams learned after the Armistice that bomb damage at Bous and Wadgassen, for the entire war period, amounted to 8,261 marks (£ 413), a total that exactly matched the figures reported by the British survey party.[146] According to the latter, "no material damage from bombs was recorded at this place" but "anti-aircraft dropping on the office of the factory" caused 3,000 marks (£ 150) in damages.[147] The 41st Wing had attacked the two localities by day on 21 October 1917, with 11 DH4s of No. 55 Squadron dropping 2,464 pounds of bombs.[148]

113

Of four raids on the Carl Foundry at Thionville, only the 21/22 January 1918 attack caused notable damage. German records show that only one of 17 bombs landed near the target area. "One bomb thrown. The bomb apparently bursted in front of a house in the foundry street on the telephone wires. Glass damage."[149] The remaining 16 British bombs apparently fell well outside any built-up areas; the local authorities did not record their existence in the column "No. of Bombs Outside Foundry Grounds."[150]

Overall, in its campaign against enemy iron and steel works, 41st Wing made little headway. Major Paul, the air intelligence officer for the strategic bombing program, conducted a postwar survey of the effects of bombing German blast furnaces. "In no case can the material results achieved by any one single raid on a blast furnace be said to have been very striking. Indeed, with one or two exceptions, the amount of material damage wrought has been decidedly disappointing." "Other raids carried out on the BURBACH Works give an average result of about 8,000 Marks, or about £ 400 per raid."[151]

Major Paul's survey parties also conducted extensive interviews of plant managers. The opinions of these industrial executives proved to be consistent with Paul's conclusions.

> Generally speaking, the Directors did not attach much importance to air raids.
>
> They were ready to admit the justifiability of bombing from a military point of view, but condemned the Allies' principle of attacking workmen's colonies.
>
> With few exceptions, the Directors asserted that the material damage had been insignificant and had not affected the war one way or the other. Such damage had invariably been repaired at once without any difficulty, and in very few cases had any stoppage of work resulted.
>
> Our shooting, they considered, was very erratic both by day and night. They were anxious to know what portion of the Works was aimed at; the vital points, the buildings, the workmen's cottages or the Works as a whole.[152]

In a dozen day and night attacks, British aircrews flying 70 machines claimed to have dropped 26,553 pounds of bombs (20,027 pounds by night) on enemy blast furnaces. This undertaking represented 44.5 percent of the total bomb pound-age delivered by 41st Wing between October 1917 and January 1918. In the considered opinions of air intelligence teams and German officials, material results were incommensurate with effort.

Nor did material results at German munitions and chemical works entirely fulfill British expectations. Although aircrew reports habitually refer to "Mannheim," their objectives, the enormous "Badische Aniline und Soda Fabrik" (BASF) complex and its annex at Oppau, were in fact located across the river in Ludwigshafen. Throughout the war, the Germans made every effort to keep these works amply supplied with raw materials, especially coal, "of which 1700 tons were used daily."[153] Investigators noted that "the buildings of these two Works are of the most massive type. The walls of some are three feet thick."[154] In two attacks, by day on 24 December 1917 and on the night of 24/25 January 1918, 41st Wing aircrews were unable to drop any ordnance within the grounds of the BASF or Oppau factories.[155] Aircrews, however, reported numerous observed bursts inside the industrial perimeters on both missions.[156] American investigators were told by local authorities that Ludwigshafen proper had incurred damage from 41st Wing raids on the two occasions.

Dec. 24, 1917	Raid lasted from 12.50 A.M. to 1.20 A.M. 2 bombs were dropped in this city, the balance in Mannheim.
Jan. 2, 1918	Raid lasted from 9.00 P.M. to 9.45 P.M. 3 bombs were dropped. One bomb fell between Ludwigshafen and Mannheim, damaging the telephone line which was repaired at a cost of 42.84 Marks (approximately £ 2).[157]

At Kaiserslautern, after the 1 November 1917 raid, in which enemy action turned back half the attacking force of 12 DH4s, all military and industrial objectives survived untouched. Bomb damage to civilian and municipal property amounted to just 100 marks (£ 5).[158] German authorities refused permission for British and American survey teams to enter Karlsruhe, south of the "bridgeheads" of the Allied occupation zone. Records of air raids on that city do not include the 41st Wing day mission of 14 January 1918.[159]

Newall's force attacked enemy munitions and chemical targets on four occasions, with 29 machines dropping 7,710 pounds of bombs (6,366 pounds by No. 55 Squadron in daylight). At the BASF and Oppau works in Ludwigshafen and at Kaiserslautern, the attacks did absolutely no damage of strategic significance. At Karlsruhe, lack of evidence precluded definite conclusion.

Forty-first Wing directed over half its operational efforts (57.4 percent of bomb poundage, 53.5 percent of sorties) against blast furnaces and chemical/munition centers, two categories of particular interest to the War Cabinet. Actual results proved to be disappointing at best, far less than the estimates in wartime evaluations and public releases.

With respect to 41st Wing attacks on the German railway system, little data on specific targets is available. Railroad targets, the favorite objective of night-flying "Fees" of No. 100 Squadron, accounted for 33 percent of the totals of bombs dropped and sorties flown. "The results of the bombing of stations have been consistently moderate. On rare occasions only can they be said to have [been] really satisfactory. . . . a certain amount of success was achieved, but not so much as might have been hoped." "Unfortunately, there is nothing on record to show what the effects of bombs would have been on railway bridges. Judging by the effects of bombs on solid buildings, it is doubtful whether much damage would have been done by any bomb of less weight than 1650 lb."[160] One must remember that, in this extract, Major Paul was summarizing the cumulative effects of the entire British campaign of strategic bombardment between October 1917 and the Armistice. The 1,650-pound aerial bomb did not reach active service until October 1918; fewer than a dozen were dropped on Germany before the end of hostilities.[161]

Available information on a limited number of rail objectives tends to support Paul's conclusions. German records indicate that St. Avold and Bensdorf stations, reported by 41st Wing to have been bombed on the nights of 24/25 and 29/30 October 1917 and again on 16/17 and 21/22 January 1918, in fact sustained no damage of any sort on those dates.[162] At Zweibrücken, bombed on 5 December 1917 by one of two DH4 formations forced by weather to divert from Mannheim, British aircrews reported that at least 12 bombs hit "the Railway Station and Sidings."[163] Local records show only that nine bombs caused 13,743 marks' (£ 687) worth of damage to civilian property within the town that day.[164] In fact, railways in the vicinity of Zweibrücken were never hit by Allied bombs.[165] According to the 41st Wing war diary, 16 bombs "were dropped on the Factories immediately West of SAARBRUCKEN" (also hit on 5 December 1917 as a weather-divert target).[166] German records available to the British survey team listed different results. "SAARBRUCKEN was attacked at 2.25 p.m. on Dec. 5th, 1917. About 11 bombs were dropped. A house and drug store were seriously damaged. Two bombs fell near a repair shop in SAARBRUCKEN Station, damaging telegraph and telephone wire."[167] Local authorities, basing their opinion on the damage inflicted, concluded that British planes had been trying to hit railways rather than blast furnaces at Burbach. These examples of 41st Wing rail attacks seem to be typical for the period October 1917–January 1918. Frequently, night bombing tactics employed by No. 100 Squadron scattered ordnance in the vicinity of several stations without significantly disrupting rail traffic.

This geographical separation of railway targets attacked on a single night also suggests that Newall's force did not seriously attempt a sustained, systematic offensive against them. Despite assurances given by the French, by Haig, and by the War Cabinet, 41st Wing never cooperated to any noticeable extent in French bombing plans. The British consequently bombed on an ad hoc basis.

The consensus of opinion of our bombing by the German officials is summed up in the word "annoying." Judging from observations and conversations with German officials, this statement is neither an exaggeration nor an underestimate.

They considered our shooting was moderate, but pointed out that it varied very much. As regards the stoppage and dislocation of traffic, they maintained that damage had never been so great as to entirely isolate a station for a period of long duration.

They stated that attacks on trains running on open lines between stations had been frequent, but this was outside their own experience and they professed not to know what effect it had.[168]

Opportunities rather than firm priorities appeared to govern the actual targets of 41st Wing night-bombing aircrews, particularly when weather or inexperience made navigation difficult.

Three missions, the Pirmasens attack of 30 October 1917 and the night and day raids on Treves on 24/25 and 27 January 1918, merit comment. They exemplify the disparity that existed, even under good conditions, between aircrew observations and the actual effects of bombing.

Major Baldwin, commander of No. 55 Squadron's raid on the tanning factories at Pirmasens on 30 October, a "bright and fine day," reported on the mission.

Two machines were damaged by A.A. fire which was more accurate although not so heavy as usual. Observers in the first raid saw at least two bursts in the centre of town close to factory No. 4, besides at least six others in the town and outskirts. . . . Capt Stevens M.C. saw the smoke rising from what he thought was fire at or near No. 4. . . . Lt Mackay, Lt Marshall's observer, saw two bursts on railway sidings, bracketing railway station, one burst on or near gas works near factory No. 4 and claims they were his own bombs. 2/Lt Castle also confirms one burst on factory and one on or near gas works. The remaining bursts were seen in the outskirts to the northern end of the town.[169]

Captain Paul's intelligence report for this mission reiterated these observations and noted that "No E.A. (enemy aircraft) seen throughout operation."[170] At 41st Wing headquarters, Newall scribbled "Good effort" across Baldwin's summary and forwarded its details up the chain of command. The next morning, *The Times* printed the GHQ dispatch: "This morning, at 11 a.m., 12 of our machines went further afield, and attacked the munitions works and gasworks at Pirmasens, 20 miles beyond Saarbrucken. Bombs were seen to burst in the factories and on the gasworks, with excellent results."[171] Since other periodicals also reprinted the dispatch, with "munitions works" rather than "boot factories" as the target, it is likely that Haig's headquarters was responsible for the original error.[172]

After the war, the British survey team visited Pirmasens. On the 30 October 1917 mission, when neither enemy aircraft nor appreciable antiaircraft fire was present over the target, aircrew observers emphatically claimed at least eight hits within the city limits, two in the center of town and others near the railway gas works. In contrast, German bomb-plot diagrams show two distinct bomb patterns that particular day, one a mile southwest of town and the other scattered across the outskirts and fields northwest of the city. No bombs fell in the vicinity of the factories and gas works. American investigators in Pirmasens learned also that on 30 October 1917, only nine of 20 dropped bombs had detonated; one person was killed.[173]

Unlike the Pirmasens operation, which took place on one of the best flying days of the period, deteriorating meteorological conditions influenced two 41st Wing raids on Treves. In the first attack, 16 FE2bs of No. 100 Squadron took off at 5 P.M. on 24 January 1918 to bomb Treves barracks and railway station, as well as targets at Thionville. Engine trouble forced five machines to abort, but four "Fees" persisted to claim these results at Treves, a city of 50,000: "Very good bursts being observed in the Northern portion and in the centre of Town, and a very large fire being caused in the N.E. corner of the Town, which was observed later by other pilots."[174]

Three days later, two formations of six DH4s from No. 55 Squadron attacked Treves. Weather dictated the conduct of the raid.

Although the sky was quite clear, the ground was obscured by a very thick mist practically the whole way. In consequence both formations passed the objective and flew about 15 miles North of it where there was a gap in the clouds, in order to ascertain their whereabouts. On returning the first formation passed over the objective and recognized it by the River showing up through the mist. They dropped 1 - 230 lb. and 8 - 112 lb. bombs, but could not observe the bursts as the mist was so thick. Only one pilot of the second formation was able to recognize the target, and he dropped 1 - 230 lb. bomb, the effects of which were also unobserved, although he caught a glimpse of the target for a very short period.

The first formation returned to the Aerodrome at 2.5 p.m. and the second at 2.10 p.m., having encountered no E.A., and only experiencing slight A.A. fire on crossing the lines.

9 photographs were exposed which, however, were useless owing to the mist.

Total bombs dropped:
          2 - 230 lb
          8 - 112 lb   = TOTAL 1,365 lbs.[175]

The US Bombing Survey, however, reported different results from these two raids. German records failed to support the wartime reports:

> German records of these two attacks differ from the wartime reports submitted by 41st Wing. Jan. 24, 1918. Raid lasted from 7.35 P.M. to 8.35 P.M. 2 bombs fell in village of Seyen, just outside of Trier, damaging fourteen houses and buildings, on which claims of 406.55M. about 20 were paid, of which amount 180M. was paid by insurance companies. 1 man failed to report damage.

> Jan. 27, 1918. There was no raid on Trier this day but anti-aircraft fire damaged property of 46 people, on which claims to the extent of 994.56M. approximately 50 were paid, of which 917.35M. was paid by insurance companies. 34 people who carried insurance failed to report damage.[176]

The mayor of Ehrang, a town four miles north of Treves, noted that at 1 P.M. on 27 January, "one bomb fell close to the Russian prison camp but did no damage."[177] This projectile probably belonged to the only pilot in the second formation to bomb on that day; besides their proximity, Ehrang and Treves lie in the Moselle valley, with little to distinguish between them from the air.

Thus, under weather conditions varying from unlimited visibility to solid overcast, 41st Wing aircrews experienced difficulties in hitting targets smaller than a large town. This inability to bomb accurately, even when the proper objective had been reached, plagued the British force throughout the war.

The question of accuracy has generally been investigated in terms of apparatus rather than attitude. Considerable investigation has been done concerning different designs and tolerances of the mechanical and optical bombsights of the period. Neville Jones devoted several sections of *The Origins of Strategic Bombing* to the development, description, and operation of the Central Flying School (CFS) 4B bombsight, the Wimperis "drift" sight, and the negative lens sight, all used by 41st Wing or their successors.[178]

These various instruments represented different approaches to the problem of accuracy in bombing under operating conditions. Less technically, in *First of Many*, Alan Morris asserts that planners "knew" that bombs salvoed from a formation at 1,500 feet had a circular error probable (CEP) of 308 yards radius on the ground. Similarly, "toggling" bombs individually yielded a CEP of 425 yards.[179] Both analyses assume that the degree of accuracy is imposed by design limitations of the bombsight.

However, aircrew accounts—quite apart from evidence on German bomb-plot diagrams—reveal that pilots and observers developed their own techniques for bomb-aiming. In a paper prepared for the first course at the new Royal Air Force Staff College at Cranwell, Wing Commander Baldwin, who commanded No. 55 Squadron and succeeded Newall as commanding officer of 41st Wing in early 1918, said of bomb-aiming:

> Simplicity in operation allied to reasonable accuracy is what is needed in a two-seater bomber. In the last war the mirror sight was by far the most useful and most popular. Even with this simple sight, pilots worked out still simpler methods of their own. For example, it was found that bombing down wind on a DH4 at a target such as a munition factory, if one released the bombs as the centre of the target disappeared under the leading edge of the bottom plane in line with the port inside bay strut, this coincided with the moment when the target appeared on the intersection of the wires of your mirror sight.[180]

Baldwin's approach to the problem enjoys the virtue of extreme simplicity; his narrative hints that other pilots evolved their own solutions, undoubtedly of comparable accuracy, to the bombing problem. Lt William Armstrong, a DH9A pilot in No. 110 Squadron of the long-range bombing force, expressed another common view of available bombsights.

> Fellows who had been overseas told me they never used their bomb-sights. And if my own experience counted for anything, they were a waste of money. There were two kinds; the Farnsborough model and the Aldis. The former was a simple thing of wires and a spirit level. The Aldis was more complicated and had a large lens in the aircraft floor. "It's no good," one of the men from France told me: "all we used it for was to look through and be sure our bombs had

gone." And I am afraid that it came in for no more use than this—anyway, so far as my own squadron was concerned.[181]

A natural reluctance on the part of aircrews over enemy territory to concentrate their attention on any device inside the cockpit for more than a second or two obviated efficient use of any bombsight. The wide cockpit separation of the DH4 made timely coordination difficult even for conscientious pilots and observers. At night, reduced visibility generally offset the advantages of lower bombing altitudes. Targets from almost any height seem to be "impossible to miss." In the light of such attitudes and tactical constraints, it seems pointless to debate the technical merits of various bombsights.

Major Paul also investigated this matter of bombing accuracy under combat conditions in the final volume of his bombing survey. Considering the British campaign from October 1917 to November 1918, he advanced four hypotheses to account for the poor aiming demonstrated by bomber aircrews.

> It is submitted that shooting, in so far as it was moderate, chiefly owed its failure, in the case of day squadrons, to the high altitude and, on occasion, to the heavy barrages put us by the enemy over vital points. But the following causes may, perhaps, have also contributed in a small degree towards making shooting less accurate than it might have been:
>
> Lack of interest on the part of many pilots since they were not expected to aim independently when flying in formation.
>
> Failure on the part of some squadron commanders and flight commanders to grasp the importance of military, as apart from material, damage.
>
> In the case of night pilots it would appear, judging by results, that there was a tendency at times to drop an odd bomb or two on objectives of their own choosing. The night pilot has a considerable advantage in altitude over the day pilot and, if visibility is good, can probably pick out his objective with reasonable certainty; but this advantage is entirely neutralized if, as happens on rare occasions, he elects to aim at a theatre, or even at a cathedral, in preference to a railway station or munition factory.[182]

In his postwar lecture to the Royal United Services Institute, Air Commodore Brooke-Popham also addressed the matter of bombing performance. His explication, also spanning the entire period of British strategic bombing, suggested several factors indicative of training deficiencies.

> I should like to say one or two words about bombing. The first point is that during the war, we really never got going with bombing on an extensive scale, partly for lack of suitable bombs, but chiefly owing to want of suitable machines. In addition to this, the bombs were not always dropped in the most effective manner, partly owing to a lack of time for training pilots and observers in the use of bomb sights, and partly because the ground personnel were not sufficiently trained in the handling of bombs, with the result that quite a large portion of them were badly assembled as regards their detonating components and failed to explode when dropped. Another reason was the lack of military training of pilots and observers. This may seem rather far fetched, but the effect was that they did not appreciate in many cases the military significance of their particular mission, and were inclined to drop their bombs on some neighbouring and more attractive target, failing to realize its comparative unimportance compared to that of their original objective.[183]

Major Paul enumerated four shortcomings, each related to the lack of training which Brooke-Popham blamed for mediocre bombing results during the war. Paul's "lack of confidence" in bombsights and "lack of interest" in accuracy are the operational manifestations of the organizational "lack of time for training pilots and observers" to which Brooke-Popham attributed such moderate results. Similarly, Brooke-Popham's second hypothesis, "the lack of military training of pilots and observers," is congruent with Paul's complaint that aircrew failed to "grasp the importance of military, as apart from material, damage." Finally, both comment at length on the tendency for aircrews to select their own targets despite having assigned objectives. Significantly, Brooke-Popham referred to lack of time, rather than lack of resources or techniques, as the major constraint in instructing students in the skills and attitudes required for active operations. The difference between Paul's and Brooke-Popham's assessments lies primarily in their respective operational and organizational orientations; they agree that aircrews were insufficiently trained for the demands of active service flying.

In this regard, the policies of the Royal Flying Corps must bear most of the responsibility. The offensive philosophy meant the steady influx of replacements would be ill-prepared for the demands of combat operations. Eventually, the vicious cycle developed: casualties replaced by inexperienced crews who became casualties. There wasn't enough time to train aircrews to survivable standards. In the field, the consequences of the offensive policy meant that squadrons received new pilots and observers lacking the tactical skill or organizational motivation to do a first-rate job consistently.

In mitigation, one must acknowledge that the political and military chain of command responsible for long-range bombardment never clarified the goals of the campaign for the commanders in the field. Despite Paul's and Brooke-Popham's complaints that aircrew often ignored assigned targets, no firm priorities or target lists were ever formulated, despite the French example. This confusion, as well as the impetus to present 41st Wing operations as indubitable successes, originated with the War Cabinet and Lloyd George.

The lack of required indicators for evaluating the campaign's progress, plus the pressure to report only victories, reinforced the habit of selectively interpreting what little information about bombing results was available. Trenchard at HQ RFC seemed particularly susceptible to optimism. As with No. 3 Wing, ambiguity and frustration encouraged all levels of command to assume that bombing effects, though unknown, could be estimated by the intensity of operational activity. Hours flown, sorties launched, and bombs dropped were accepted as proof of worthwhile results. Very little indication to the contrary existed, and no one in the chain of command had anything to gain by adopting a skeptical stance.

This state of affairs eventually created an inflated expectation of the potential for strategic bombing. The purported achievements of 41st Wing were widely publicized, with political approval. More significantly, official reports were edited to convey the same impression to those responsible for supervising the bombing campaign. Whitehall developed an unwarranted confidence in the strategic efficacy of 41st Wing, as did the British public. These high hopes would make it increasingly difficult in the future to reevaluate the concept of long-range bombardment as a significant or decisive weapon. The air authorities in particular would find it extremely difficult to examine their own wartime data critically.

Notes

1. H. A. Jones, *The War in the Air: Being the Story of the Part Played in the Great War by the Royal Air Force,* 6 vols. (Oxford: Clarendon Press, 1937), 165.

2. Andrew P. Boyle, *Trenchard* (London: Collins, 1962), 227–28.

3. Public Records Office (PRO), Air Ministry Records (AIR) 1/678/21/13/2102, Trenchard to Air Policy Committee, 28 November 1917.

4. Jones, *War in the Air,* vol. 6, 172.

5. Neville Jones, *The Origins of Strategic Bombing: A Study of the Development of British Air Strategic Thought and Practice up to 1918* (London: Eimber, 1973), 147.

6. Ibid., note 28, 227. N. Jones bases his opinion upon AIR 8/167, "Private Interview with Lord Trenchard. Dictated Notes by H. A. Jones, 11 April 1934."

7. Ibid., 147–48; and Boyle, 227–28.

8. Cyril Falls, *Military Operations, France and Belgium, 1917* (London: Macmillan and Co., 1940–48), 504–5; and Brian Bond, *War and Society in Europe, 1870–1970* (Bungay, England: Richard Clay, 1984), 123–24.

9. N. Jones, *Origins of Strategic Bombing,* 148–49.

10. Oddly, this Final Dispatch of 1 January 1919 did not appear in the appendices volume of the official history. H. A. Jones quoted from it selectively in *War in the Air,* vol. 6, 135–37. For its full text, see *Aeroplane,* 8 January 1919, 129–31.

11. AIR 1/1649/204/95/6, file, "Organisation Correspondence, VIII Brigade, October 1917–December 1918," letter to HQ, RFC (CRFC 1937/55Q), 6 October 1917.

12. Ibid.

13. War Diary of Eighth Brigade, Newall Papers, B392; and Maurice Baring, *Flying Corps Headquarters, 1914–1918* (London: Bell, 1920), 255.

14. War Diary of Eighth Brigade; and Baring, 255.

15. War Diary of Eighth Brigade, 15 and 29 October 1917; and Baring, 255.

16. AIR 1/1649/204/95/6, Trenchard to Haig, 13 November 1917.

17. US Air Service aerodromes occupied mainly the Toul-Verdun rear areas. Maurer Maurer, ed., *The U.S. Air Service in World War I,* vol. 1, *The Final Report and a Tactical History* (Maxwell Air Force Base [AFB], Ala.: Air Force Historical Research Agency [AFHRA], 1978), 29–32.

18. War Diary of Eighth Brigade, 29 November and 4 December 1917.

19. War Diary of Eighth Brigade, November–December 1917.

20. PRO, AIR 1/1649/204/95/6, Trenchard to Haig, 4 December 1917; and A. R. Kingsford, *Night Raiders of the Air: Being the Experience of a Night*

Flying Pilot Who Raided Hunland on Many Dark Nights during the War (London: Hamilton, 1930), 103, describes Ochey airfield as it appeared in the winter of 1917–18. Ochey is presently a large French air base.

21. Leonard Miller, *The Chronicles of 55 Squadron, R.F.C. and R.A.F.* (London: Unwin, 1919), 59.

22. AIR 1/1649/204/95/6, Trenchard to Haig, 4 December 1917.

23. Ibid., Trenchard to QMG, GHQ, 26 December 1917.

24. Maurer Maurer, ed., *The U.S. Air Service in World War I*, vol. 2, *Early Concepts of Military Aviation* (Maxwell AFB, Ala.: AFHRA, 1978), 141.

25. Ibid., 151. Colonel Gorrell fondly hoped that America could "take the initiative in bringing about such a coordination" for joint bombing program.

26. In Gorrell's "Early History of the Strategical Section," in "History of the Air Service, AEF" (the so-called "Gorrell History" comprising 280 volumes), B-6, 371-401, January 1919. Reprinted in Maurer, *Early Concepts of Military Aviation*, 152.

27. Ibid.

28. Gorrell's initial proposals for the American bombing program drew heavily upon British estimates of German industrial vulnerabilities. See Maurer, *Early Concepts of Military Aviation*, 143, 145.

29. Ibid. This personnel policy for aviation units was the antithesis of Pershing's doctrinal refusals to permit piecemeal infusion of American soldiers into understrength Allied armies as replacements for British and French casualties.

30. Numerous American aviators gained their experience with RFC and RAF squadrons before returning to the US Air Service. One, Capt. Charles L. Heater, transferred from No. 55 Squadron, RAF to the American 11th Aero Squadron to replace its commander, who had been lost on operations on 18 September 1918. See *The U.S. Air Service in World War I*, vol.4, *Postwar Review*, ed. Maurer Maurer (Maxwell AFB, Ala.: AFHRA, 1979), 94; and Miller, 77.

31. Maurer, *Early Concepts of Military Aviation*, 153.

32. Baring, 262.

33. Ibid., 272.

34. Trenchard, Final Dispatch, 1 January 1919.

35. "The Independent Force," Draft of R.A.F. Staff College lecture, sent to Brig-Gen C. L. N. Newall by Brooke-Popham, November 1923, Newall Papers (B405), Royal Air Force Museum (RAFM), Hendon, England, 3.

36. PRO, AIR 1/2085/207/5/1, bound volume "I.F. H.Q. Communiqués, June–November 1918," has map of aerodrome areas in 1:600,000 scale, dated 20 September 1918, apparently used by staff for planning purposes. Tactical Pilotage Charts (TPC) E-2C and E-2D (1:500,000), Director of Military Survey, Ministry of Defence, United Kingdom, Her Majesty's Stationery Office (HMSO), 1979, have topographical information based on 500-ft contour intervals for the region. See "Carte Topographique" No. 23, "Nancy, Bar-le-Duc" (1:100,000), Institut Geographique National (Paris), 1981, for area details based on 10-m. contour intervals. In May 1984 a

first-hand ground and aerial reconnaissance of the aerodrome area confirmed the conclusions of map study.

37. Ibid.

38. War Diary of Eighth Brigade, Newall Papers, B392; and Philip J. R. Moyes, *Bomber Squadrons of the R.A.F. and their Aircraft* (London: Macdonald, 1964).

39. Bruce Robertson, *The Army and Aviations: A Pictorial History* (London: Cassell, 1978), 18.

40. Ibid.

41. Miller, 61, 92–93, gives aviators' opinions of these nonflying technicians.

42. C. Gordon Burge, *Annals of 100 Squadron* (London: Herbert Reach, 1919), 9; and W.R. Read Papers, private diary no. 7, entry for 2 September 1918, London: Imperial War Museum (IWM), 82/76/2.

43. W. R. Read Papers, 2 September 1918, IWM, 72/76/2.

44. J. E. A. Baldwin, "Experiences of Bombing with the Independent Force in 1918," in *A Selection of Lectures and Essays from the Work of Officers Attending the First Course at the Royal Air Force Staff College, 1922–1923* (London: HMSO, Air Ministry, December 1923), 2–5, details these tactical responsibilities.

45. J. M. Bruce, *The Aeroplanes of the Royal Flying Corps (Military Wing)* (London: Putnam, 1982), 49–61; and W. M. Lamberton, *Reconnaissance and Bomber Aircraft of the 1914–1918 War* (Warwick, England: Warwick Printing, 1962), 36–37.

46. H. A. Jones, *War in the Air*, Appendix 27, between 130–31; and Baldwin, 3.

47. George E. A. Reinburg (Commanding Officer [CO], 2d Day Bombardment Group, US Air Service), "Lessons Learned," in Maurer, *Early Concepts of Military Aviation*, 87.

48. Lamberton, 13.

49. Ibid.

50. Baldwin, 2–5.

51. War Diary of the Eighth Brigade, entry for mission to Pirmasens, 11 December 1917, Newall Papers, B392. Attacking force consequently diminished from 12 aircraft to seven.

52. War Diary of Eighth Brigade, Newall Papers, B392; Kingsford; and Burge.

53. Bruce, 414.

54. Ibid.

55. Lamberton, 64.

56. H. A. Jones, *War in the Air*, Appendix 27, 30–31.

57. Kingsford, 212.

58. Miller, 19.

59. Ibid., 117.

60. Burge, 50, 57.

61. Kingsford, 105, 122.

62. Ibid., 211–13.

63. War Diary of Eighth Brigade, 11–17 October 1917.

64. No reliable, comprehensive operational summary exists for 41st Wing activities. Data were compiled from a number of sources: R.A.F. Hendon, B392 (Newall Papers), War Diary of Eighth Brigade; B393 (Newall Papers), Detailed Raid Reports Submitted by Eighth Brigade R.C/RAF to Independent Force Headquarters on Bombing Operations, October 1917–June 1918. Some of the latter are also in PRO AIR 1/2266/209/70/26, Reports of Bombing Operations of Ochey Squadrons. See also AIR 1/1986/204/273/111, Intelligence Reports of Raids before 15 June 1918, Maj H. W. M. Paul (41st Wing, RFC) to Air Ministry; AIR 1/2085/207/5/3, Approximate Results, 41st Wing, RAF 17 October 1917–11 November 1918. Data from logbooks, diaries, and memoirs of aircrew also provided useful cross-checks.

65. Take-off and landing times are in AIR 1/2085/207/5/3, Approximate Results.

66. Detailed Raid Report for 1 November 1917, Newall Papers, B393.

67. "Report by Captain Lambe after Visit to "A" Naval Squadron at Ochey," 31 October 1917, PRO, AIR 1/640.

68. W. R. Read Papers, unpublished autobiography, IWM, 72/76/1, 38; W. R. Read Papers, private diary no. 7, entries for 17, 23, August 1918, IWM, 72/76/2; E. D. Hardings et. al., *History of Number 16 Squadron (known as "A" Naval Squadron) Royal Naval Air Service Renumbered 216 Squadron Independent Force, Royal Air Force* (London: H. W. Hill & Son, 1923), Appendix C, 65; and in draft at PR; and AIR 1/184/15/219/1.

69. Denis Winter, *The First of the Few: Fighter Pilots of the First World War* (London: Allen Lane, 1982), 36.

70. Mason M. Patrick, "Final Report of Chief of Air Service, A.E.F.," *Air Service Information Circular (Aviation)* 2, no. 180 (15 February 1921). Reprinted in *Postwar Review*, ed. Maurer Maurer, 110.

71. Wilkins Papers, flying log book no. 2, 5 December 1917–February 1919, IWM, P394.

72. Aeroplane Diary, 1918, miscellaneous box 34, item 616, IWM, contains daily tally of replacement machines shipped oversees.

73. H. A. Jones, *War in the Air*, vol. 6, 92.

74. Robertson, 23.

75. H. A. Jones, *War in the Air*, vol. 6, 91.

76. H. R. Brooke-Popham, "The Air Force," *Journal of the Royal United Services Institute (JRUSI)*, February 1920, 49.

77. Alan Morris, *First of the Many: The Story of the Independent Force, RAF* (London: Jarrolds, 1968), 168–69.

78. Burge, 182–84.

79. Morris, 169.

80. PRO, AIR 1/1972/204/273/1, "Casualty Statistics, June–November 1918," IF Form No. A-8.

81. B. E. Sutton, "Some Aspects of the Work of the Royal Air Force with the B.E.F. in 1918," *JRUSI* 67, no. 46 (May 1922): 344.

82. War Diary of Eighth Brigade, B392.

83. B. E. Smythies, "Experiences during the War, 1914–1918," in *A Selection of Lectures and Essays from the Work of Officers Attending the First Course at the Royal Air Force Staff College, 1922–1923* (London: HMSO, Air Ministry, December 1923), 89.

84. James Clay Thompson, *Rolling Thunder: Understanding Policy and Program Failures* (Chapel Hill, N.C.: University of North Carolina, 1980), 95.

85. Robert B. Rhoads, "Lessons Learned," in *Postwar Review*, ed. Maurer Maurer, 219; and Smythies, 88, complain that the tendency to exaggerate in post-mission reports was widespread.

86. Private diary no. 7, entry for 23 August 1918, IWM, 72/76/2.

87. Ibid., entries for 16 September and 5 October 1918; and W. R. Read Papers, unpublished autobiography, IWM, 72/76/1, 33, 28–40.

88. Last aircraft serviceability data is in Approximate Results dated 17 January 1918.

89. War Diary of Eighth Brigade, entry of 17 October 1917, B392.

90. *Times*, 18 October 1917, 6; and *Flight*, 25 October 1917, 1120. The *Times* article noted that this was the first time in the war "on which the objective in a raid into Germany has been specifically identified in the reports of General Headquarters."

91. PRO, AIR 1/1986/204/273/111, "Further details of bombing raid on BURBACH WORKS and SAARBRUCKEN carried out by No. 55 Squadron, R.F.C. 17/10/17," Capt H. W. M. Paul, 19 October 1917.

92. *Times*, 22 October 1917, 8; 31 October 1917, 6; 1 November 1917, 6; 2 November 1917, 6; 26 December 1917, 6–7; 15 January 1918, 6–7; *Flight*, 25 October 1917, 1120; 8 November 1917, 1181; 13 December 1917, 1323; 3 January 1918, 21; and 24 January 1918, 107.

93. *Times* and *Flight*, dates cited.

94. *Flight*, 1 November 1917, 1148, reprinted GHQ Dispatches of 25 and 26 October 1917 on the Saarbrücken raid; 3 January 1918 issue, 21–22, reprinted GHQ and War Office reports of 24 and 29 December, respectively.

95. *Flight*, 3 January 1918, 21–22.

96. Ibid, 13; War Diary of Eighth Brigade entry of 24 December 1917, B392, lists aircrew losses.

97. *Times*, October 1917–January 1918. GHQ dispatches were generally released between 9:30 and 11:30 P.M. on the day of the raid.

98. Miller, 48, reprints excerpt from French news article that appeared on 18 October 1917, giving details of 41st Wing's mission to Saarbrücken the day before.

99. *Times*, 18 October 1917, 6.

100. Ibid.; 26 December 1917; and 15 January 1918, 6–7.

101. "Oberbillig" in *Times*, 26 January 1918, 6; and *Flight*, 31 January 1918, 133, versus "Oberbilig" in 41st Wing War Diary, 24 January 1918; "Munitions works" in *Times*, 31 October 1917, 6; and *Flight*, 8 November

1917, 1181, versus "tanning industries" in 41st Wing War Diary, 30 October 1917.

102. PRO, AIR 1/1649/204/95/6, Robertson, CIGS, War Office to Haig, letter, 27 October 1917.

103. War Diary of Eighth Brigade, B393, preprinted instructions on each sheet of form.

104. AIR 1/2266/209/70/26, file, "Reports of Bombing Operations of Ochey Squadrons, Nancy area," correspondence on Kaiserslautern raid, 1 November 1917, shows this routing.

105. Ibid.; Trenchard at HQ RFC to Newall, letters, 29 and 30 October 1917.

106. Detailed Raid Reports, copy no. 2., 26 June 1918, Newall Papers, B393.

107. AIR 1/1968/204/273/111, "Intelligence Reports of Bombing Raids on German Towns, Aerodromes, etc. Raids before 15th June 1918," Maj H. W. M. Paul.

108. Ibid., "Further Details," Capt H. W. M. Paul, 19 October 1917.

109. Ibid.; PRO, AIR 1/2087/207/8/37, "Air Ministry Office Memos Issued Periodically by Secretary Air Ministry." Memo No. 37 has organizational chart with names, duties, room, and telephone numbers for the various directorates.

110. Bodleian Library, Oxford, "Summary of Air Intelligence," with Supplements (London: HMSO, Air Ministry, 1918), serials 1-8.

111. AIR 1/2085/207/5/3, "Approximate Results, 41st Wing, R.A.F., 17 October 1917–11 November 1918."

112. Ibid. Report dated 12/13 April contains distribution list. For corrections, see Report of 24/25 March 1918.

113. War Diary of Eighth Brigade, 5 December 1917, B392.

114. Detailed Raid Report, 5 December 1917, Newall Papers, 393.

115. *Times*, 6 December 1917, 6; and *Flight*, 13 December 1917, 1323.

116. "U.S. Bombing Survey," in *Postwar Review*, ed. Maurer Maurer. Hereafter cited as US Bombing Survey.

117. Ibid., 454.

118. War Diary of Eighth Brigade, Newall Papers, B392; and Detailed Raid Report, 6 December 1917, Newall Papers, B393 entries. Hereafter cited as Detailed Raid Report.

119. US Bombing Survey, 438–39.

120. War Diary of Eighth Brigade, 11 December 1917, Newall Papers, B392.

121. Detailed Raid Report, 11 December 1917.

122. US Bombing Survey, 455–56; and AIR 1/1998/204/273/266, "Reports as to the Effect of Various Types of Bombs on Buildings, Streets, etc., and General Conclusion," Maj H. W. M. Paul, 26 February 1919.

123. H. A. Jones, *War in the Air*, Appendix 27, between 30–31.

124. Detailed Raid Report, Capt. A. Gray, commanding No. 55 Squadron, to Headquarters, 41st Wing, 11 December 1917.

125. AIR 1/2266/209/70/26, "Summary of Work Carried out by the Royal Flying Corps in the Field during the Month of October 1917," HQ RFC to the War Cabinet, 5 November 1917.
126. War Diary of Eighth Brigade, entries for October 1917.
127. Ibid.
128. Ibid., 24 October 1917.
129. AIR 1/2266/209/209/70/26, "Summary of Work Carried out by the Royal Flying Corps in the Field during the Month of November 1917," HQ RFC to the War Cabinet, 4 December 1917.
130. US Bombing Survey, 457–59.
131. Detailed Raid Report, 2 November 1917.
132. US Bombing Survey, 456.
133. War Diary of Eighth Brigade, 1 November 1917.
134. Detailed Raid Report, 2 November 1917.
135. War Diary of Eighth Brigade, 14 November 1917.
136. Ibid., 31 October 1917.
137. US Bombing Survey, 437.
138. Ibid., 439.
139. AIR 1/1999/204/273/269, "Report on the Effects of Bombing German Blast Furnaces," Maj H. W. M. Paul, 26 February 1919.
140. War Diary of Eighth Brigade, 17 October 1917.
141. US Bombing Survey, 438.
142. War Diary of Eighth Brigade, 24 October 1917.
143. Ibid., 5 and 6 December 1917.
144. Detailed Raid Reports, 5 and 6 December 1917.
145. US Bombing Survey, 438–39.
146. AIR 1/1999/204/273/269, "Blast Furnaces," Maj H. W. M. Paul, 26 February 1919.
147. US Bombing Survey, 445.
148. War Diary of Eighth Brigade, 21 October 1917.
149. US Bombing Survey, 403, 406.
150. Ibid., 406.
151. AIR 1/1999/204/273/269, "Blast Furnaces," Maj H. W. M. Paul, 26 February 1917.
152. Ibid.
153. AIR 1/1999/204/273/268, "Report on the Results and Effects of Bombing German Chemical and Munition Factories, 1917–1918," Maj H. W. M. Paul, 26 February 1919.
154. Ibid.
155. Ibid.
156. War Diary of Eighth Brigade and Detailed Raid Reports, 24 December 1917 and 25 January 1918.
157. US Bombing Survey, 463, 466.
158. Ibid., 456.
159. Ibid., 460; and AIR 1/1999/204/273/268, "Chemical and Munitions Factories," Maj H. W. M. Paul, 26 February 1919.

160. AIR 1/1998/204/273/262, "Reports of British Bombing Raids on German Railways, Railway Stations and Railway Objectives, 1918," Maj H. W. M. Paul, 26 February 1919.

161. "Card Index of I.A.F. Raids into Germany, giving Units, Aircraft Type, Targets, Number of Raids, Casualties and Weight of Bombs Dropped, October 1917–November 1918," Newall Papers, 391.

162. US Bombing Survey, 446–47.

163. War Diary of Eighth Brigade, 5 December 1917.

164. US Bombing Survey, 454.

165. Ibid.

166. War Diary of Eighth Brigade, 5 December 1917.

167. AIR 1/1998/204/273/261, "Raids on German Railways," Maj H. W. M. Paul, 26 February 1919.

168. Ibid.

169. Detailed Raid Report, Maj J. E. A. Baldwin, commanding No. 55 Squadron, to Headquarters, 41st Wing, 30 October 1917.

170. AIR 1/1986/204/273/11, "Further Details," Capt H. W. M. Paul, 19 October 1917.

171. *Times*, 31 October 1917, 6.

172. *Flight*, 8 November 1917, 1181.

173. AIR 1/1998/204/273/266, "Effects of Bombs," Maj H. W. M. Paul, 26 February 1919; and US Bombing Survey, 456.

174. Detailed Raid Report, 25 January 1918.

175. Ibid., 27 January 1918.

176. US Bombing Survey, 421–22.

177. Ibid., 432.

178. N. Jones, *Origins of Strategic Bombing*, 72–77, 166–69.

179. Morris, 132.

180. Baldwin, 10.

181. William Armstrong, *Pioneer Pilot* (London: Blandford Press, 1952), 36–37.

182. AIR 1/1998/204/273/266, "Effects of Bombs," Maj H. W. M. Paul, 26 February 1919.

183. Brooke-Popham, 54–55.

Chapter 4

Eighth Brigade and Independent Force (February–November 1918)

Under newly promoted Brig Gen C. L. N. Newall, 41st Wing continued operations in 1918 much as it had since October 1917. Renamed Eighth Brigade on 1 February, with no appreciable increase in combat strength, the 41st constituted the nucleus of Independent Force RAF in early June 1918. Service flying and aerodrome development proceeded throughout the spring and summer. M. J. D. Cooper summarized the activities of Newall's units in the first half of 1918.

> With the influence of the parent service still strong, VIII Brigade tended at times to favour targets more in line with army bombing policy (such as railways and aerodromes near the front) than the more distant munitions and population centres originally intended as its objectives.[1]

Owing largely to an absence of realistic guidance from Whitehall, the British air command in France controlled the daily prosecution of the aerial offensive—including long-range bombardment—as it had done since 1916.

In London, authorities tended to dwell upon the future potential of the British bombing fleet rather than on rectifying its difficulties. They paid only sporadic attention to Newall's Ochey squadrons—at the end of a communication line that included GHQ and HQ RFC. The War Cabinet felt it had persuaded the military hierarchy in France that civilians exercised ultimate control over the long-range bombing program.

During the last year of the war, a compromise developed. The military continued to oversee daily activities of the bombardment force while the War Cabinet occupied itself with programs of expansion and strategy. Within this polarity, the new Air Ministry exerted negligible influence. Despite the Royal Flying Corps and the Royal Naval Air Service being combined into the Royal Air Force in April, British direction of the air war did not cohere during 1918.

With the benefit of hindsight, one can identify three competitive forces shaping British bombing policy and strategy during the last year of the war: the War Cabinet's continued wish to exert effective control; the Air Ministry's creation to assist this political direction (among other considerations); and Trenchard's influence (first as chief of the Air Staff from 18 January to 12 April, then as GOC, Independent Force, from 6 June until the Armistice).

Using War Cabinet direction, the government wished to translate schemes into action in implementing Smuts's recommendations. Already, classified reports seemed to indicate that the accomplishments of Newall's three squadrons merely foreshadowed the achievements of the projected force of 60 squadrons. Public opinion reinforced this political optimism, and the War Cabinet cultivated Franco-American goodwill for the bombing fleet it hoped to create. The secretary of state for War, Lord Milner, concerned himself with all aspects of the newly founded Air Ministry and Royal Air Force.

From the outset, Milner had paid particular attention to proposals for attacking Germany from the air. In October 1917, Rear Adm Mark Kerr submitted a memorandum to the Air Board warning of the need to preempt enemy long-range aerial supremacy.[2] Though exaggerated and alarmist, Kerr's warnings were underscored by the German "Harvest Moon" raids that month.[3] On 11 October, in a "private and confidential" letter to Lord Milner, Lord Robert Cecil advocated the formation of an Air Ministry and recommended Lord Weir to be its Secretary of State.[4] The minister's reply two days later expressed his agreement on both points. He later concurred in the arguments of Winston Churchill, the Secretary of Munitions, calling for an independent aerial arm and outlining the grave effects of German bombs on the output of munitions.[5] By virtue of his position, Milner could play a key role in overcoming any lingering doubts among his colleagues about the urgency for large-scale strategic bombing.

Once the decision had been taken to create a unified air service, Milner kept in touch with its principal architects. His aide memoir of 11 November 1917 detailed the bombing proposals of Lord Weir and Maj J. C. Baird, the parliamentary undersecretary: "there seems at present to be no answer to the heavy night-flying bombers except retaliation."[6] Milner monitored the emergent Air Ministry very carefully; most likely, he instigated most of the War Cabinet's requests for information on 41st Wing operations during the winter of 1917.

Milner's queries, however, were not always welcomed by the military chain of command. On 17 December 1917, Lord Rothermere, the ministerial appointee for the Air Force, wrote to Trenchard, his newly selected chief of Air Staff:

> Yesterday morning, after you had left, Lord Milner came to see me and said that he felt great anxiety about the adequacy of the preparations for the long range bombing offensive. He considered it a matter of vital importance, and he felt that the War Cabinet should be kept fully informed of the situation.[7]

Trenchard's reply, from HQ RFC in France on 20 December, illuminated his attitude toward independent aerial operations and his reluctance to leave his field command for a staff billet:

> I am uneasy about other people being uneasy about the adequacy of preparations for long range bombing. I am responsible for it, and of course you will be, but if they cannot trust me, then I cannot see any object in your asking me to come as C.I.G.S. [sic, C.A.S.].[8]

As Trenchard's peevish tone attests, the new CAS felt at odds with his civilian superiors, particularly Lord Rothermere.

As Secretary of State for War, Lord Milner did not rely solely upon the established hierarchy. He sought his own sources of information, a shrewd habit which must have been disquieting to the chain of command. One week after his visit to Lord Rothermere, Milner interviewed Major Lord Tiverton, a staff officer who had just completed a second inspection tour of the 41st Wing base area.

> He (Tiverton) has just come from Ochey, where he has been visiting our aerodromes with Paine (Fifth Sea Lord, responsible for naval aeronautical).

> The position is that 5 aerodromes are being prepared for 5 squadrons each—all bombing machines. Aerodromes roughly about 1,000 yards by 1,000 yards. Coolie labour being employed, almost 2,500 at present. It is intended to bring the number up to 10,000 and expect to have the aerodromes ready by March 1918.* (*3 other sites have been

135

chosen, but no work had yet been done. Ultimate number contemplated, 40 squadrons!)

As compared with what he found on his last visit (27th November), Tiverton says that there is now much greater activity. He also thinks that our aerodromes are too far forward. The French have lately been drawing theirs further back.

The commander of our Cmd is Colonel Newall. It is still under Trenchard at G.H.Q. Newall is well thought of.

Tiverton still thinks that the contemplated number of squadrons is inadequate for an attack on Germany on a great scale. He says that it is quite inaccurate—and that Paine admitted this—that there is plenty of room for aerodromes for 5,000 machines in this neighbourhood.

The base chosen for our aerodromes is Troyes. The number of men required to serve each machine *in the field* T. estimates as low as 7½, i.e., 15,000 men for 2,000 machines.

The machines wh. it is contemplated to place in the 25 squadrons are partly Handley Pages and partly D.H.

Tiverton's address in Paris is 16 Avenue Kléber. Liaision between English and French for all technical work is "fair."[9]

On several other occasions, Tiverton communicated directly with Lord Milner. The cabinet minister did not discourage this correspondence.

Tiverton was ideally placed and qualified to comment on the bombing program. A barrister since 1906, Lord Tiverton had begun his war service on 1 August 1915 as a lieutenant aboard HMS *Revenge* off the Belgian coast.[10]

His considerable knowledge of mathematics and scientific principles . . . enabled him to undertake a detailed and systematic study of strategic bombing and the problems which it involved.[11]

In early 1916, as armament training officer in the Air Department of the Admiralty, Tiverton investigated ballistics and its application to bomb-aiming accuracy. In May 1916, while armament officer of No. 3 Wing at Luxeuil, he qualified sufficiently as a pilot (at age 36) to carry out practical work in fitting the Sopwith 1½ Strutter with a suitable bombsight. When the Luxeuil wing was disbanded, Tiverton returned to England. By October 1917 he was back in France as the technical member of the British Aviation Mission in Paris. Early in that month he had alerted Rear Admiral Kerr that "nothing has been done to prepare for the reception of the bomber force in the Verdun-Toul district."[12] This news prompted Kerr's complaint to the Air Board on 11 October 1917.

In early 1918, Major Lord Tiverton headed FO3a Section in room 223, FO3 Branch of the Directorate of Flying Operations, at the Air Ministry. He was responsible for "all detail questions of strategic bombing and liaison with Technical and Training Directorates in relation thereto," including the collection of target data and information on "the strength, composition, and development" of the British strategic bombing force.[13] Until the Armistice, he submitted reports and memoranda to his superiors inside and outside the Air Ministry; most of these were highly critical of the aerial offensive. Lord Tiverton's position and expertise thus made him a useful conduit to Milner.

Milner also solicited other opinions on long-range bombardment, particularly after it became apparent that force deployments would not meet projections. His 7 March 1918 request to members of the Air Council for "independent summary" concerning "our situation and prospects" on strategic bombing prompted an extensive response from Sir Henry Norman, a member of Parliament, on 25 March.

Sir Henry Norman's analysis can be taken as a contemporary political appraisal of the bombing effort. In contrast to the military view, Norman did not suggest that the campaign be scaled to match the available forces; instead, he argued that increased output of bombing machines had to receive the highest priority: "The future of our race and Empire may depend upon whether or not we rise now—though it be at the eleventh hour—to this conception."[14]

Once Cowdray's surplus air fleet materialized, Norman advocated its use in overwhelming incendiary attacks upon Essen, Cologne, Frankfurt, Düsseldorf, Stuttgart, and Mannheim. He calculated that such a force could deliver 20 tons of bombs hourly on each of two targets for 10 consecutive hours, so that "our victory in the war would be in sight" within a month.[15] However, Norman conceded that at present this scheme was unrealistic, since 41st Wing had taken five months to drop just 48 tons of bombs on German objectives, less than the quantity he wanted to "have been able to drop in *one hour*"[16] The government, in his view, had grossly underestimated the force required to inflict significant damage. Furthermore, moral effect could be a two-edged sword.

A brief consideration of the subject appeared to show that, <u>contrary to confident public expectation</u>, we shall not be in a position to carry out bombing operations in Germany upon a scale likely to have an appreciable influence upon the course of the war before next Autumn (i.e., fall of 1919), if even then.

<u>Public expectation of great reprisals against German towns this spring and summer is doomed to disappointment</u>, for the simple reason that we shall have no machines to execute great reprisals with.[17]

Clearly, public opinion represented a very sensitive factor in any political decision to curtail or abandon bombing. The government found itself constrained by its previously reported successes and a conditioned citizenry.

On the question of effective command and control, Norman argued for a "Supreme Strategical Council" to formulate a coherent program. Though the Air Ministry and the Royal Air Force had been created expressly for those purposes, Norman felt that they had yet to exercise effective supervision over aerial matters.

He then analyzed the actual effort of 41st Wing during its first three months (through January 1918), using data provided by the military. The discrepancies between his figures and the actual state of affairs illuminate the extent to which civilian policy makers were misled. Norman noted that Newall's force had launched a total of 31 raids, with the following outcomes by aircraft type:

Sorties flown/Machines missing		Machines with engine trouble
D.H.4:	107/5	1
F.E.2.b:	84/4	13
H.P.	10/0	3
Totals:	201/9	17

He noted that 59,585 pounds of bombs dropped in 173 successful sorties implied that each 41st Wing sortie dropped an average of 344 pounds of bombs,[18] and he criticized the short distance of these raids: "none being nearly so far as the German raids on London." He also criticized the "trifling average weight of bombs carried per machine" and concluded that these raids "do not even approach an offensive sufficient to have an appreciable effect upon the duration of the war."[19] Norman's conclusions would have been even more pessimistic had he enjoyed access to other information.

Norman either overlooked or never learned of the two Handley Pages that went missing on "A" Naval Squadron's maiden mission to Saarbrücken on 24/25 October 1917 or of the Handley Page "completely wrecked" in a landing accident upon its return from the same raid.[20] Similarly, Norman recorded one DH4 from No. 55 Squadron forced to abandon their mission owing to engine trouble in December 1917; the actual count was five. Engine trouble resulted in a total of nine DH4s failing to complete their sorties, a fact of which the Air Council was apparently never informed. Likewise, Norman recorded 13 FE2bs of No. 100 Squadron aborting their sorties in January 1918 owing to engine problems; the actual number was 20.

Nor did Norman's analysis fully appreciate the adverse effects of weather and other limitations. Only 95 of 118 DH4s setting out on missions during this period managed to bomb successfully—an 80.5 percent success rate. Equivalent figures for night operations are 90 of 125 for a 72.0 percent success rate. Overall, 185 aircraft of 41st Wing (of 243 launched) dropped 59,678 pounds of bombs on assigned targets, secondary targets, and targets of opportunity. Thus, 58 machines failed to complete their missions—more than twice the number (26: 9 missing, 17 aborted) reported to Sir Henry. On the other hand, bomb totals gleaned from official records agree within one-tenth of 1 percent with the figure supplied to Sir Henry (59,678 actual pounds *versus* 59,585 reported).

Sir Henry Norman concluded that new types of aircraft were necessary. They should be capable of mounting mass raids to deliver one hundred tons of bombs, and they should be able to sustain that pace week after week. He argued for priority production of these new types of aircraft: "Our situation and prospects appear to require immediate reconsideration."[21]

Milner and the War Cabinet were clearly concerned with the conduct and magnitude of the air war against Germany. But as before, the political direction clashed with the priorities and concerns of the field commanders. These fundamentally incompatible outlooks also collided within the new Air Ministry, in the persons of Lord Rothermere, secretary of state for the Air Force ("Royal Air Force" after March 1918), and his chief of Air Staff, General Trenchard.

Lord Rothermere aggressively supported the augmented bombing campaign. In this, he enjoyed public support and encouragement. Responding to a toast in his honor as the Air Minister in December 1917, Rothermere presented his philosophy unambiguously.

> At the Air Board we are wholeheartedly in favour of air reprisals. It is our duty to avenge the murder of innocent women and children. As the enemy elects, so it will be the case of "eye for an eye, and a tooth for a tooth," and in this respect we shall slave for complete and satisfying retaliation. . . . We are determined, in other words, that whatever outrages are committed on the civilian population of this country will be met by similar treatment on his own people.[22]

The editor of *Flight* hailed this outlook as an "admirably clear explanation" of the air policy to be expected in the near future.[23] His editorial, entitled "Our Own Policy of Reprisals," called for massive bombing, linking Rothermere's assault on German morale with the military necessity to defend Britain.[24] He conceded that it was tempting to agree with the Air Minister.

> [We should] place our policy of counter raids on no higher a plane than that of avenging the murders of our defenseless civilians. But we think the matter goes far beyond that. In the first place, the duty is laid upon our authorities of defending our shores, and if that can only be done—as we believe to be the case—by raiding the enemy's towns from the air until he cries for mercy, then let us raid them as often and as heavily as need be. . . . We regret the necessity, but we cannot get away from the fact that the necessity has been forced upon us by the prior action of an enemy who has adopted frightfulness as his creed in the belief that he was the only one with a stomach for it.[25]

In this fusion of moral and strategic effects, reprisals became acceptable for two reasons: Germany, the first to adopt terror tactics, deserved punishment; further, such a counteroffensive handily complemented the related issue of home defense.

Rothermere forcefully voiced the same sentiments in private. Sir Almeric Fitzroy, following his conversation with the Air Minister, recorded Rothermere's thoughts in his diary.

> December 28th.— Lord Rothermere's ideas on air reprisals are not lacking in force or comprehensiveness; he is satisfied that no adequate effect will be produced in Germany unless the thing is done on a scale which, in point of thoroughness and terror, has not hitherto been dreamed of. His intention is, for every raid upon London, absolutely to wipe out one or two large Germantowns, either on the Rhine or in its affluent valleys. Frankfort itself does not lie beyond the bourne of his imaginings. For this purpose he contemplates the possibility of an attack in three divisions comprising each from 100 to 150 aeroplanes and carrying bombs enough to lay the place attacked level with ground in the course of a few hours. In favourable circumstances a sufficient number of machines may be at his disposal by the month of June. It is estimated that, among a people ravaged by hunger and despair, the panic will be instantaneous and complete.[26]

In this regard, Rothermere merely echoed the demands of the population and the government for immediate and overwhelming retaliation. However, the chief of Air Staff did not share his outlook.

Trenchard, a reluctant CAS, did not get on well with his minister, either personally or professionally. He felt that he had been forced by Rothermere and Lord Northcliffe into accepting the staff post to protect Haig.[27] He complained to the field marshal that Rothermere habitually took advice from other than his "professional advisers" while ignoring problems of less appeal but greater immediacy to concentrate on reprisals.[28] Trenchard fulminated in a post he did not want under a superior whom he did not respect or trust.

On 13 January 1918, the impatient CAS handed a memorandum on bombing directly to the Prime Minister, bypassing Rothermere.[29] Trenchard emphasized the disjunction between the aspirations of the new Air Staff and Newall's small force at Ochey.

> It is worth noting that the bombing of Germany which has taken place in 1917, involving the dropping of about 20 tons of bombs in a few weeks in winter, has been done by this limited force, for though the figures of additional bombers about to be set out are meagre and disappointing, they represent some power of doing substantial mischief.[30]

Planners, claimed Trenchard, had lost sight of the fact that Germany was being bombed by only a single day squadron and two night squadrons, one of which could do "short-distance night flying only." Although aerodrome accommodations for 40 squadrons would be complete by July 1918, Trenchard estimated that only nine squadrons "will be actually at work" by that date.[31] He urged goals commensurate with the force.

> This memorandum does not attempt to discuss why the figures are not larger, but the figures themselves cannot be successfully challenged. It is far better to know what can really be done so as to be able to count on it than to indulge in more generous estimates which cannot be realized.[32]

This pragmatic analysis ran counter to widespread political and public assumptions that a strategic bombing force could be quickly expanded to any desired size. Trenchard's proposal more closely matched the abilities of the fleet in being; however, it also rested upon several key assumptions:

> It is intended to attack, with as large a force as is available, the big industrial centres on the Rhine and in its vicinity, in accordance with an organized plan. If the French do any long-distance bombing I am hopeful they will attack the targets we suggest.

> It is intended, when the weather is unfit for long-distance bombing, to attack nearer targets such as the big steel works near Briey, Saarbrucken, &c. This will be a development on a larger scale of work already successfully undertaken. It will be carried out under the orders of the French who will select, from time to time, the particular objective.[33]

The doubtful ability of 41st Wing to penetrate Germany to the Rhine valley has already been analyzed, as well as the wing's barely discernible cooperation in the French bombing program. Trenchard did not address these two points in detail, but his narrative minimized them as operational obstacles. In these matters, the CAS was less than candid with his prime minister. While Trenchard's memorandum to Lloyd George appeared to outline a more plausible concept than huge reprisals, its propositions were likewise undercut by the results of 41st Wing efforts.

During Trenchard's stormy tenure at the Air Ministry, little was done to implement even his proposed policy. Personal antagonisms and professional differences between him and his air minister made failure inevitable. S. F. Wise summarized the turbulence.

Controversy surrounded the first appointments to the Air Ministry, including that of the first Air Minister, Lord Rothermere. An Air Council under his presidency was established on 3 January 1918; its vice-president was Sir David Henderson. Trenchard was prevailed upon to become Chief of the Air Staff and was given Rear-Admiral Mark Kerr as his deputy. Within a few weeks of the official birth of the Royal Air Force, on 1 April 1918, not one of these men remained at his original post. Kerr had disagreed with Trenchard, and Brigadier-General R. M. Groves had been appointed in his place. Rothermere had given way to Sir William Weir; Trenchard had resigned, to be replaced by his old rival Major-General Fredrick Sykes; Henderson had left, finding it impossible to work with Sykes.[34]

Personalities aside, much of the difficulty and paralysis at the new ministry arose from its organizational and staff arrangements. These shortcomings contributed significantly to its general ineffectiveness. Based on years of experience, the two senior services had developed staff systems that united the crucial functions of operations and intelligence. For example, the deputy chief of Naval Staff (DCNS), who was in charge of both the Division of Naval Intelligence and the Operations Division, constituted the unifying link in the Admiralty chain upward to the chief of Naval Staff (CNS) and the First Sea Lord.[35] In the army's case, the two responsibilities were combined within the War Office in the Military Operations and Intelligence Directorate, whose head was directly responsible to the chief of the Imperial General Staff.[36] Both older services concentrated intelligence and command within a single staff position subordinate to the service chief. Compared to these departmental establishments, command and staff relationships within the new Air Ministry suffered from structural disunity.

Within the Air Ministry, control of the interlocking functions of intelligence and aerial operations were split between the Directorate of Flying Operations (DFO) and the Directorate of Air Intelligence (DAI). These discrete staffs coalesced only at the highest military echelon: chief of the Air Staff.[37]

This bifurcation contributed significantly to Air Ministry disjointedness throughout 1918. After June 1918, it hindered Air Staff in its supervision of Trenchard, the strong-willed GOC of the Independent Force, when he ignored or altered directives to conform to his own notions of how the bombardment should be waged. Ironically, the institutional and working relationships that caused these difficulties were initially formulated during Trenchard's brief tenure as the first chief of Air Staff (18 January–12 April 1918).[38] A combined Operations and Intelligence Directorate emerged after the Armistice, reflecting a belated acknowledgment of previous shortcomings.[39]

Under Trenchard, an energetic and forthright CAS, these structural flaws were comparatively unimportant. His vigor and personality—his "command presence"—cut across paper boundaries to dominate staff machinery; he personified the nexus of control.[40] When he abruptly vacated his position on 12 April 1918 (the result of a last-straw squabble with Rothermere), effective control departed with him.

For his part, the unfortunate Rothermere never enjoyed widespread support or sympathy within his ministry. It appears that he was at odds with the institution from the beginning. On the day prior to his becoming air minister, Rothermere visited Sir Almeric Fitzroy, who noted that he "had much to say on the swollen staff he had found at the Hotel Cecil, where 4,000 men and women are engaged, including 600 commissioned officers!"[41] Rothermere "resolved to apply drastic measures" to relieve this "biggest scandal"; he attributed staff size to "petticoat influence," asserting to Sir Almeric that there were "only four trained civil servants in direction of this huge staff."[42] Rothermere's management problems were compounded by lack of active support from his CAS. He resigned on 26 April 1918, barely a fortnight after Trenchard's departure, to be succeeded by William D. Weir. Amidst the German Lys offensive and Haig's "backs to the wall" order, Britain had to replace the top men in its air establishment.

Maj Gen Fredrick Sykes, the new CAS, lacked the overbearing but charismatic temperament of his predecessor; he inspired neither the confidence nor the respect which had characterized Trenchard's relationships. The two, longtime rivals, represented the antipodes of leadership: while Trenchard exemplified the warrior who inspired by example, Sykes epitomized the calculating manager who valued logic above loyalty.

Trenchard loathed Sykes, whom he regarded as an opportunist.[43] What's more, most of the Royal Air Force agreed with Trenchard's harsh opinion.[44] Sykes had inherited a "one-man" department in terms of effective management; however, Sykes never became that man.

Sir William D. Weir, the new secretary of state for the Royal Air Force, assumed his position on 27 April 1918 and remained in office until 14 January 1919. A shrewd Scots businessman, he convinced Trenchard to accept the position of GOC, Independent Force.[45] Haig intended to have Trenchard back in France, either as his "advisor on all matters relating to the employment of aircraft," or "to command an Infantry Brigade."[46]

Weir, however, had no intention of losing Trenchard. On 30 April 1918, he offered Trenchard a choice of three positions:

1. The Bombing Command in the South of France.
2. Settling our relations and our policy with America, particularly with reference to a long range bombing enterprise from an English base.
3. Co-ordinator of air forces in the Mediterranean and Middle East with land and naval work and anti-submarine operations.[47]

With respect to choice number 1, Weir pointed out that it possessed "the advantages of independent Command, wherein the man in charge devotes his entire energies to the development of bombing."[48] In his reply, Trenchard pointed out that number 2 and number 3 could be handled quickly and easily by officers already in position. He objected to number 1 on the grounds that Newall was already in charge: "the whole point is whether he should work under Salmond (i.e., H.Q., R.A.F. in the Field, the present command arrangement) or under the Air Ministry."[49] Trenchard asserted that Air Ministry supervision "will mean a great waste of man power, overlapping of work in workshops, etc., etc."[50]

Weir then offered Trenchard the post of Inspector General Overseas of the RAF, overseeing all air work except operations. When Trenchard rejected this post too, Weir's patience wore thin.[51] On 6 May 1918, he made his exasperation evident and called for a prompt decision.

I am really at a loss to understand your view that such work is not of "real value." However, since our last talk, I appreciate more fully your desire to have a position as a Commander rather than to act in a supervisory or advisory capacity.[52]

The Air Ministry then offered four positions, including Inspector General Overseas or in the Home Establishment and "command of all Air Force units in the Middle East," as well as "*independent command* of long range bombing forces in France."[53]

Now, I trust I have made it clear that I will not create a position specially for you. The above are positions requiring men, and I want you to accept one of them so that your experience may contribute to the success of the Royal Air Force, and not on any ground of quelling what you term "the agitation."[54]

Trenchard replied two days later. He summarized his objections to the post but concluded, "I can only say I will accept command of the long distance bombing force and do my best to make it a success as far as possible."[55]

On 13 May 1918, Bonar Law announced to the Commons that General Trenchard "has been offered and has accepted the command of a very important part of the British Air Force in France."[56] The Air Ministry then notified the War Cabinet:

I am commanded by the Air Council to inform you that they are of the opinion that the time has arrived to constitute an Independent Force, Royal Air Force, for the purpose of carrying out bombing raids on Germany on a large scale. This will be organized as a separate command of the British Royal Air Force under Major-General Sir Hugh Trenchard, who will work directly under the Air Ministry.[57]

The message also asked that arrangements be made so that Trenchard "should be able to deal direct in this subject with the necessary French military authorities."[58] On 17 May, Trenchard crossed to France. After visits with Haig at GHQ and Salmond at HQ RAF, he assumed tactical command of the Eighth Brigade, renamed Independent Force, on 6 June 1918.[59]

In negotiating for the position, Trenchard had stipulated that as commander of the Independent Force he would work directly for—and take orders solely from—Weir. He explicitly confirmed this agreement in a telegram to Weir.

> We have notified H.Q., R.A.F. I am prepared to take over administration of all R.A.F. units in Independent Force today. From this date Independent Force will deal direct with you on all matters.
>
> I.F. R.A.F. 1020 pm.[60]

This deviation would have serious repercussions for the command that Sykes (as CAS) nominally exercised over the Royal Air Force.

In practical terms, the agreement between Trenchard and Weir bypassed the chief of air staff. Trenchard, if he wished, need not consult Sykes concerning Independent Force bombing policy. Weir, Sykes' superior in the Air Ministry, ensured that Trenchard enjoyed autonomy. The Air Council, whose members devoted more of their 1918 agenda to selecting uniforms for the new service than to Independent Force operations against Germany, paid only fitful attention to the aerial offensive.[61]

> [There was no] substantial flow of correspondence between the Independent Force staff and the Air Staff in London. Instead, Trenchard chose to report directly to Weir on a monthly basis. Sykes' staff chafed over this situation, but the Chief of Air Staff did not elect to assert his authority.[62]

Trenchard, as GOC of the bombing force in the field, did not intend to let "any officer in London" direct its operations.

While Trenchard's pact with his Air Minister invalidated Sykes' authority, it also deprived the GOC IF of expert assistance from others within the CAS Department. To maintain bureaucratic independence, Trenchard had to assemble his own counterpart of the Air Staff organization at IF Headquarters at Autigny-la-Tour, four miles northeast of Neufchâteau. This self-imposed duplication of effort constituted a significant portion of the "great unnecessary waste of man power, time and energy" of which Trenchard periodically complained in his private diary.[63]

The Department of the Chief of Air Staff represented a considerable pool of technical ability and combat experience upon which the GOC IF could profitably have drawn.[64] Some of the staff officers had been selected and appointed during Trenchard's tenure as CAS. Two staff groups had been established solely to support strategic bombing:

1. FO3 Branch, Strategic Bombing and Independent Force Operations, within the Directorate of Flying Operations.
2. AI1B Section, Bomb Raids and Targets, AI1 Branch, Receipt and Distribution of Intelligence, within the Directorate of Air Intelligence.

On 27 May 1918 the head of FO3, Lt Col R. J. Armes, suggested to Brig Gen P. R. C. Groves, the director of Flying Operations, that he add another officer to the branch.

> A most useful officer as S.O.3 in F.O.3 section would be Captain H. McClelland, D.S.C.
> Has been with 8th Brigade at Ochey, since its inception.
> Before that Eastern Mediterranean and took part in the raids on Constantinople.
> In the first part of the war was night flying in England, and flying instructor.[65]

Captain McClelland joined FO3 soon after this request and remained there until the Armistice.[66] Among his tasks were "analysis and filing of all reports and records. Circulation and summaries &c., of operations of Independent Force. War Diary of Independent Force."[67]

Upon his arrival at the Hotel Cecil, McClelland probably had more long-range night bombing experience than anyone in the building. He had been in charge of the first group to proceed to France as part of Newall's hastily formed 41st Wing in October 1917. He flew the unit's first mission to the Burbach Works on 24/25 October 1917. On 24/25 March 1918, McClelland commanded one of two Handley Pages assigned to raid Cologne.

> Having crossed the lines his engines boiled and he was forced to return. A second start was made and when near Metz one of the engines cut out entirely. He dropped his bombs at Courcelles and returned on one engine.[68]

(The other pilot, Flight Commander F. T. Digby, DSC, managed to reach Cologne and earned the DSO for his achievement.)[69]

McClelland flew nine raids with Newall's force—a considerable accomplishment that gained him a niche in the unit's unofficial history as one of the aviators who completed the most missions during the war.[70] His arrival increased FO3 to three officers, of whom he was the junior.

His colleagues and their duties in FO3 also deserve comment. Major Lord Tiverton, the SO2, was the Air Ministry expert on target selection and related technical questions. He had the experience and background to act as a useful interface between HQ IF and establishments in England, but Trenchard never requested such assistance. Like McClelland, Tiverton remained for the duration, resigning from active service three months after the end of the war.[71] Lt Col J. A. H. Gammell replaced Lt Col R. J. Armes sometime after 3 June, very likely in August.[72]

> [FO3 was responsible for] allocation of aircraft to Independent Forces. Policy as regards the conduct of all aerial operations by these Forces and all general questions relating thereto. Formulation of plans for future operations by Independent Forces. . . . Policy with regards to the selection of bomb targets. Preparation in so far as concerns operations by Independent Forces of all information and operation papers for the War Cabinet and of periodical summaries and comments for issue through D.D.A.I. to Press Bureau. . . . Liaison with Independent Forces and with the Allies in regard to their development.[73]

In short, FO3 was responsible for plans and support of the strategic bombardment program. In this respect, it was co-equal with FO1 and FO2, which were charged with supervising air forces assigned to the army and navy.

Besides FO3, one other group at Air Staff level was concerned with the bombing campaign. Section AI1B of Branch AI1, Bomb Raids and Targets, had responsibility for collecting and evaluating information about possible targets and enemy countermeasures, active and passive, in the IF area of operations. Even though Tiverton had the specific task of "liaison with DDAI regarding bomb targets," no one in the Directorate of Air Intelligence was charged with the reciprocal duty to coordinate with him.[74] However, surviving documentation shows that Tiverton kept in close touch with AI1B.[75]

Except for such initiatives between subordinate staff officers two floors apart in the Hotel Cecil, no organizational provision for coordination of operations and intelligence existed below the level of Sykes himself. To a large extent this disjointedness contributed to the frustration that followed upon the command arrangement between Weir and Trenchard. The Department of the Chief of Air Staff could not act unless the IF specifically requested assistance. The initiative lay completely in the field.

Returning to Section AI1B, it was a constituent staff of Branch AI1, one of seven branches in the Directorate of Air Intelligence. They looked after tasks ranging from analysis of foreign aviation (AI2) to control of RAF propaganda and censorship (AI6).[76]

> [AI1B was responsible for] compilation of all information regarding Bomb Targets in all enemy countries. Information regarding location of enemy A.A. [i.e., anti-aircraft] defences of all types. Records of results of Bomb Raids. Records of location of P. of W. [Prisoner of War] camps in districts coming within the scope of allied Bomb Raids.[77]

This office consisted of three officers: Capt A. R. (Archibald Robert) Boyle, M. C., 2Lt G. H. Carbutt, and Maj W. de L. Willis. Capts C. W. Curd and F. D. Taylor joined them prior to October 1917,[78] and these five intelligence officers remained in the AI1B until the end of the war.

Soon after the Armistice, the section was redesignated as Section AI3C, Bomb Targets, Results of Raids, and AA Defenses. Capt W. J. Salaman and Lt M. C. Caley were added while Major Willis resigned from the RAF.[79] AI3C came under the jurisdiction of Branch AI3, responsible for "Relations with Foreign Countries." These facts strongly indicate that these six staff officers were responsible for analyzing postwar evidence from occupied Germany on the effects of British aerial bombardment.

By June 1919, all AI1B/AI3C officers except A. R. Boyle had departed active service. Boyle, who had been promoted to major and SO2, advanced to the head of AI1. He remained in the intelligence network of the Air Ministry throughout Trenchard's second stint as CAS, eventually retiring as an air commodore in 1940. He retained his post during the change of regimes at the Air Ministry as well as the reductions in force imposed upon the peacetime Royal Air Force.[80] Of all the officers who had served in FO3 or AI1B during the existence of

Trenchard's Independent Force in 1918, A. R. Boyle was the sole survivor on active service at the beginning of 1920.[81]

The creation and purposes of the CAS Department's propaganda office, Section AI6B, testify to the new service's preoccupation with its public image and prestige. Less than two weeks after Sykes had become chief of Air Staff, Col E. H. Davidson, the deputy director of air intelligence (DDAI), wrote to him concerning a proposal for a new group within the DAI.

> Attached are the broad instructions upon which I propose conducting Air Propaganda.
>
> Will you please see if you approve.
>
> If approved I propose informing Directorates of this scheme and asking them to notify me of any subjects which they may wish taken up from time to time. This will ensure that our propaganda is comprehensive.[82]

This project, though initiated during Trenchard's term as CAS, had to be brought to his successor's attention for final approval.[83]

Davidson enumerated the duties of his proposed group and also foreshadowed its future utility, arguing that "propaganda must not only deal with the present war conditions but must be to a certain extent in retrospect and more important still, must deal with the future."[84] Therefore, he asserted, the "education" of the public about aviation was a major concern, and propaganda for "home consumption" (via the media of "cinematograph, photographs and exhibitions") had to be produced.[85] As specific objectives of this public indoctrination, the DAI included "questions of bombing policy," "strategy of the air" and the "forthcoming fight for commercial supremacy in the air," concluding prophetically that "Command of the Air" will be as essential to this country after the war as "Command of the Sea."[86] Davidson's comprehensive proposal foreshadowed most of the issues and techniques of RAF publicists after the Armistice.

After Sykes' approval, Section AI6 moved into two rooms on the fifth floor of the Air Ministry. Consistent with the DDAI's original scheme, their assigned tasks included "Educational publicity. Liaison with Ministry of Information . . . Production and issue of matter for the Press . . . Articles of propaganda value and Lecture organisation."[87] A Captain Dawson was in charge of AI6B; Crichton moved up a rung to become chief of the Censorship and Propaganda Branch.[88] In essence, the organization functioned as the first public relations bureau of the Royal Air Force.

This apparent digression into the organization of the Air Ministry, particularly its CAS Department, clarifies some of the command and staff relations underlying London's supervision of Trenchard. The apparatus existed at the Air Ministry, on charts and in fact, to enable Sykes, as chief of the Air Staff, to oversee the Independent Force in the field. His Department, staffed by competent officers, diligently carried out their duties within DFO and DAI.

On the other hand, Sykes' executive control over Trenchard's IF suffered because staff channels to formulate and coordinate policies merged only within his own office. Although both War Office and Admiralty provided models, the advantages of unifying operations and intelligence below the desk of the CAS escaped the Air Ministry planners. Sykes' relatively low stature among political superiors and military subordinates, who generally did not like, respect, or trust him, multiplied his difficulties. Ineffective staff work, at times preoccupied with peripheral details or unrealizable schemes, characterized this organization.

The largest obstacle to CAS control of strategic bombing was the agreement between Weir and Trenchard, which simply obviated Air Staff supervision. Sykes became extraneous to the British bombing offensive. Trenchard was neither professionally nor personally inclined to consult his rival on matters touching his field command.

Though rendered powerless by this situation, the midlevel staff officers in DFO and DAI performed to the best of their abilities. The paucity of information forwarded by their IF counterparts limited them severely. Nonetheless, their reports and analyses are extremely valuable as contemporary critiques of Trenchard's independent command.

After he became chief of the Air Staff, Sykes initiated the Strategic Council to oversee details of the government's bombing plan. The new CAS wished to develop a system to "consider questions of policy in their strategic aspect and the best utilization of aerial resources," though on a less grand scale under Weir than under Rothermere.[89] On 22 April 1918, at its inaugural session, this Strategic Council considered the future of the bombing offensive.[90] At the time, General Newall's Eighth Brigade fell under the supervision of Haig's GHQ and Salmond's HQ RAF in the field; Trenchard had not yet accepted command of the Independent Force.

The Strategic Council represented the first definite organizational attempt to translate policy into achievable goals. In this regard, as Neville Jones has observed, this Air Ministry group necessarily maintained a close liaison with the Air Council:

> The Air Council might lay down the policy of bombing a German Key Industry; the Strategic Council would settle what number of bombs were necessary to obliterate any particular factory, the force necessary to obtain this number of direct hits and hence the order in which such factories should be destroyed, having regard to the force available at the time, and with what number of machines, and what system, this should be carried out.[91]

Such a charter allowed the Strategic Council to fill the gaps between sweeping directives and particular objectives; however, it was not always possible for the Air Staff to avoid becoming bogged down in trivia at times. Rather than attempting to obliterate enemy cities wholesale, as Rothermere and Norman had urged, the Strategic Council held that the proper object of bombing should be the selective destruction of key German war industries.

In two memoranda to the War Cabinet, Sir William Weir endorsed the diminution of the schemes of his predecessor. He also established the independent existence of the Air Ministry and its right to allocate all aerial resources.

His first document, outlining main policies of the Air Ministry, acknowledged legitimate claims by the army and navy upon some portion of aircraft production.[92] However, the new Air Minister cautioned against losing the advantages of bombing raids.

> The continuous bombing of German industrial centres presents very important possibilities, and valuable results may be achieved by its rapid progressive development.[93]

153

He asserted that, upon request from the other services, the Air Ministry "will detach temporally sufficient resources to carry out the operation required, but such Forces will be under the control of the Air Ministry for re-allocation."[94] In other words the Air Ministry planned to conduct an independent aerial offensive.

Weir soon found himself obliged to defend this policy in the face of War Office and Admiralty objections. In mid-August 1918, he cut their proposed air program, "owing to the demands made by the several branches of the service."[95] His plan, the "Amended Provisional Programme of Development to September 30th 1919," provided a total increment to the army and navy of just 56 1/3 squadrons; in the same period, the Independent Force alone would increase in size from five squadrons to 58 squadrons.[96] RAF's sister services requested detailed justification of this proposal.

In a subsequent session of the Air Policy Committee, the Air Minister disclaimed "any intention of criticizing the submarine strategy" of the navy by reducing their request. He also reminded the CIGS that squadrons assigned to Trenchard's IF lay outside Foch's control, while those with Haig could come under the Generalissimo's orders.

> Lord Weir called attention to the following paragraph of G.T. 5495, the C.I.G.S. Memorandum: "The Effect of the Air Ministry's proposal to increase the Independent Air Force will be able to give General Foch control of a number of squadrons at the expense of the British Army in France" and pointed out that Marshal Foch does at present control all aviation, except the I.A.F. in France and could, subject to the concurrence of Sir Douglas Haig, at any time move British Flying Squadron from the British to the French line if he thought it necessary. On the other hand the I.A.F. could be removed from France and would not then be under Marshal Foch's orders.[97]

Weir assured his colleagues that in the current situation it seemed likely that Monsieur Georges Clemenceau would agree to leave the Independent Force as "an independent command."[98] Bombers allocated to Trenchard would remain British in any case. The Air Ministry sought to defend the IF from the predations of Allied claims for support as well as from demands from its sister services for scarce aviation assets.

Weir also defended reductions in the overall allocations by using a statistical consideration of wastage effects. Such losses normally averaged between 33 percent and 50 percent monthly in each unit.

Lord Weir reminded the Committee that these figures were made out on the basis of not only maintenance of squadrons but also *allowing for wastage which basis has never been taken into consideration before* and which made, undoubtedly, a very considerable difference in the total strength allocated to the two Services.[99]

Surprisingly, no one remarked on the fact that wastage had at last been acknowledged in force projections. (It had been the largest single factor eroding aerial strength in three years of war.) The Air Policy Committee approved the Air Minister's allocations.

The accompanying document for Milner on 23 May 1918 presented Weir's concept of strategic bombardment. With an eye toward Allied involvement, the Air Minister requested the "support and assistance" of his colleagues in ensuring the "progressive development of long range bombing of Germany," stressing the need to "obtain as much preliminary experience as possible" in this sphere.[100] Weir acknowledged that Trenchard's new command at present consisted of only four squadrons.

> Arrangements are well in hand to bring this Force up to at least 24 ["30" was lined out in the original] squadrons by the end of October, and the most energetic steps are now being taken to assure this strength.

> When the force has reached the strength indicated, it will be possible, apart from weather limitations, to carry on continuous day and night bombing.

> I desire to emphasize the definite character of these proposals and the heaviness of the blow which may be anticipated. At the same time, such a proposal, to achieve success, would entail the complete and thorough co-operation of America and France, together with their full sympathy and support.[101]

Accordingly, Weir asked the War Cabinet to obtain from the Supreme War Council a "confirmation" of the independent status of Trenchard's bombing command and its "ultimate development" into an inter-Allied force under a British GOC.

He concluded by asking that Clemenceau be requested "to obtain the support of the French Army Authorities to this scheme"—an attempt on the Air Minister's part to guarantee future cooperation of the French despite their past ambivalence.[102]

As Weir had requested, the War Cabinet discussed the Independent Force at Versailles. Sykes, who was at the conference, informed Trenchard that Clemenceau had agreed to provide assistance.

> Mr. Lloyd George stated that he had spoken to Mr. Clemenceau with reference to the numerous difficulties which might be encountered by General Trenchard and the Independent Force, and had asked for all possible assistance from the French; that M. Clemenceau had agreed and had told General Duval that everything should be done by the French to assist the Independent Force.
>
> M. Clemenceau heartily endorsed this statement, and added that, if any difficulty were to arise, I was to go and see him on the subject.[103]

It should be noted that French logistical support to British bombing units in the field had already been substantial.

The French, in fact, continued to assist the new independent bombing command just as they had previously done for Newall's 41st Wing and Eighth Brigade. Trenchard himself seems initially to have secured qualified approval from his Gallic counterparts, thus confirming the amicable relationship that had developed in late 1917:

> You may like to know that I got on very well with my interview with the French yesterday on the bombing programme. They are quite prepared to help me in practically everything I ask for, but it takes a little tact to get it all done.[104]

This material support continued, though the French began increasingly to express reservations about the wisdom of a strategic bombing force operating independently of Allied control.

French authorities interpreted the Clemenceau–Lloyd George agreement to cover logistical assistance exclusively, not as a blanket endorsement of the Independent Force. Within those limits, they were willing to cooperate. Trenchard recorded the heartening outcomes of his conferences with French military commanders in his official diary.

25 June 1918: Lunched with General Castelnau. Had a very interesting lunch with him and General Hello his Chief of Staff. They were most anxious to help in every way. They had sent on my letters asking for more aerodromes to G.H.Q. and were pressing very hard for it. They were very keen to help and to bomb Germany.[105]

The following day, after a luncheon with General Petain at French General Headquarters, the French commander "said he would help the I.F. all he could."[106] However, command and control of British forces was quite another matter.

In this matter of unity of command, Allied goodwill generated by the Admiralty's No. 3 Wing under operational control of the French Air Service had largely vanished. Further, and ironically, Trenchard discovered that his earlier insistence that all bombing be under one responsible agency now recoiled upon him.

In May Sykes had drafted a proposal to give Trenchard command of an inter-allied independent bombing force to include French and American as well as British units. Presented to the Supreme War Council in June, the proposal met from Foch almost precisely the same arguments previously employed by Haig and Trenchard when they had attacked the idea of independent air operations. Not until 24 September was agreement reached to establish an inter-Allied Independent Air Force. Even then the Supreme War Council laid down that the IAIAF was to engage in independent operations only after "the requirements of battle" had been met; during periods of "active operations" of the armies its prime function was to supply bombing support for the ground battle. Trenchard was not finally confirmed as its commander until 29 October 1918.[107]

No effective coordination of Allied bombing proved possible before the Armistice, despite the energy and memoranda dedicated to achieving unity of command.

Why, then, did the British eventually accept an inter-Allied bombing force controlled from Foch's headquarters? As GOC of such a force, Trenchard would have been able to employ the combined national bombing fleets legitimately, and autonomously, against targets selected by his IF planning staff. However, Lord Tiverton, in a letter to Milner, identified a less altruistic rationale.

If the matter was a simple above board transaction one would understand this view (i.e., "to let the I.F. come under Foch"). It is, however, a typical "wrangle" of the worst and stupidest character. It is hoped by this move to get an inter-allied I. F. under Trenchard consisting of British, Americans and Italians. It is then thought that Foch can be put off when he asks for squadrons by giving them Americans and Italians, thus reserving the British intact for Sykes' long distance bombing schemes, while apparently giving way. This can only lead to very bad feeling without any results. It is not a time to be frightened of speaking out and the truth is that no one has the courage to stand up to Trenchard who is over here and is simply doing things as he wants them.[108]

Finally, the development of 27 Group, RAF at Norfolk, a unit of the Independent Force flying the gigantic new Handley Page V1500, promised to give Britain an independent strategic bombing capability from its home soil. Weir had intimated as much in countering CIGS objections to a French-based IF at the Air Policy Committee session on 23 May 1918. With such reservations, it is doubtful that effective, harmonious control of an inter-Allied force would have emerged, even had the war lasted into 1919. Certainly, Trenchard encountered considerable obstacles as GOC IF in soliciting Allied cooperation—or at least noninterference—in his bombing operations.

Trenchard met General Duval, chief of the French Air Service, on 18 June, two weeks after the Lloyd George–Clemenceau agreement at Versailles. His privately recorded assessment was that Duval "was very difficult to deal with as he openly said to me 'what would you have said a year ago?'" The question was a pointed reference to Trenchard's earlier opposition as GOC, RFC in the field, to all independent operations.[109] When Trenchard visited the US Air Service at their headquarters two days later, he met the same skepticism. His reply on that occasion revealed deep reservations about his own independent force.

I pointed out to them that the difficulty was to reconcile that irresponsible newspapers had forced our Government into adopting an unsound organization and that my task was to carry out the sound policy of bombing Germany on an unsound organization.[110]

To undercut French and American objections, Trenchard sought to convince his counterparts that the freedom of action he enjoyed would enhance, rather than disrupt, their own plans.

He carefully distanced himself from any vestige of cross-channel accountability and complained when his position was undermined.

> 3 July 1918. The Air Ministry are starting to publish our communiques as from the Air Ministry and not from the Independent Force. This of course will lead to the very thing the Air Ministry want to avoid, that is, to make it appear as if the Independent Force is directly under the Air Ministry which will stop the Americans and French joining in.[111]

His success in this delicate role can be ascertained from the comments of Brig Gen Benjamin D. Foulois, assistant chief of the US Air Service.

> Fortunately, for the operations of this Independent Air Force, it was placed under the command of Major General Hugh Trenchard, an officer of the highest practical knowledge and experience, not only as regards Air Service operations, but military operations in general, and an officer who was well known and liked by all American officers with whom he had associated. In my opinion the success of the operations of this force, during its period of service, was due entirely to the personality and judgment of General Trenchard, and not to the policy which created this force and placed it under the direct control and orders of the British Air Ministry.[112]

Trenchard's reputation and prestige overcame American and French doubts and allayed their suspicions concerning management of British strategic bombing. In this matter, he proved relatively more successful than his government's ministers.[113]

To reinforce this independent stance, Trenchard duplicated the Department of the Chief of the Air Staff under Sykes. This organization mirrored almost exactly its London parent. Known officially as the "Air Staff Branch, H.Q., I.F.," it consisted of four staff groups, including operations and intelligence sections.[114] While self-sufficiency allowed HQ IF to function without recourse to Sykes and convinced skeptical Allied commanders of Trenchard's autonomy, it also isolated him from expert staff groups at the Air Ministry. Considerable disjointedness, inefficiency, and ill will resulted.

Their isolation forced IF staff officers at Autigny-la-Tour to relearn lessons (such as the impact of weather and the need for training) already absorbed by their Air Ministry counterparts. Finally, their autonomy made them liable. An undertone of frustration came to characterize Air Staff memoranda dealing with Independent Force affairs during this period, largely in response to Trenchard's cavalier treatment of DFO and DAI staffs.

In May 1918, when joint Allied bombing operations had seemed feasible, Tiverton circulated a paper citing the technical difficulties of such undertakings. He emphasized the urgent need to begin contingency planning.

> Sufficient data have been obtained to make a comparison between various targets on the question of their vulnerability. However, such factors as the number of bombs necessary, the effect of formation flying on the error curve . . . the actual choice of targets, the type of machine, are so intimately connected with this question and with one another that the whole matter must be treated as one large and complex question. It must of necessity take some time to solve and therefore cannot be taken up too soon.[115]

As the joint scheme was predicated upon mistaken forecasts for aircraft production, it had to be altered when those projections proved specious.

The Air Staff accordingly produced yet another bombing program, using Tiverton's estimates; as N. Jones noted, this new plan "could be put into operation by a force of aircraft considerably smaller than that originally planned for."[116] Tiverton's memorandum of June 1918 (Notes on Targets) in fact set target priorities that Sykes later incorporated into his own futile guidance to the Independent Force.[117] These strategic schemes illustrate Air Staff views on strategic bombing.

Soon after the war, Sykes was to summarize the targets of this offensive as the chemical bottlenecks of the German warmaking industry.

> [They were] the centre of the chemical industry at Mannheim and Frankfurt; the iron and steel works at Briey and Longwy and the Saar Basin; the machine shops in the Westphalian district and the magneto works at Stuttgart; the submarine bases at Wilhelmshaven, Bremerhaven, Cuxhaven, and Hamburg, and the accumulator factories at Hagen and Berlin.[118]

Sykes had presented this scheme, in considerably more detail, to the War Cabinet on 28 June 1918 as "the policy of the new Air Staff" for bombing Germany's "root industries."[119] With respect to forces available and operating areas, the new CAS noted that submarine bases and factories which supplied U-boat accumulators could be reached by No. 27 Group operating from English airfields.

> It will be seen from a map that three of the main industrial centres were situated near the west frontier of Germany; and, therefore, one portion of the striking force was based at Ochey, which lies within a few miles of the Saar Basin, within 180 miles of Essen, and within 150 miles of Frankfurt. Another portion was based on Norfolk, where a group of super-Handley Page machines were established for the specific purpose of attacking Berlin, a distance of 540 miles, and the naval bases within 400 miles. It was obvious that though aircraft from England would have to cover greater distances, they would not expose themselves to the strong hostile defences in the rear of the battle front.[120]

Trenchard was specifically prohibited by the Air Staff scheme from activities such as reconnaissance or attacks on enemy aerodromes and railways. Though Sykes did not expect long-range bombing to "be in really effective operation" until June 1919, "it is urged that much may and must be done this year."[121] The German chemical industry constituted Sykes' primary objective for the Independent Force.

Upon War Cabinet approval, the Air Staff plan was forwarded to HQ IF. Sykes ordered that no other targets be attacked until enemy chemical plants (suppliers of raw materials for explosives, propellants, and poison gas) could be "completely crippled."[122] The Lorraine steel works could be raided only when poor weather precluded attacks further into Germany. Understandably, the CAS was concerned with Trenchard's possible deviations from this plan. In the meantime, his Air Staff continued to refine this scheme.

Tiverton, again in the forefront of strategic planning at Hotel Cecil, appended a caveat to the plan that Sykes had transmitted to the GOC IF. Given the present size of Trenchard's force, he cautioned that it should adhere strictly to Air Staff priorities and concentrate solely on German chemical plants. Attacks upon such attractive targets as magneto and aero-engine factories (which the enemy could duplicate beyond bomber range) should be postponed until the IF was large enough to destroy them in one or two raids.

If it were possible a very much larger force than is at present available should be allocated to carry out this policy. . . .The desired result can therefore only be obtained by employing the Independent Force strictly for the purpose which is in view and resolutely refusing its services in other directions however desirable they may appear in themselves.[123]

Tiverton was acutely aware of the need for realistic targeting priorities.

Evidence of a divergence between Air Staff plans and Independent Force operations soon became apparent. As early as mid-June, less than two weeks after Trenchard had taken over the IF, a memorandum to the DFO from FO3 Branch protested against the practice of HQ IF issuing daily press releases containing details of IF raids and their results.

I have carefully read all the Minutes from the War Office and I have considered D.D.A.I. Minutes to you on the matter.

I reluctantly come to the conclusion that I see no excuse whatever for giving publicity to the particular targets at which we are aiming. I do not see in the least any use in telling the public of what we are intending to do, and I see every reason from a military point of view in keeping this information to ourselves. . . . It would be of the greatest value to the Germans to have a certain knowledge of what we were aiming at.

If it once becomes a question of giving information in some cases and withholding it in others it will not please the public and it will still be giving a hint to Germany that there is something we wish to conceal.

For these reasons I am most strongly of the opinion that the public should not be told of the particular target which we were attacking on any particular date.[124]

The ubiquitous press releases that so concerned the Air Staff had characterized all British strategic bombing campaigns since No. 3 Wing in 1916 and 1917. However, publicizing the Independent Force's activities far outstripped these earlier endeavors. Within two hours of assuming command, the GOC IF sent his first release, containing details on objectives, bombs dropped, and results.

For Press Communique aaa Night of 5th 6th June 5 tons of bombs dropped on Metz Sablon Railway Station and Triangle and in the Railway Siding at Thionville with good results although visibility was indifferent aaa In the morning of the 6th the Railway Station at Coblentz was heavily attacked by our machines and good bursts were observed on the Railway line aaa All our machines returned safely.

repeated GHQ France and GHQ RAF

GOC Independent Force RAF[125]

As a matter of historical interest, this communication preceded Trenchard's telegram to the Air Ministry in which he announced that he had officially taken charge of the Independent Force.

> I established my Headquarters today at AUTIGNY-LA-TOUR, 4 miles N.E. of NEUFCHATEAU and sent my first press communique at 4.30 pm. I would be obliged if you would inform me what time you received this telegram so that I can see if it gets home in time to get into the next morning's press.

/s/Trenchard[126]

In subsequent correspondence with London, Trenchard complained whenever his press releases had not been followed *verbatim*, or not printed at all, in major English newspapers. All this exchange indicates that publicity extolling his new command held significant and continuing interest for Trenchard. Tiverton's memorandum reveals it was also an issue from the perspective of the Air Staff.

As Trenchard continued to wage his news campaign, the Air Staff's misgivings over IF press returns mounted. In mid-September 1918, when the aerial offensive was well underway, the head of F03, Colonel Gammell, complained to General Groves, the DFO.

> Everything should be done to foster in all units in the Independent Force the idea of the importance of direct hits on objectives as opposed to the policy of merely dropping so many tons of bombs on the German side of the lines. . . . Would it be possible to alter the form of the communication to the Press into terms of actual number of hits scored as opposed to the amount of bombs dropped. . . . Should not the Independent Force give the lead by adopting the only system of reports which gives the real value of results achieved.
>
> Even if it were inadvisable to adopt this policy in reports for the Press would it not be desirable to omit all references to weight of bombs dropped by individual squadrons or other units *in all R.A.F. communiques*. In this way the importance of actually hitting objective would be emphasised.[127]

However, as with conduct of operations, the initiative lay with HQ IF at Autigny-la-Tour; the Air Staff lacked the ability to influence the matter.

This disagreement over press releases was symptomatic of fundamental differences in philosophy between London and the field. Working relationships between Sykes' subordinates and their counterparts in the IF continued to deteriorate throughout 1918.

By July 1918, less than one month after the creation of the Independent Force, a "we-they" state of affairs had developed between the two staffs. Tiverton was particularly disturbed.

1. The somewhat disquieting analysis of last week's bombing raids has led me to analyse the work of the 8th Brigade since its inception. The accompanying chart [not included] shows that a definite class of targets has been selected by this Brigade which confirms:

   (a) Neither the class of target against which the Independent Force was created.

   (b) Nor to any class of target from which reasonable results may be expected.

2. Before going into any further criticisms it will be as well to face actual facts.

There was a reconstruction of the staff, of which everyone is aware, and, however unpalatable it may be to read, the sole result has been up to date that:

   (a) The 8th Brigade has continued to attack what the new staff believes to be wrong and useless objectives, and the new staff have taken no action.

   (b) There is no official systematic list of objectives giving their priority and the new staff have not insisted upon any such list being prepared.

   (c) On paper an immense amount of work has been done. In fact, nothing has been accomplished.[128]

Tiverton concluded his critical brief with an implicit reference to Trenchard and a warning of future hazards.

It may be advisable up to a point to sacrifice personnel, material, policy and personal good name in order to obtain the good will of one officer, but it must be remembered that the good will of many others will be alienated in the process and it therefore logically follows that the success of such policy may be too dearly bought.[129]

Tiverton's acerbic evaluations of Independent Force policy and targeting priorities reveal the extent to which Trenchard departed from the spirit and letter of Sykes' directive.

In early August Tiverton handed General Groves an eight-page study of bombing policy and the prospects for gaining

Allied participation. Lord Milner, secretary of state for war, also received a copy of Tiverton's paper.[130] The Air Staff expert summarized the approved policy of the "new staff."

> [The policy is] the systematic obliteration (afterwards modified to "dislocation") of the German industrial and munition works by
>
> (1) The creation of an Independent Force.
> (2) Increasing the force allocated for long distance bombing.
> (3) The systematic choice of targets according to their effect upon Key industries.
> (4) The systematic use of bombs, sights, etc. having regard to the nature of the target, all of which necessarily involved an intensive training in the knowledge of targets, navigation, and the knowledge of the essential districts.[131]

Tiverton then explained that two forces had been dedicated to this policy. One force, developed from the 41st Wing, RFC, and Eighth Brigade, RAF, was based in eastern France; the other, No. 27 Group flying the "V-Type Handley Page," was based in Norfolk. The latter had already fallen well behind schedule, owing to strikes, crashes, and general mismanagement.

> A systematic choice of key industries was begun upon paper and the chemical targets definitely chosen for priority. In fact the I.F. have not systematically attacked them, or even attempted to do so. No systematic use has been made of the right type of bomb so that both the Technical Department and the technical officers of the Independent Force are in despair. Although models of all targets have been offered by the War Trades Intelligence, no intensive training in knowledge of such targets has been undertaken. In fact, therefore, nothing has been done to carry out the promised policy more than would have been done in any case. The policy put forward in April as the essential policy of the new staff has not in fact been carried out in any way. The very opposite policy has persistently been carried out with all the material available.[132]

Tiverton substantiated these accusations in detail. As he had warned previously, "certain targets could not be bombed until sufficient strength was collected to obliterate them." However, one of these targets, the Bosch magneto works, had already been attacked by the IF, even though "the miserably small amount of aeroplanes which visited Stuttgart were not all employed against the works." Moreover, complained the Air Staff officer, "This was not done fortuitously, as the G.O.C. I.F. made it one of the main objects of his July programme."[133]

The Independent Force had raided Stuttgart proper on the last two nights of the month with four Handley Pages of No. 216 Squadron. Of eight launched on 29/30 July, one machine claimed hits on a "factory" with half its payload (986 pounds of bombs) from an altitude of 8,000 feet.[134] Its companions struck individual targets between Maizieres and the Rhine valley. On the following evening, three Handley Pages (of four launched) dropped 4,480 pounds of bombs on the city from 6,400 to 7,000 feet, with 2,912 pounds falling on the railway station and the Bosch factory.[135] On these two nights, just four of the 12 aircraft that bombed successfully claimed hits on the magneto factory. Postwar survey teams were unable to assess actual damage to the works or the city.[136] These bombing returns substantiate Tiverton's assertion that the IF had ignored the government's directives.

He also complained about the quality of aerial intelligence conducted by HQ IF and its implications for the bombing campaign.

It has often been pointed out that the pilots must be trained to know their targets, and yet on August 8th a raid was solemnly reported as having taken place on the Rombach explosive works. A.I.1.b. say that they have no knowledge of any such works. Either some knowledge is in the possession of the I.F. which ought to be in the possession of the Intelligence, or the Intelligence of the I.F. is wholly wrong, or the pilots cannot have known what target they really were attacking, in which latter case it would be impossible for any pilot to pick out the vital spot in the particular works.[137]

Raid returns from No. 55 Squadron show that the unit had one of its more successful missions on the day in question. Ten DH4s were launched, all bombed, and all returned without mishap. Aircrew listed their target as the "Wallingen Factory," northeast of town of Rombach; German documents examined after the war confirm that on 8 August 1918 a total of 24 bombs fell in the vicinity of the blast furnaces there. One bomb was blind, one fell outside the plant perimeter, and the remaining 22 fell on the works but caused no casualties among the work force.[138] However, the target was a blast furnace complex, not a gunpowder factory, and crews undoubtedly identified it correctly. As with the earlier incident in which GHQ transformed tanneries at Pirmasens into munition

166

factories, someone above squadron, wing, and even Eighth Brigade level changed the description of this target before releasing it to the press.

Attached to the appendix was a map graphically representing three key target districts identified by the Air Staff and the number of RAF raids on each during the period April–July 1918. Of 245 attacks, only 32 had been directed against these objectives. Tiverton admitted that some raids had been diverted or "abandoned for weather conditions," but he argued that the "vast majority were undertaken against railway sidings and enemy aerodromes."[139]

Tiverton's map sheet was apparently in wide use for planning purposes. It shows distances to German objectives from eastern England as well as from the Nancy-Ochey region. The difficulty imposed by neutral Holland upon routes to targets is made clear. From this perspective, the primary advantage to basing units of the IF in Britain would be their freedom from Allied interference.

Following this analysis, Tiverton examined the doctrinal basis for strategic operations. He concluded that the British had little justification to present to the Supreme War Council (the Allied forum deciding the issue). Quite apart from French arguments that "all operations should be under the Generalissimo in command of the Armies," the British had not used the IF in a demonstrably independent role.[140] Trenchard's target selection lay at the root of the difficulty.

> [Employing the]Independent Force for the dislocation of Army transport and Enemy aerodromes which is clearly a policy that must be in the province of the Generalissimo. We therefore approach the Conference either from a wholly illogical standpoint or with the inherent weakness of arguing from what we mean to do in the future, but have never succeeded in doing in the past.[141]

To such a position, Tiverton postulated the French reply.

> Either you will continue in the future your present policy in which case you should be under Marshal Foch, or you want independence to do something which you don't know yet that you can do.[142]

Until the IF demonstrated that it could conduct a strategic campaign, arguments justifying its existence could not be tenable. Its machines would be better employed in a unified plan under Foch, as its current targets largely overlapped those on the Allied tactical lists. Tiverton also explicated the adverse consequences of widespread publicity on this matter.

The "method of propaganda is equally instructive" in both nations. In Britain, the result of extensive press coverage "has been to leave an impression in the mind of the public that all is going well with the bombardment of Germany, and that the present authorities are satisfied."[143] Consequently, said Tiverton, the people were "more or less satisfied with what they believe is being done," and would not object if Foch were to assume overall control of the IF. In France, however, using French names for towns in the operating area—at French request—has given "to their people the idea that England is bombing French towns."[144] Here again, he claimed, putting Foch in charge seemed logical; "the French people undoubtedly have a spirit of irritation in the matter which would be set at rest by such a policy."[145]

In concluding his memorandum, Tiverton asserted that the authorities had lost sight of the whole point of strategic bombing.

> The object must always be borne in mind. It is not the producing and maintenance of so many squadrons. It is the systematic obliteration of Key industries. And squadrons wrongly used because the pilots do not know their targets, because wrong bombs are used, because wrong targets are chosen, are wasted effort which does not damage Germany in the way intended and discredits every effort to do so.

> If there is not sufficient strength to carry out such a policy then there can be no legitimate argument [against] handing over all command to marshal Foch.[146]

Tiverton would repeat this argument inside and outside the Air Ministry until the Armistice.

The recent characterization of Tiverton as a "self-confessed extremist" and "a devoted advocate of 'terror bombing' as an Air Staff officer in 1918" seems not only harsh but misplaced.[147] Preoccupied As he was with technical and experimental means of conducting an effective bombing campaign, his criticisms about the character and capacity of IF operations, and about strategic policy and inter-Allied organization, is undeniable.

But there were weaknesses in his position. He seems to have underestimated the practical difficulties of dealing with a dominant personality such as Trenchard. Either he was unaware of or discounted the special agreement between the GOC IF and Weir. Had the Air Minister informed only Sykes and no one else in his department of the command arrangement for the IF, Sykes' reluctance to confront Trenchard, his apparent subordinate, becomes understandable. The frustration of his staff officers managing Independent Force affairs would also increase accordingly. The Directorate of Flying Operations was particularly chafed by the situation.

Within the DFO, Tiverton continued to inveigh against Trenchard's command, and many of his memoranda found their way into Milner's files. In a 20 August 1918 paper sent to both DFO and Milner, Tiverton argued that the Versailles Council afforded an "opportunity . . . of laying down definitely a campaign against German munitions . . . which can be used in the future to stop once and for all the useless waste of effort which is at present going on."[148] Against "all expert advice," he said, the IF bombed German towns indiscriminately instead of concentrating on "targets recommended by the trade experts."[149] The following day, he complained to the same authorities that no one had yet empirically calculated the specific types or quantities required to "demobilize the German Army by destroying a certain definite number of targets."[150]

The matter could not escape official notice. Tiverton's studies provided sufficient ammunition for the DFO to forward a lengthy memorandum to the CAS on 11 September 1918. General Groves contended that Air Staff policy approved by the War Cabinet was in fact being ignored.

The DFO demonstrated that bomb payloads allocated to the top classes of designated first-priority objectives (chemical factories and iron or steel works) had declined during June, July, and August 1918. However, the tonnage dropped on enemy aerodromes, targets favored by Newall as well as by Trenchard, had increased sharply:

The percentage of attacks carried out on Chemical Factories has dropped from 14% in June to 9.5% in July and to 8% in August. Similar attacks on steel and iron works show a decrease from 13.3% in June to 9% in July and to 7% in August. Examination of the figures show that this decrease has been caused chiefly by an increased activity against hostile aerodromes, the number of attacks rising from 13.3% in June to 49.5% in August.[151]

Groves conceded that the on-scene commander "must be the judge of what counter–offensive against enemy flying establishment is necessary to enable our own machines to work without undue interference." He emphasized, however, that this tactical contingency per se did not fully account for the decreased effort directed against chemical, iron, and steel targets.[152]

The DFO was also convinced that far too much ordnance had been expended against enemy "railway objectives which are placed by the Air Staff as third in order of importance on the priority list of targets."

The percentages of attacks on railway targets were 55% in June, 46% in July, and 31% in August. It is submitted that this percentage, although decreasing, is still far too high, and that every effort should be made to concentrate upon root industries, since to carry out the destruction of these industries is the object [for] which the Independent Force was created.[153]

Then the DFO appended a third argument to his memorandum (a point which did not appear in the draft). This addition clarified his assertion that shifts in targeting policy resulted from a deliberate decision by the GOC IF.

It may be argued that weather conditions have, on many occasions, prevented attacks being carried out on factories, and that railways and sidings have been given as alternative targets within easy reach. In this connection I would point out that there are 24 iron and steel works, 4 chemical and 2 munition factories and 9 important miscellaneous industrial targets within a radius of 75 miles from Nancy, and that of the total number of raids on railways 66% have been carried out within this radius.[154]

On 16 occasions, when a neighbourhood containing a railway objective has been visited, bombs have been directed wholly or partially against the railway target. It may be put forward that these attacks on railways and other targets have some connection with intended operations in the area in which the Independent Force is working. It is considered that this contention cannot be advanced in defence of a policy carried out over a period of three months.[155]

Finally, Groves concluded that Independent Force operations contravened military and political guidelines for the campaign.

> I would submit that the policy pursued at present amounts to the diversion of maximum effort against targets of subsidiary importance. Such a dissipation of Air Force is at variance with the policy laid down by the Air Council in the above-mentioned letter (Secretarial Letter No. 11555/1918, 13 May 1918) and with the views put forward by you in the declared policy of the Air Staff submitted to the War Cabinet in a printed paper on June 17th (G.T. 4622).

> Moreover, I consider that if the G.O.C., I.F. continues to pursue his present policy it will be difficult to justify the allocation of Air Forces as between the Army, Navy, and the Independent Force, in which the War Cabinet has recently concurred.[156]

To his paper, "I.F., R.A.F. 'Policy'," Groves attached a tabulation of raid returns and the relative percentage of effort devoted to each target category to support his conclusions. The matter then cooled on the desk of the chief of the Air Staff. Sykes, though sympathetic, was unwilling and unable to alter the situation.

> The Chief of the Air Staff supported General Groves' contention that the bombing operations should be made to conform with the Air Ministry plan, but it seems that he could do nothing to bring this about.[157]

Jones argues that Trenchard, though opposed in principle to strategic bombardment and desiring independence from British command structure, was quite willing to commit his machines to support tactical requests from the French. However, such an argument appears self-contradictory. While IF and Eighth Brigade units supported ground offensives by attacking designated tactical targets during the spring and fall of 1918, such diversions were limited in scope and duration. And aside from these undertakings, Trenchard functioned independently of everyone. Jones then hypothesizes that Trenchard believed French goodwill was essential to the continued vitality of his command.[158] This, perhaps, is inferring too much. The French did continue logistically to support the campaign throughout the war, but they never ceased to have doubts concerning the strategic supervision and orientation of British bombing.

Jones' explanation does not give sufficient weight to the institutional consequences that followed from the pact between Trenchard and Weir. Sykes was circumvented, thus giving Trenchard maximum latitude. Air Staff contact with the Independent Force continued to diminish even as the prestige and reputation of the IF increased.

At the end of September, Tiverton prepared his last major memorandum on bombing policy. He sent this paper, "The Possibilities of Long Distance Bombing from the Present Date until September 1919," to Colonel Gammell, head of FO3, who forwarded it to General Groves, DFO, on 1 October 1918.[159] Tiverton also sent a copy, with cover letter, to Milner on 30 September, the dates indicating that he may have been in the habit of writing to the War Minister whenever he sent reports through the formal chain of command.[160]

After an extended summary of Independent Force operations, which he felt "has not justified its original promise," Tiverton presented his "less ambitious programme" for the next 12 months.[161] He did not alter former Air Staff target priorities, retaining chemical and steel objectives as the top two categories. However, due to the limited force available, "the number must be cut down ruthlessly." Accordingly, just five chemical plants and a dozen steel works were selected as the "Essential Guts of the whole munition industry." To destroy this short list, Tiverton insisted that each attack be carefully planned "by the joint brains of all those who know the question from the commercial, the political, the flying, and the technical points of view."[162] Furthermore, he pointed out the critical importance of thoroughly briefing aircrews.

> Until the pilots and observers know intimately every building in every works and its value, and until they realise that bombs dropped anywhere else are of no value, effort will continue to be wasted without diminishing the risk of casualties. On the programme put forward below, there are under 20 targets, this training therefore, is not an impossibility.[163]

Tiverton supported his scheme with estimates of the bombs required to destroy each target. He also determined the number of large raids possible per month between October 1918 and September 1919. Tiverton concluded that, through April 1919, "the very moderate obliteration suggested should be easily accomplished during the year."[164] His final bombing plan represented a change in magnitude but not in direction from his initial proposals to Sykes in May–June 1918.

So far as strategic planning in the field by Newall and Trenchard is concerned, very little documentation has survived. What exists demonstrates that actual guidance of bombing operations remained on an ad hoc basis throughout 1918. Two sets of Eighth Brigade/IF documents, one dating from May–June 1918 and the other from October 1918, confirm the consistently low priority field headquarters gave to coherent strategic policy.

The first set, two memoranda prepared by Newall as GOC, Eighth Brigade on 12 and 27 May and one by Trenchard as GOC IF on 23 June 1918, underscores the lack of substantive thought which followed the stormy creation of the Independent Force. Careful comparison of these plans, written under different circumstances, reveals that they are virtually identical. Each is merely a transcription of its predecessor.

In fact, Trenchard's "very secret" five-page paper for Lord Weir, "Memorandum on the Tactics to be Adopted in Bombing the Industrial Centres of Germany," was copied entirely from Newall's report on 27 May, "The Scientific and Methodical Attack of Vital Industries."[165] Except for short paragraphs setting out personal views on bombing and moral effect, Trenchard's scheme mirrors Newall's memorandum to Sykes, transmitted via Salmond at HQ RAF the previous month.[166] In its turn Newall's paper of 27 May was a minor revision of his scheme of 12 May, "The Scientific and Continuous Attack of Vital Industries."[167] These three documents are easily confused or overlooked, particularly since they are scattered throughout the official archives.

What unambiguously emerges is that Newall had formulated field policy guiding strategic bombing by mid-May 1918, well before creation of the IF and the arrival of its GOC. Trenchard contributed nothing of substance to Newall's initial concept of operations.

Newall's original paper of 12 May was completed the day before the Air Council announced creation of the Independent Force. Trenchard, its GOC, had been unemployed since resigning as CAS on 12 April, although he had been, as discussed earlier, negotiating with Weir since 30 April for a suitable new assignment. On 8 May 1918, he had concluded his special agreement with the Air Minister for the IF. He crossed to France on 17 May, five days after Newall had prepared his strategic scheme.

Trenchard arrived at Newall's headquarters on 20 May and remained in the vicinity of Eighth Brigade Headquarters until his departure on 6 June for Neufchateau to assume tactical command of the Independent Force. At the time, the IF consisted of four squadrons (with supporting elements) from Newall's Eighth Brigade, plus the headquarters echelon that Trenchard was assembling at Autigny–la–Tour, northeast of Neufchateau. Trenchard therefore was in Newall's area on 27 May 1918 when Newall rewrote his previous memorandum, slightly altering the title ("Scientific and Continuous Attack of Vital Industries" became "Scientific and Methodical Attack"). It is unthinkable that Newall would have transmitted this policy statement without obtaining the approval of the GOC IF. Trenchard's *nihil obstat* is further indicated by his copying massive sections of Newall's memorandum verbatim and forwarding this "work" directly to Weir, representing it as his own program, on 23 June 1918.[168]

Thus the Air Ministry learned of the plans of its bomber commanders from Newall to Sykes through usual channels on 27 May and from Trenchard's confidential memorandum to Weir on 23 June. Significantly, despite events during the six weeks following Newall's original report on 12 May, neither London nor the field modified the originally proposed bombing plan for Independent Force.

Newall's memorandum of 27 May 1918 constituted a comprehensive approach to the question of how best to attack Germany. Largely copied from his 12 May paper, his proposal seems to represent the Eighth Brigade's bid to secure institutional stability. Newall and his subordinates wished to establish acceptable criteria and priorities for their strategic activity. They worked, as usual, independently of the Air Staff.

As the memorandum's title suggests, Newall considered that objectives for aerial assault had to be both vital ("being of great importance, if not essential," to the enemy war effort) and vulnerable ("being located within an area which will admit of their being attacked more or less continuously").[169] In his estimation, "the line COLOGNE-FRANKFURT-STUTTGART," some 125 miles behind the trenches, marked the practical limit for "systematic attacks" on these targets:

(a) The iron and coal mines.
(b) The iron ore "bassins," where most of the blast furnaces are to be found, and where the iron ore is made into pig iron, which forms the basis for steel.
(c) The chemical production.
(d) The explosive production.
(e) The miscellaneous production, viz. railway material, rolling stock, aircraft, internal combustion engines, submarine parts, magnetoes and tanning industries.[170]

This plan, emphasizing iron and coal centers and including "railway material, rolling stock . . . and tanning industries," had very little in common with Air Staff and War Cabinet schemes. Chemical and ammunition factories in the Rhine valley, of primary concern to London, stood third and fourth on the Eighth Brigade target list. Newall's priorities also retroactively justified objectives that his squadrons had hit during the first five months of 1918. He selected targets which he knew from experience his aircrews could find.

Newall analyzed these bombing categories from the perspective of operational feasibility and material effects. In a passage that flatly contradicted bombing priorities formulated in Whitehall, he justified efforts directed against enemy railways.

It is generally known and admitted throughout GERMANY that her principal danger lies in the lack of railway material and rolling stock. As far as munitions are concerned GERMANY will always be able to produce sufficient to enable her to carry on, but she will be unable to produce the increasing needs in rolling stock and material.[171]

At present numerous targets exist about which no information can be got as to their manufactures.

As data is lacking it is difficult to determine which target, whether the most important or not, should be attacked. Provided the target is not too small and within range, it should be attacked continuously both by day and by night.[172]

When the memorandum reached London, Tiverton rebutted Newall.

General Newall advocates the bombing of rolling stock where possible, but I have grave doubts as to this being the most economical use of bombing squadrons. The whole paper displays a strange lack of information which is available from Intelligence. For instance, apparently he has been given no information that the Bayer works, Leverkussen [near Cologne], and Meister Lucius, at Hoeschst [near Frankfurt] are both in the same order of importance as the Badische Anilin & Soda Fabrik, at Mannheim.[173]

Newall's 27 May memorandum presented his revised evaluation of what his squadrons could be expected to accomplish. It reflected his original paper of 12 May 1918, but it differed from his earlier plan in two additions. Here, one detects Trenchard's slight influence: the necessity to bomb enemy aerodromes in order to retain the initiative in the air war and a brief examination of the "moral effect of bombing."[174]

Regarding the latter, the passage quoted below appeared in the respective narratives of each commander.

The further an objective is located from the battle area the greater will be the moral effect, of an attack on the industries.

The industrial population must be made to realise that they are not immune from the effects of War owing to their being possibly indespensible [sic] to the manufacture of munitions. If thoroughly bombed they will become far more rapidly demoralized than those working within the sound of the guns of the battle area. They must be made to realise that they are subject to attack at any moment. The anxiety as to whether an attack is likely to place is probably just as demoralizing to the industrial population as the actual attack itself, provided that they have previously been given the opportunity of experiencing aerial bombardment.

So far as Newall was concerned, this adequately covered the topic. Trenchard, however, in the *only* portion of his 23 June 1918 paper that did not copy Newall's concept word for word, included four additional paragraphs on the importance of moral effect.

The GOC IF also added moral effect to the list of reasons for attacking vital German industries.

It must be remembered that the moral effect at present is far greater than the material effect, so it is of the utmost importance to utilise to the utmost both moral and material effect. It is more often the moral effect that makes the enemy immobilize a large number of his means of warfare such as Aeroplanes and Anti-Aircraft Guns than material effect.[175]

Trenchard's belief in the primacy of enemy morale as a target also emerged from his proposed method of attack. He noted that if one town were to be continually attacked (the Air Staff and War Cabinet concept), "all the other towns are feeling fairly safe." The GOC IF, dismissing this principle of concentration, decided to scatter his aerial assault in order to reap maximum moral effect.

> Therefore, it stands to reason that if attacks are spread out all over Germany for a period and then perhaps concentrated on one objective for three of four days, then scattered again and afterwards concentrated, the whole of Germany will be uneasy as each town will be expecting a three or four day of [sic] attack at any moment.[176]

Contrary to his orders, and to most military thought, Trenchard intended to dissipate his scarce bombing machines in an effort to undercut German morale. The scheme had two advantages: (1) any claimed results could not readily be contradicted or criticized; and (2) the bombing of nearly any portion of enemy territory at any time was rationalized. Material damage counted for less than moral effect, in the opinion of the IF commander.

In the same light, Trenchard shuffled Newall's target categories, though without altering Newall's analysis; the first classes became chemical works, iron/steel works, and aero–engine/magneto works. He also added submarine and shipbuilding works, large gun shops, and engine repair shops to his list, objectives that Newall had included under "miscellaneous." For all of these latter categories, Trenchard merely stated, "Details will be filled in later."[177] The depth of his evaluation for his "special long distance" objectives revealed simply that large gun shops could be found in "Essen (home of the Krupp Works) and Rhohr [sic] Valley Group," while the engine repair shops he intended to bomb were "scatterd [sic] over Germany."[178]

Trenchard's strategic plan, as communicated to Weir, was unworthy of his experience, reputation, and integrity as general officer commanding, Independent Force, RAF. Targets ostensibly selected because of their strategic importance in reality provided blanket justification for aerial assaults aimed at German morale. In the case of Essen, this policy was to have disastrous consequences for the IF on the evening of 16/17 September 1918. However, when Weir wrote to Trenchard on 29 June 1918, he offerred no objections to this superficial program and commented only on the vulnerable construction of most German industrial centers.[179]

In point of fact, Trenchard's 23 June memorandum to Weir also differed significantly from his "Operation Order No. 1," issued to his subordinate commanders on 20 June, three days *before* he wrote to Weir.[180] His field directive, "intended as a guide in detailing operation orders to the units under your command," dictated a different set of target categories.[181]

20 June (Opn. Order 1)	23 June (Paper to Weir)
1. Chemical works.	1. Chemical works.
2. Iron and steel works.	2. Iron and steel works.
3. Railways.	3. Aero engine/Magneto works.
4. Aero engine/Magneto works.	4. Submarine/Shipbuilding works.
5. Aerodromes.	5. Large gun shops.
	6. Engine repair shops.

The targets Trenchard assured Weir that he planned to attack were not the same objectives he ordered his commanders to raid. The GOC IF concealed from his superior the fact that he intended to assault tactical targets, enemy railways, and aerodromes. Trenchard ignored Sykes and the Air Staff, and was less than candid with Weir.

Succeeding operation orders for June through August demonstrate the extent to which Trenchard operated in defiance of Whitehall. For the period 29 June–2 July, he ordered his squadrons to conduct strategic reconnaissance (an activity which Sykes had prohibited) of the enemy rail network near Thionville and Saarbrücken. "For this purpose two machines may be withdrawn from bombing operations."[182] Operation orders for the remainder of July, with one exception, designated enemy aerodromes as primary objectives. Short-range FE2bs in No. 100 Squadron were modified in the field to attack German airfields with incendiary bombs "on the first suitable opportunity."[183] Aerodromes and railways again constituted the majority of assured targets during August.[184] On two occasions, long-distance objectives (Mannheim and Stuttgart on 7

July, Frankfurt on 6 August) were designated for attack once conditions seemed favorable. At Frankfurt, consonant with Trenchard's targeting of morale, specific aiming points included the "central portion of the city" on each side of the bridge, as well as the main railroad and goods stations on the outskirts.[185]

As the DFO pointed out to Sykes in his memorandum of 11 September 1918, returns from the field betrayed Trenchard's departure from Air Staff and War Cabinet bombing policy. Further, two categories of targets (aerodromes and railways) that Trenchard had not mentioned even in his confidential paper to Weir, received the preponderance of IF attention between June and August 1918:

	June	July	August
Aerodromes	13.3%	28.0%	49.5%
Railways	55.0%	46.0%	31.0%
Total	68.3%	74.0%	80.5%[186]

In September, strikes against aerodromes and railways accounted for 84.6 percent of total IF bombing effort, verifying that the upward trend continued into autumn. The GOC IF did indeed set his own bombing policy.

By mid-October 1918, when negotiations were well under way to organize an Inter-Allied Independent Bombing Force under his control, Trenchard produced another paper embodying his latest target doctrine. The memorandum, "Order of Importance and Types of Targets and Reasons for Importance," identified target categories without ever reaching any firm conclusions.[187] Classes of objectives included "Chemical, Poison Gas, Explosive, Munition, Powder Works, Aviation, Blast Furnaces, and Railway Stations."

The GOC IF also betrayed his bias against independent aerial operations in favor of supporting the ground campaign.

The order of importance of the above targets depends on (a) The size of works or Station (b) The output and the number of hands employed (c) The locality (d) The temporary importance with regard to operations (e) Paper importance.

The first three considerations simply mean that any large industrial complex within range could theoretically constitute a worthwhile objective for the IF. The fourth criterion ties bombing priorities firmly to ground activity, as Trenchard's amplification made clear.

(d) By the temporary importance is meant: The Germans may be making great use of Poison Gas shells or many troop trains may be passing through a particular station during operations.

Hence by virtue of our positions, raids can be carried out on some of the most important Chemical and railway centres with a view to, if possible, reducing the output or hindering the traffic.[188]

Trenchard's final point merely reasserted his independence from London, particularly the Air Staff.

(e) Information and reports based on pre war knowledge enable the Higher Command to decide on the relative importance of the military objectives in Germany, but this only affects the policy in so far that it gives the Commander of the Force some idea on which to base his bombing programme.[189]

A three-page list, giving "some of the most important objectives within range," though in no specific priority, closed this extraordinary document. External agencies could only offer advice, not influence IF policy. The fruits and costs of that policy can now be assessed.

Notes

1. Malcolm Cooper, "British Air Policy on the Western Front, 1914–1918" (PhD diss., Oxford University, 1982), 313–14.

2. Rear Adm M. E. F. Kerr, CB, MVO, memorandum to President, Air Board, subject: War Cabinet, Air Policy, 11 October 1917, Milner Papers, Bodleian Library, Oxford, England, dep. 357, fols. 84–85.

3. S. F. Wise, *Canadian Airmen and the First World War*, vol. 1, *The Official History of the Royal Canadian Air Force* (Toronto: University of Toronto, 1980), 283n. Wise, official historian of the Royal Canadian Air Force, considered it "scarcely credible that such a memorandum should have been written by a responsible staff officer."

4. Milner Papers, Cecil to Milner, 11 October 1917, dep. 357, fols. 98–102

5. Ibid., fols. 103, 115–16.

6. Milner Papers, dep. 357, fol. 73.

7. Trenchard Papers, correspondence with Lord Rothermere, 17 December 1917, Royal Air Force Museum (RAFM), Hendon, England, MFC 76/1/89, sheet 1 of 2.

8. Ibid., 20 December 1917.

9. Milner Papers, dep. 357, "Note of Conversation with Tiverton, 25.12.17."

10. Public Record Office (PRO), Air Ministry Records 1/467/15/312/160, pt. II, Tiverton's request for Award of the 1915 Star.

11. Neville Jones, *The Origins of Strategic Bombing: A Study of the Development of British Air Strategic Thought and Practice up to 1918* (London: Eimber, 1973), 112.

12. Lord Tiverton to Rear Adm Mark Kerr, 8 October 1917. Cited in Jones, 152.

13. Ibid., 175; AIR 1/2087/207/8/37, Secretary Air Ministry, Air Ministry Office, memorandum, subject: Matters relating to Air Ministry Staff, Office Memorandum No. 37, 3 June 1918 and List of Staff and Distribution of Duties, October 1918.

14. Milner Papers, "Long Range Bombing," Sir Henry Norman, MP, 25 March 1918, dep. 358, fols. 191–220 (also in PRO, AIR 1/2422/305/18/17).

15. Ibid., fol. 196.

16. Ibid., fol. 197. Norman's data are consistent with Commons reply to William Joynson-Hicks by Mr. MacPherson, Under-Secretary for War, on 20 March 1918. MacPherson stated that Newall's bombing force had dropped 48 tons of bombs while losing just 10 machines on 250 sorties during the preceding five-month period. He also announced that the "accuracy . . . beyond all shadow of a doubt" of aircrew reports had been confirmed by aerial photographs. *Aeroplane*, 27 March 1918, 1152, 1154.

17. Milner Papers, dep. 358, fols. 191, 194, emphases added.

18. Milner Papers, dep. 358, fol. 198.

19. Ibid.

20. AIR 1/640, Capt Lambe to Admiralty, 31 October 1917.

21. Milner Papers, Norman Report, dep. 358, fols. 201–6, 213.

22. Ibid.

23. Lord Rothermere at Gray's Inn, December 1917, quoted in *Flight*, 20 December 1917, 1325.

24. Ibid.

25. *Flight*, 3 January 1918, 4.

26. Sir Almeric William Fitzroy, *Memoirs*, 2 vols. (London: Hutchinson, 1923), 667–68.

27. Andrew P. Boyle, *Trenchard* (London: Collins, 1962), 260.

28. Ibid., 261.

29. AIR 1/522/16/12/5, "The Bombing of Germany," Trenchard to Lloyd George, 13 January 1918. Reprinted in H. A. Jones, *War in the Air: Being the Story of the Part Played in the Great War by the Royal Air Force* (Oxford: Clarendon Press, 1937), Appendix 5, 22–24.

30. Ibid., 22.

31. Jones, *War in the Air*, Appendix 5, 23.

32. Ibid.

33. Ibid., 23–24.

34. Wise, 284.

35. Admiralty (Naval Staff), Cmd. 1343, Distribution and Duties of the Naval Staff, June 1921.

36. Brian Bond, British Military Policy between the Two World Wars (Oxford: Clarendon Press, 1980), Appendix 2, 398; and F. H. Hinsley, British Intelligence in the Second World War: Its Influence on Strategy and Operations, 3 vols. (London: Her Majesty's Stationery Office [HMSO], 1979), vol. 1, 9.

37. AIR 1/2087/207/8/37, Secretary, Air Ministry, Air Ministry Office, memoranda, issued periodically for 3 June 1918 and October 1918.

38. Air Ministry, Air Historical Branch, Members of the Air Council and Air Force Board of Defence Council, 1918 (London: HMSO, September 1973), 5A. Dates of office are in Ministry of Defence.

39. AIR 1/2087/207/8/3, Air Ministry Office Memorandum No. 105, 20 June 1919; and C. G. Grey, A History of the Air Ministry (London: G. Allen & Unwin, 1940), facing 304, depicts the combined Directorate and Air Ministry reorganization as of 1921. In this resepect F. H. Hinsley (British Intelligence in the Second War) errs when he claims that "when the Air Staff was set up in 1918 . . . the Air Intelligence Branch was made a subordinate part of the Directorate of Operations and Intelligence," 9.

40. Maurice Baring, Flying Corps Headquarters, 1914–1918 (London: Bell, 1920), illustrates Trenchard's temperament and style of staff management.

41. Fitzroy, 666.

42. Ibid., 666–67.

43. Trenchard's antipathy did not abate with time. See comments in MFC 76-1-542, "Note by Lord Trenchard on Reading From Many Angles by General Sir Fredrick Sykes, 1943," 19 January 1943.

44. Sykes suffered by his professional proximity to Trenchard. For differing evaluations, see Boyle; H. R. Allen, The Legacy of Lord Trenchard (London: Cassell, 1972); and F. H. Sykes, From Many Angles: An Autobiography (London: Harrap, 1942).

45. King George V sent Lord Stamfordham to Lloyd George "to protest on behalf of the King about Trenchard being superseded," Stephen W. Roskill, Hankey, Man of Secrets, vol. 1, 1877–1918 (London: Collins, 1970), 519. For debates on the Air Ministry, Rothermere and a new position for Trenchard, see Hansard, 1918, cv. 1306–1368 (29 April), 1710 (2 May), 1978 (7 May) and cvi. 30 (13 May). Reprinted verbatim the Parliamentary "Air Force Debate: of 29 April 1918," Aeroplane, 1 May 1918, 1588–1596.

46. PRO, AIR 1/433/16/12/121, Haig to Trenchard, 17 and 25 April 1918.

47. MFC 76/1/20, Trenchard Papers, Weir to Trenchard, 30 April 1918.

48. Ibid.

49. Ibid., Trenchard to Weir, 1 May 1918.

50. MFC 76/1/20, Trenchard to Weir, 1 May 1918.

51. Ibid., Trenchard-Weir exchange, 3, 5 May 1918.

52. Ibid., Weir to Trenchard, 6 May 1918.

53. Ibid., Weir to Trenchard, emphasis added.

54. MFC 76/1/20, Weir to Trenchard, emphasis added.

55. Ibid., Trenchard to Weir, 8 May 1918. An official summary prepared by the Air Ministry in September 1929, *A Short History of the Royal Air Force* (AP 125), does not mention Trenchard's first tenure as CAS. It leads one to believe that he went directly from GOC, RFC to GOC, IF on 6 June 1918 (383).

56. *Hansard*, 1918, cvi, 30.

57. PRO, Cabinet Office Records (CAB) 24/51, GT 4553, Constitution of Independent Force, RAF for carrying out bombing raids on Germany, 13 May 1918.

58. CAB 24/51.

59. Boyle, 329–30; Wise, 296–97; and Newall Papers, War Diary of Eighth Brigade, B392.

60. PRO, AIR 1/461/15/312/104, Trenchard to Weir, letter C4/10, "Miscellaneous Correspondence: Independent Air Force," 3 July 1918.

61. PRO, AIR 2/12, 13,17,18 contain Air Council minutes for this period. Approximately twice as much time was devoted to uniforms and rank titles for the new RAF as to its strategic bombing role.

62. Wise, 298.

63. MFC 76/1/32 Trenchard Papers, Private Diary, June–November 1918, entry for 10 June.

64. PRO, AIR 1/2087/207/8/37, Air Ministry Office Memoranda issued periodically by Secretary, Air Ministry, 3 June 1918, October 1918.

65. PRO, AIR 1/461/15/312/107, file 130, Gammell to P. R. C. Groves, 27 May 1918.

66. Air Ministry, *The Monthly Air Force List*, October–December 1918.

67. PRO, AIR 1/2087/207/8/37, Air Ministry Office Memorandum No. 37, June 1918; and List of Staff and Distribution of Duties, October 1918.

68. E. D. Harding et al., *A History of Number 16 Squadron (known as "A" Naval Squadron) Royal Naval Air Service Renumbered 216 Squadron Independent Force Royal Air Force* (London: H. W. Hill & Son, 1923), 5–6, 9, 16.

69. Ibid., 16, 24.

70. Ibid., 64.

71. Air Ministry, "Monthly Air Force List" for February 1919 does not show them on active service.

72. PRO, AIR 1/460/15/312/97, letter 14/44 to Gammell as FO3 head, 15 October 1918.

73. PRO, AIR 1/2087/207/8/37, Air Ministry Office Memorandum No. 37, 3 June 1918.

74. PRO, AIR 1/2087/207/8/37, Air Ministry List of Staff and Distribution of Duties, October 1918.

75. PRO, AIR 1/452/15/312/24 and AIR 1/461/15/312/107, contains details of such interoffice coordination.

76. PRO, AIR 1/2087/207/8/37, Air Ministry List of Staff and Distribution of Duties, October 1918.

77. Ibid.

78. Ibid., June 1918, October 1918.

79. Ibid., June 1918, October 1918, November 1918. Air Ministry, "Monthly Air Force List," February 1919.

80. Air Ministry, "Monthly Air Force List," July 1920.

81. Ibid., January 1920.

82. PRO, AIR 1/31/15/1/60, Propaganda Section Formation in Air Intelligence Directorate and Policy of, DDAI to CAS, letter, 22 April 1918.

83. PRO, AIR 1/31/15/60. Trenchard's resignation as CAS (tendered to Rothermere in March) was not accepted till 12 April 1918. Correspondence on the proposed Propaganda Section was initiated on 5 March 1918.

84. PRO, AIR 1/13/15/1/60, Propaganda Section Formation in Air Intelligence Directorate and Policy of, DDAI to CAS, letter, 22 April 1918.

85. Ibid.

86. Ibid.

87. PRO, AIR 1/208/207/8/37, Air Ministry List of Staff and Distribution of Duties, June 1918, October 1918.

88. Ibid.

89. PRO, AIR 1/450/15/312/4, "Proposed Minute on the formation of a Strategic Committee Dealing with Air Matters," 19 April 1918.

90. PRO, AIR 1/2087/207/8/37, Air Ministry List of Staff and Distribution of Duties, October 1918. Later the Strategic Council, with the same membership, was known as the Strategic Committee.

91. PRO, AIR 1/450/15/312/4, Documents relating to the Strategic Council in Neville Jones, *The Origins of Strategic Bombing*, 174.

92. Milner Papers, dep. 357, fols. 142-46, Weir, memorandum to Milner, subject: Certain Lines of Policy Regulating the Conduct of the Air Ministry, 23 May 1918. Reprinted in H. A. Jones, *War in the Air*, Appendix 7, 26–28.

93. Ibid.

94. Ibid.

95. Milner Papers, dep 357, fols. 164–69 (GT 5425), Lord Weir, memorandum, subject: War Cabinet Allocation for Royal Air Force, 13 August 1918.

96. Ibid. Enclosure to G.T. 5424, 13 August 1918.

97. Milner Papers, dep. 357, fols. 164–69, enclosure to GT 5424.

98. Ibid.

99. Ibid. Emphasis added.

100. Milner Papers, dep. 357, fols. 147–49, Weir, memorandum to Milner, subject: Independent Air Force Command for Long Range bombing of Germany, 23 May 1918.

101. Ibid.

102. Ibid.

103. MFC 76/1/68, Trenchard Papers, Major-General Sykes, memorandum to Trenchard, subject: Conversation between Mr. Lloyd

George, M. Clemenceau, and Himself, at Versailles on Monday, 3rd June 1918, sheet 2 of 2.

104. MFC 76/1/89, Trenchard Papers, Trenchard, HQ RFC in the field, to Rothermere, Air Ministry, 23 December 1917, sheet 1 of 2.

105. MFC 76/1/30, Trenchard Papers; and PRO, AIR 1/1985/273/107.

106. Ibid.

107. Wise, 308; PRO, AIR 1/1997/204/273/251, "Formation of the Inter-Allied Independent Air force" file, contains correspondence with Allied political authorities and their military chiefs; and H. A. Jones, *War in the Air, Appendices*, 8–11; Sykes to War Cabinet, "Notes by the Chief of the Air Staff on the Independent Royal Air Force, and the Proposed Inter-Allied Strategic Bombing Force," 7 August 1918.

108. Milner Papers, dep. 357, fols. 217–18, Tiverton to Milner, 30 September 1918.

109. MFC 76/1/32, Trenchard Papers, Private Diary, June–November 1918, entry for 18 June 1918.

110. Ibid., entry for 20 June 1918.

111. Ibid., entry for 3 July 1918.

112. "Air Service lessons learned during the present war," postwar report of Foulois to Pershing, commander in Chief, AEF, 20 January 1919, par. 128. Reprinted in Maurer Maurer, ed., *The U.S. Air Service in World War I*, vol. 4, *Postwar Review* (Maxwell AFB, Ala.: AFHRA, 1979), 27.

113. The Air Council was particularly tactless in notifying Haig about the Independent Force. On 11 June 1918 they announced that IF would be "administered direct by the Air Ministry." Specifically, "The Field Marshal C. in C. British Armies in France will exercise no control over the Independent Force, R.A.F." Quoted in Air Commodore R. W. Brooke-Popham, "The Independent Force," lecture, RAF Staff College, November 1923, Newall Papers, B405.

114. MFC 76/1/68, Trenchard Papers, "Composition of Headquarters, Independent Force, Royal Air Force. Corrected to 8th October 1918. *Confidential.*" This detailed booklet, at the Air Historical Branch (AHD No. 204/273/258) while the RAF official history was written, was not transferred to the Air Ministry files at the Kew PRO.

115. PRO, AIR 1460/15/312/101, "The Urgency of Decisions for the 1918 Programme," Tiverton to CAS through DFO, 22 May 1918; and AC/2, Halsbury Papers, box 3, 16a.

116. N. Jones, *Origins*, 181.

117. AIR 1/460/15/312/97, "A List of Targets in Germany," Tiverton to DFO, 2 July 1918; and AC 73/2, Halsbury Papers, box 3, 24.a. In *Origins*, N. Jones discusses Tiverton's plans in detail, 181–83.

118. F. H. Sykes, *Aviation in Peace and War by Major-General Sir F. J. Sykes* (London: Edward Arnold, 1922), 90.

119. "Review of Air Situation and Strategy for the Information of the Imperial War Cabinet," Sykes to War Cabinet, 28 June 1918. Reprinted in Sykes, *From Many Angles*, Appendix 5, 550–54.

120. Sykes, *Aviation in Peace and War*, 90–91.

121. Sykes, "Review of Air Situation and Strategy," 28 June 1918.

122. PRO, AIR 1/462/312/16, "Operation Order for the Guidance of the Independent Force," n.d., probably early July 1918.

123. AIR 1/460/15/312/97, "Paper on Targets within Easy Reach of Ochey," Tiverton to DFO, 3 July 1918; and AC 73/2, Halsbury Papers, box 3, 24c.

124. AIR 1/461/312/107, "On the Inadvisability of Giving Publicity to Particular Targets," Tiverton to DFO, 18 June 1918; and AC 73/2 Halsbury Papers, box 3, 22c.

125. PRO, AIR 1/461/15/312/104, file C4/5, Trenchard to Air Ministry, telegram 4:45 P.M., 6 June 1918.

126. Ibid., Trenchard to Air Ministry, 6 June 1918; and Official Diary of IF, entry for 6 June 1918, MFC 76/1/30, Trenchard Papers. This latter source also records that, on the day after drafting his first press release, Trenchard "drew up the organization for the Independent Force" (entry for 7 June 1918).

127. AIR 1/461/15/312/107, file 08/90B, F03 to DFO, 18 September 1918.

128. AIR 1/461/15/312/107, "An Analysis of One Week's Bombing Raids," Tiverton to DFO, 4 July 1918; and AC73/2, Halsbury Papers, box 3, 25.a.

129. Ibid.

130. Milner Papers, dep. 357, fols. 179–87; and "Review of Operations (April to July, 1918)," Tiverton to D.F.O., n.d., probably mid-August 1918, AC 73/2, Halsbury Papers, box 3, 27.

131. Ibid.

132. Ibid.

133. Ibid.

134. War Diary of Eighth Brigade, entries for July 1918, B392, Newall Papers.

135. Ibid.

136. US Bombing Survey, in Maurer, *Postwar Review*, 365.

137. "Review of Operations (April to July 1918)," Tiverton to DFO, n.d.

138. War Diary of Eighth Brigade, entry for 8 August 1918, B392, Newall Papers; AIR 1/1999/204/273/269, Report on the Effects of Bombing German Blast Furnaces, Maj H. W. M. Paul to Air Ministry, 26 February 1919; and US Bombing Survey, in Maurer, *Postwar Review*, 494.

139. "Review of Operations (April to July 1918)," Tiverton to DFO, n.d.

140. Ibid.

141. Ibid.

142. Ibid.

143. Ibid.

144. Ibid.

145. Ibid.

146. Ibid.

147. Wise, 307 and photo caption between 229–30. Wise seems to have misinterpreted Tiverton's memorandum to the DFO, "On the Advantages to F.O.3 of a Personal Bombing of Germany," 21 June 1918, AC 73/2, Halsbury Papers, box 3, 23.b.

148. Milner Papers, Tiverton to P. R. C. Groves, 20 August 1918, dep. 357, fols. 190–92.

149. Ibid.

150. Ibid., fol. 189, 21 August 1918.

151. AIR 1/460/15/312/97, file 14/39, "I.F., R.A.F. 'Policy,'" DFO to CAS, 11 September 1918.

152. Ibid.

153. AIR 1/460/15/312/97. Underlined portions indicate differences between Groves' draft and final versions. In the draft "far" was omitted, and "that every effort . . . was created" was originally rendered as "that is should be still further decreased and effort directed more against chemical works and steel factories." Groves' final narrative emphasizes the assigned duties of the IF to a greater degree than his first draft. N. Jones, *Origins*, 189–90, cites the draft version.

154. Ibid.

155. Ibid.

156. AIR 1/460/15/312/97.

157. N. Jones, *Origins*, 190.

158. Ibid., 190–91.

159. AIR 1/460/15/312/101, file PL2/23, Tiverton to DFO, 1 October 1918; and AC 73/2, Halsbury Papers, box 3, 10a.

160. Milner Papers, Tiverton to Milner, cover letter, 30 September 1918, dep. 357, fols., 218–22.

161. Ibid.

162. Milner Papers, dep. 357, fols., 218–22.

163. Ibid.

164. Ibid.

165. PRO, AIR 1/2422/305/18/11, Trenchard to Weir, 23 June 1918; and AIR 1/460/15/312/101, Newall to Sykes, 27 May 1918.

166. AIR 1/460/15/312/101, Salmond's cover letter, 27 May 1918, for Newall's memorandum to the CAS.

167. PRO, AIR 1/1986/204/273/114, GOC, Eighth Brigade, 12 May 1918.

168. In his accompanying memorandum Trenchard stated, "On the next paper I have discussed the tactics to be adopted in the bombing of those industrial centres in Germany." AIR 1/2422/305/18/11, Trenchard, memorandum to Weir, subject: Memorandum on the Bombing of Germany, 23 June 1918.

169. AIR 1/460/15/312/101, Newall to CAS, 27 May 1918.

170. Ibid.

171. Ibid.

172. Ibid.

173. AIR 1/460/15/312/101, "Criticism of a Paper by General Newall," Tiverton to DFO, 6 June 1918; and AC 73/2, Halsbury Papers, box 3, 19b.

174. AIR 1/460/15/312/101, Newall to CAS, 27 May 1918.

175. AIR 1/2422/305/18/11, Trenchard to Weir, 23 June 1918.

176. Ibid.

177. Ibid.

178. Ibid. The GOC, IF's phrasing ("scattered over Germany") and spelling "Rohr" for "Ruhr") duplicate that in Tiverton's paper to the DFO, "Strategic Bombing: Objectives in Order of Importance," May 1918, AC 73/2, Halsbury Papers, box 3, 9b.

179. AIR 1/2422/305/18/11, Weir to Trenchard ("secret and confidential"), 29 June 1918.

180. AIR 1/1649/204/95/3, "Operation Order No. 1 by Major General Sir H. M. Trenchard, K.C.B., D.S.O., Commanding Independent Force, Royal Air Force," 29 June 1918.

181. AIR 1/2422/305/18/11, 23 June 1918.

182. AIR 1/1649/204/95/3, IF Operation Order No. 2, June–2 July 1918.

183. Ibid.; and IF Operations Orders No.'s 3, 5–7, 7–27, July 1918.

184. Ibid.; IF Operation Orders No.'s 12, 16–18, 6–24 August 1918.

185. Ibid.; IF Operation Order No. 12, 6 August 1918.

186. AIR 1/460/15/312/97, DFO to CAS, 11 September 1918. Percentages for June–August based on data in the Tabular Summary (discussed earlier) are somewhat higher: 83.5 percent in June, 80.9 percent in July, and 88.9 percent in August.

187. AIR 1/1986/204/273/5, GOC, IF, 15 October 1918.

188. Ibid.

189. Ibid.

Chapter 5

Eighth Brigade and Independent Force Operations

The magnitude of Eighth Brigade and Independent Force operations between 11 February and November 1918 increased substantially as new bombing units augmented the force. During May and late August, three DH9/9A daylight squadrons reinforced No. 55 Squadron. In August also, three Handley Page squadrons joined the long-range night effort as No. 100 Squadron converted to Handley Pages from the agile but obsolescent FEs. By September, Trenchard's command totaled nine active bombing squadrons—a level maintained until the Armistice.

The magnitude of strategic bombing activity during the last year of the war is best evaluated in the aggregate. Trends and conclusions drawn from cumulative results yield considerably more insight than a descriptive summary of daily raids. Data extracted from chronological records help provide raw materials for further evaluation. Target categories developed earlier (blast furnaces, munition/chemical works, aerodromes, the rail system, and miscellaneous) are particularly illuminating in this context. They provide the indices to measure the full discrepancies between policy and reality as the British independent bombing campaign continued into 1918. The belated expansion of Independent Force inexorably determined the scope and pace of its active operations.

During the spring and summer of 1918, three daytime bombardment squadrons equipped with DeHavilland 9 and 9A machines arrived in the Nancy–Ochey area. Externally, the DH9 resembled the dependable but aging DH4. Compared to its predecessor, the DH9 shifted the pilot's cockpit rearward, sandwiching the two main fuel tanks between the engine and an internal compartment in which bombs were hung vertically. Its wings, rear fuselage, landing gear, and tail unit were identical to those of the DH4.[1] In the air, the DH9 represented a regression in performance: a service ceiling of 17,500 feet versus 23,000 feet for the DH4, and a cruising speed at altitude of 91 miles per hour versus 122.5 miles per hour for the DH4.[2] Although the DH9 relocated the pressurized fuselage fuel tank that had bedeviled the pilot and observer in the DH4, the low power and unreliability of its liquid-cooled 230-horsepower Siddeley Puma engine hampered it tactically.

The Siddeley–Deasy Motor Company of Coventry had modified the Beardmore-Halford-Pullinger (BHP) six-cylinder engine for mass production. It also featured an adjustable underslung radiator that could be lowered into the slipstream beneath the machine for cooling.[3]

This feature contributed to a number of DH9 losses; Germans attacking DH9 formations tended to fire low, whether by accident or design, so that the extended radiator was frequently holed.[4] Coolant leakage caused the engine to seize and forced the crew to land behind enemy lines. As one pilot noted, low temperatures at altitude sometimes had the same results as enemy fire.

> Engines were however very unreliable things then, and this (Siddeley Puma) was no exception; it was always giving trouble; and if not the engine itself, then the installation or the water-cooling system. The exposed part of the radiator sometimes froze up and ruptured during high flying in very low temperatures. Then we came lower, the ice would melt, we would lose the water, and there would be a seize-up of the whole engine soon afterwards.[5]

Altogether, the DH9 did not provide the improved performance for which the air arm had hoped. It had been ordered in quantity when, partially in response to the German daylight raid on London on 13 June 1917, the War Office decided to enlarge the size of the Royal Flying Corps by 92 squadrons (from 108 to 200), mostly bombing units. Its numerous shortcomings did not appear until the type came into large-scale production. As one aviation historian has observed, the DH9 "was rashly substituted for the 'Four' in the contracts."[6]

By November 1917, when both Haig and Trenchard bitterly inveighed against further production of the DH9, the logistic situation was such that they had to make do with the "Nine" or nothing at all.[7] No. 99 and No. 104 Squadrons joined the Eighth Brigade on 3 May and 20 May respectively, and flew the DH9 almost for the duration.[8]

The chronic problems experienced with the Siddeley Puma version of the 230-horsepower BHP engine apparently stemmed from fundamental design flaws. To simplify construction, J. D. Siddeley had altered some basic structural features of Frank Halford's power plant, which had been derived from a contemporary Hispano–Suiza model.[9] In July 1917, early in the program, it was discovered that 90 percent of the aluminum cylinder blocks were defective. Later, problems arose with the exhaust valves.[10]

Such continuing difficulties with the DH9 power plant seriously degraded the tactical effort of No. 99 and No. 104 Squadrons. Mechanical problems throughout 1918 constituted a significant handicap to their participation in the long-range daylight bombing campaign.

In its first two missions to the railway triangle at Metz–Sablon on 21 and 22 May, No. 99 Squadron launched six DH9s each day; all six managed to bomb successfully.[11] For the remainder of May, the squadron suffered aircraft aborts for engine trouble on every mission, except for an operation diverted by weather from Thionville to Metz–Sablon on the last day of the month. On six missions, 14 DH9s (of 60 launched) were unable to bomb owing to engine problems. Nine other planes aborted because of adverse weather.

During May, 23 of 77 aircraft launched by No. 99 Squadron proved unable to bomb their primary targets, alternate targets, or targets of opportunity—an abort/launch ratio of 29.9 percent. Inexperience partially accounts for this high failure rate, but it never became negligible.

Thirty-one of 161 DH9s launched by No. 99 Squadron during June 1918 aborted with engine difficulties; on just three missions did every machine that took off manage to complete the operation. In July, on 11 missions for which data are available, 14 of 109 DH9s dropped out of formation with engine problems. On only two missions during the month did the squadron launch 12 planes and suffer no mechanical troubles. In August 1918, 16 of 64 machines launched by No. 99 Squadron had to abort because of engine problems.

No. 104 Squadron, also operating with Siddeley Puma-equipped DH9s, suffered the same sort of mechanical problems after their arrival in the Nancy-Ochey area on 20 May 1918. In No. 104's maiden mission, to the Metz–Sablon railway triangle on 8 June, two of the 12 machines had to abort because of malfunctioning engines. A third aircraft, which spun out and lost formation, was unable to bomb. The next day, engine problems forced five of 12 DH9s to abandon a raid on Hagendingen. For the remainder of June, No. 104 flew eight missions for which analysis is possible; on all eight, aircraft dropped out with mechanical difficulties. Of 89 DH9s launched, 17 returned to base with bad engines.

Tactical inexperience also contributed to No. 104 Squadron's difficulties in their first month of service flying. On 24 June, the raid leader aborted with engine trouble and two aircraft mistakenly followed him home. Twelve 104 machines left their aerodrome on 26 June to raid the railway station at Karlsruhe; three returned with engine trouble, and four aircraft failed to rendezvous with the formation before it crossed the lines. Of the five aircraft that proceeded, one went missing and one crashed in Switzerland. Only three of the dozen ships launched managed to bomb their objective.

Returns for July are incomplete, but No. 104 Squadron seems to have established a learning curve; that is, their engine situation improved somewhat. Two six-ship raids bombed without any mechanical aborts on 6 and 7 July. On 1 July, two DH9s with engine trouble dropped out of a 10-ship mission to Metz–Sablon. The next day, on a six-aircraft mission, the raid leader's machine and one other had mechanical problems. The leader's flare signal to the formation was misunderstood, and the remaining four aeroplanes mistakenly dropped their bombs early. Inexperience and mechanical unreliability continued to plague the Independent Force throughout 1918.

On 31 August, No. 110 "Hyderabad" Squadron joined the Independent Force. The only daylight unit to be equipped from the outset with DH9As, all its aeroplanes had been donated by the Nizam of Hyderabad.[12] The 9A's wing area was about 11 percent greater than that of the DH4 and DH9.[13] It had been developed to rectify the flaws of the DH9 and the BHP power plant, replacing the latter with either the 400-horsepower 12-cylinder American Liberty engine or the 375-horsepower Rolls

Royce Eagle VIII. Production of the Liberty proved disappointing; only one-third of the anticipated total delivery reached Britain.[14] Performance with the Rolls Royce power plant at best made the DH9A roughly equivalent to the DH4, the ship the DH9 originally was to supplant.[15]

So far as Trenchard's command in 1918 was concerned, each of his new daylight units had a performance roughly equal to that of No. 55 Squadron, the original day squadron in Newall's 41st Wing, in DH4s—a type first flown at Hendon in August 1916.[16]

Tactics for day bombing never evolved appreciably from the six-ship wedge and "follow the leader" procedures common in late 1917.[17] A standard mission for a single day squadron consisted of 12 planes, arranged in two formations, assembled from the unit's complement of 18 machines. This 67 percent operational commitment reflected the expected wastage and serviceability rates discussed previously. Although payload varied with distance to target, returns indicate that an individual aeroplane carried approximately 250 pounds of bombs on an average long-range sortie in daylight. Thus a typical squadron could deliver approximately 3,000 pounds of bombs on a single mission. By September, the day component of the Independent Force had the capacity to lift 12,000 pounds of bombs under average conditions.

Records of Trenchard's command during summer 1918 only indirectly detail the extent to which aircrew casualties curtailed the daylight bombing campaign. The official history, squadron publications, and postwar memoirs provide additional but incomplete information on casualties to supplement IF wartime returns. However, a comprehensive analysis of the impact of casualty rates upon the long-range bombing campaign has yet to be published.

H. A. Jones' statistics in the official history, claiming to provide the "detail of personnel casualties" between June and November 1918, are incomplete and somewhat misleading.[18] Listing operational squadrons in numerical order, rather than organizational or chronological order, Jones simply enumerated total losses to flying personnel: "K," "W," or "M" in each unit. His totals in each category are 29 killed, 64 wounded, and 235 missing; he did not further elaborate.[19] The official historian fails to provide data on aircrew killed or injured in aircraft accidents and those taken ill or otherwise unavailable for operations.

The Independent Force itself maintained daily casualty returns by squadron and submitted weekly summaries of aircrew casualties.[20] Independent Force Form IF A8 provided returns on casualties among pilots and observers between June 1918 and the Armistice, beginning every Sunday and ending the following Saturday.[21] Reports for this period, the same interval tabulated in the official history, use these detailed loss classifications:

BATTLE CASUALTIES	**OTHER PERSONNEL LOSSES**
1. Killed	6. Sick
2. Wounded	7. Home Establishment for rest
3. Missing	8. Home Establishment for further training
ACCIDENTAL CASUALTIES	9. Home Establishment for training, Pilot
4. Killed	10. Reclassified
5. Injured	11. Return to Unit

The category of "Accidental Casualties" did not include officers who had crossed the lines and then been accidentally killed or injured; such losses were reported as "battle casualties."[22] Data from IF returns (29 killed, 66 wounded, 229 missing) accord fairly well with the totals compiled in the official history (29, 64, and 235). However, H. A. Jones, by omitting eight other casualty categories that depleted aircrew strength, downplayed the magnitude and significance of operational losses.

Night operations were more demanding and dangerous than flights by day. As the wisdom of the time stated, "Flying at night is no different from flying in the daytime, except you can't see."[23] Replacement pilots or observers joining Handley Page night squadrons of the British long-range bombing campaign in 1918 ran approximately twice the risk of becoming accidental casualties as their day colleagues. However, they were four to five times *less* likely to become battle casualties. Sick rates, which tend to vary directly with the intensity of active operations, bear out these general conclusions. Handley Page squadrons, with roughly the same number of aircrew members per squadron as the day units (10 three-man crews versus 18 two-man crews) and outnumbering the day component by five squadrons to four, had less than one-third the number reporting sick between June and November 1918.

These cumulative returns justify further investigation of the losses suffered by the IF's day squadrons. Trenchard noted in his private diary that, "None of the day bombing squadrons are working at present owing to the shortage of pilots and machines."[24] It was his offensive policy, however, that precipitated these shortages between June and November 1918.

Only the original IF squadron, No. 55 in the DH4, was able to continue without prolonged interruptions during the summer and fall of 1918. All of the others (99, 104, and 110) were forced repeatedly to stand down at various times owing to heavy aircrew losses. These four squadrons joined the Independent Force (or its predecessors) between 11 October 1917 and 31 August 1918. Predictably, the less tactical experience a squadron had, the higher its casualty rates in both combat and accident.

No. 55 Squadron had amassed nearly eight months of experience in long-range bombing before the Independent Force was created on 6 June 1918. At full strength, No. 55 would have approximately 36 pilots and observers to man its 18 two-seater planes. During the six-month period from June through November, No. 55 Squadron also lost two aircrewmen killed and four injured in aircraft accidents. The unit's highest sick rate (seven) occurred in August—the month in which the squadron suffered its highest battle losses. Altogether, 20 aircrewmen reported sick in No. 55 Squadron between June and the Armistice.[25] Between July and September, despite aircrew losses totaling 125 percent, No. 55 continued to fly missions. A colleague in No. 100 Squadron noted that No. 55 was greatly in need of escorts.

> 55 had been having a bad spin, losing machines day after day, but they never wavered. . . . They were flying D.H.4's and really needed escorts, for the Hun scouts gave them a bad time.[26]

In those months, a total of 19 replacement DH4s (6 in July, 10 in August, 3 in September) were delivered to the IF so it could continue operations without interruptions.[27]

> The second day unit, No. 99, flying DH9s, joined the British bombing campaign on 3 May 1918. Its first mission, a raid on the Metz–Sablon railway triangle on 21 May, was completed with no losses.[28]

As with No. 55 Squadron, No. 99's sick rates fluctuated with operational losses: Five aircrewmen reported sick in July, four in August, eleven in September, nine in October.[29]

Casualties owing to medical unfitness for high-altitude flying, as well as influenza, plagued No. 99's pilots and observers from the outset.[30] On 23 May, three days after the squadron entered active service, a young lieutenant was pronounced "medically unfit for high flying" after a raid on Metz–Sablon from altitudes between 13,500 and 14,000 feet.[31] On 9 June, two officers returned from a mission to Dillingen at 14,000 feet complaining of "breathing difficulty." Another lieutenant suffered "faintness in the air," while the commander of "B" Flight was medically judged "unfit for high flying" owing to an old lung wound.[32] Later in June, two lieutenants were "lost to Squadron owing to sickness," and one dropped out of a mission, "having fainted in the air."[33] By 3 July, one observer in No. 99 had passed out in the air with appendicitis, and five other aircrewmen had been admitted to hospital with "influenza, which was raging at the time."[34] Losses to illness compounded casualties from enemy action during July.

Aircrew shortages forced No. 99 Squadron to cease operations at the end of July. On 30 July, a US Air Service pilot and his observer, flying with the RAF, died when their DH9 broke up in the air. Another machine landed at Azelot with the pilot shot through the foot and his observer dead in the cockpit.[35] These demoralizing incidents presaged the next day's losses.

On 31 July, 12 DH9s took off from Azelot aerodrome on a mission to bomb Mainz. Three machines aborted with engine trouble shortly after takeoff and the remaining nine ships were attacked by approximately 40 hostile scouts near Saarbrücken. Seeing that it would be impossible to reach Mainz in the face of such odds, the flight leader decided to bomb Saarbrücken. Even with this new objective, four more aeroplanes were shot down prior to bombing.

> On the return journey, three more of the five remaining machines in the formation were put out of action, and it was probably due to the appearance of two formations of 104 Squadron, which had just crossed the lines, that the two surviving D.H.9's of No. 99 . . . were able to regain the aerodrome.[36]

On the last two days of July, No. 99 Squadron lost eight aircrewmen killed, one wounded, and nine missing in action—exactly half its total operational strength.

Comparison of aircrew rosters for "A," "B," and "C" Flights shows that the unit had 42 pilots and observers available for duty on 21 May 1918. Eight weeks later, on 25 July, 20 pilots and observers remained; after the losses on 30 and 31 July, 11 remained of the original group.[37]

> These severe losses made it impossible for the Squadron to muster enough pilots and observers for a raid till reinforcements had been trained up to the necessary standard in formation flying.[38]

No. 99 Squadron did not participate in any active air operations between 1 August and 15 August, confining itself to formation practices. During this time, 27 DH9s were delivered to the Independent Force.[39]

On 15 August, the two daylight units attempted a joint raid against Boulay aerodrome, just 32 miles over the lines. The "C" Flight commander, in a commendable display of leadership on his first operation with his squadron, participated. However, No. 99's tactical fortunes did not improve significantly.

> Fourteen machines left the ground at about 2.30 p.m. Owing to very hot weather, and the inexperience of the new pilots in climbing their machines, only four actually bombed the objective, obtaining a number of hits on the edge of the aerodrome, but clear of the hangars.[40]

Bombing altitude that day was 11,000 feet, well below the theoretical service ceiling for the DH9.[41] Pattinson's narrative underscores the organizational difficulties caused by mediocre planes flown by replacements, even to an objective just 44 miles from No. 99's aerodrome.

Throughout the remainder of August, No. 99 launched only six missions, including two single-ship sorties above the cloud blanket to raid the blast furnaces near Dillingen. Major Pattinson and his observer had to abort their first sortie when they "found the weather unsuitable over the lines." On their second attempt, they dropped two 112-pound bombs fitted with 15-second delay fuses on Dillingen.

One . . . was reported by the observer as having burst on a blast furnace, and caused a very large flash of flame, and the other having hit the railway line which runs round outside the factory.[42]

The D.H.9 used for this raid was fitted with a standard 5/17 Creagh-Osborne compass, and no turn indicator was used.

This was the only single machine daylight raid carried out on Germany by a unit of the Independent Force, and also the only daylight raid successfully accomplished by navigation without any sight of landmarks on the route. A telegram of congratulations was received by Major Pattinson from General Trenchard.[43]

This feat of airmanship, carried out by a squadron commander who had first flown with his unit less than a week before, attests to Pattinson's character and leadership. At a time when his men were in low spirits, his example must have perceptibly boosted aircrew morale and confidence.

The German bomb-plot diagram of Dillingen confirms that two bombs fell into the city between 1540 and 1545 on 20 August. One bomb detonated well north of the furnace complex; the other failed to explode.[44]

Despite the relatively slow pace of active operations, losses continued through August and into September. On 13 and 15 September, four of No. 99's original aircrewmen were admitted to hospital and "finally transferred to the Home Establishment."[45]

All had been unwell for several weeks, but had continued their flying duties, and avoided the Medical Officer, till the younger pilots and observers had been trained to take their places.[46]

Toward the end of September, No. 99 Squadron also experienced several changes in its chain of command. Major Pattinson moved out to take over command of 41st Wing when Lt Col J. E. A. Baldwin was transferred to Home Establishment.[47] Capt P. E. Welchman then became commander of No. 99. On

26 September, Welchman, emulating Pattinson's habit of leading from the front, was shot down and captured.[48] Capt W. D. Thorn became the third commanding officer (CO) of No. 99 Squadron in less than a week.

The mission on which Captain Welchman was lost marked the beginning of a second stand-down period for No. 99 Squadron. That day, three of ten aircraft aborted almost immediately—two with engine problems and one because he "could not get into position."[49]

> Capt. Welchman perceived that it would be quite impossible to reach Thionville, and gave the signal for bombs to be dropped in Metz-Sablon. (Both objectives lay almost due north of Azelot, No. 99's airfield. Metz-Sablon is approximately 40 miles distant, Thionville 19 miles further north.)

> Of the seven D.H.9's which crossed the Lines, only one, piloted by Lieut. West, actually returned to Azelot, carrying the body of the observer, Lieut. Howard, who had been killed by a machine–gun bullet.[50]

On the next day, the sole survivor of this operation, Lieutenant West, received a "transfer to the Home Establishment for a change of duty."[51] No. 99 did not bomb again until 9 October, when eleven DH9s raided Metz–Sablon. No planes were lost, though one machine aborted the mission with engine problems.

That the Independent Force enjoyed a priority in logistic support is apparent from the replacement rates and aircraft types which Trenchard's command received. The IF received 14 replacement DH9s and 55 DH9As between 16 August and the end of October, the interval of highest wastage in the day squadrons.[52] During September, the Independent Force received just nine of the generally unsatisfactory—and unwanted—DH9 machines while Salmond's units found themselves with 87 of them.[53] The IF also gained 38 of the newer DH9As that month as the rest of the Royal Air Force received a total of 20.[54]

Trenchard's organization, which fielded approximately 10 percent of the total British air strength in the field, received nearly twice as many of the new DeHavilland planes as the rest of the air arm. Put another way, the IF received more than four DH9As for every DH9 they received as replacements in

199

September while Salmond's RAF had a reverse ratio—more than four DH9s for every DH9A.

October data confirm a priority of support to the Independent Force. That month, the IF received 17 DH9As and only one DH9 while Salmond's forces gained 28 DH9As and 66 DH9s.[55] Subject only to the vagaries of aircraft production, Trenchard's command unquestionably had first call on replacement machines in the last six months of the war.

Considering losses across all seven categories detailed on the IF A8 returns, No. 99 Squadron suffered 114 aircrew casualties in fewer than six months of combat flying. These losses amounted to 317 percent of the unit's normal operational complement—despite two stand-downs to gain and train replacements. In this grim regard, however, No. 99 fared somewhat better than No. 104 Squadron, which arrived in the IF sector on 20 May 1918 and flew its first mission on 8 June. No. 104 suffered 134 aircrew casualties in five months.

A total of 33 aircrewmen reported sick in No. 104, with 20 reporting ill between July and September. Ten reported sick in August, the month with the most severe battle casualties.[56] No. 104 Squadron was forced to stand-down three times because of losses, the first coming within a month of the unit's entering active service. Between 8 and 31 July, the squadron participated in no raids; over half its members had been lost in the previous four weeks.[57]

No. 104 flew five missions in the first half of August, losing machines to enemy action (seven) or to crashes (one) on every operation. On a mission to Mannheim on 22 August, seven of 12 DH9s were shot down, forcing No. 104 to stand-down for the second time. The squadron flew again on 3 September, when 12 planes took off in a joint mission with 11 aircraft from No. 99 Squadron. They bombed Morhange aerodrome and returned safely.

No. 104 was grounded for the third time in late September. On 7 September, 12 machines took off in a second attempt to reach Mannheim; three were shot down and two aborted with engine trouble. Between 12 and 15 September, in daily missions to the vicinity of Metz–Sablon, No. 104 suffered losses, weather diversions, or aborts on each one. Altogether, five

DH9s went missing and 10 were forced to return with engine trouble in this four-day period. Between 15 September and 15 October, the unit lost one machine in just two missions it managed to fly over the lines.

Details other than those available in official returns for No. 104's operations are scarce; the squadron produced no unit history or volumes of postwar memoirs. From the similarities between their casualty statistics and those of the other day squadrons in the Independent Force, one can assume that No. 104's operational fortunes were similar to those of her sister units.

No. 110 (Hyderabad) Squadron, the last day squadron to augment the IF, flew its first mission on 14 September 1918. This DH9A unit, whose aircraft were the gift of His Serene Highness the Nizam of Hyderabad, participated in active air operations for less than two months. During this brief period, the squadron was forced to stand-down twice because of air-crew losses.

The Hyderabad experienced 21 sick calls for this period; again, the month of highest battle casualties (October) also had the highest number of sick calls.[58] Altitude affected both aircrew and machine.

> Due to the fairly high altitude (between fifteen and seventeen thousand feet) at which the D.H.9's bombed, frostbite caused more casualties than the enemy and the low temperatures resulted in the wind-driven petrol pump to freeze up. As these were mounted on the lower wing, observers had to engage in some dangerous acrobatics to free them and get fuel [to] the engine again before an involuntary descent in enemy territory took place.[59]

No. 110 Squadron flew only nine missions with the British strategic bombing force before the end of hostilities. Four of these raids, directed against short-range aerodrome targets, resulted in no casualties. On the other five missions, intended to hit Mannheim, Frankfurt, and Cologne, the Hyderabad Squadron lost 17 machines to enemy action. Also, five DH9s aborted due to mechanical difficulties and four abandoned their missions because of adverse weather.[60] Even with a fairly reliable aircraft, the squadron proved unable to reach strategic objectives consistently without suffering unacceptable losses.

Two consecutive attempts by No. 110 (on 1 and 5 October) to bomb Cologne were stymied by bad weather; in the latter operation, the squadron lost four DH9As after they diverted to strike targets of opportunity at Kaiserslautern and Pirmasens. The unit did not fly again until 21 October, when 13 machines took off to raid Frankfurt. On that unfortunate mission, one machine aborted with engine trouble and seven failed to return. No. 110 squadron took part in only two more raids (short runs to Morhange aerodrome in the first week of November) before the Armistice. The history of this DH9A unit raises serious questions about the wisdom of the daylight bombing campaign against the Rhine cities.

No. 110 Squadron joined the Independent Force in late August 1918, a time when the bombing capacity of the command had approximately tripled, due largely to the arrival of three Handley Page night squadrons that month. Since June, as discussed earlier, Trenchard had been preoccupied with the moral effect supposedly gained by hitting "special long distance" objectives, such as the "large gun shops" (i.e., Krupp) located at "Essen and Ruhr Valley Groups."[61] Essen itself lay nearly 40 miles beyond the city of Cologne, which was 150 miles north of No. 110's home aerodrome at Bettoncourt. A pilot with No. 110 Squadron recalled a summer evening when Major Nicholl, the commander, outlined what the IF chain of command expected.

> Major Nicholl began to talk—to talk of Cologne.
>
> Cologne was a long way off; beyond what we had assumed to be the range of our machines. So we made our calculation, each of us; and we felt reassured—if we were very careful.
>
> We encouraged Nicholl to go on talking. He told us his great secret; we were to bomb the Krupp factory at Essen.
>
> This was going too far! We could not see how we were going to get there and back on the petrol we carried. So there was some anxious speculation, and we felt the edge of our knees wear a little thin.[62]

This bombing policy was reaffirmed a few days later, when General Trenchard visited Bettoncourt aerodrome.

> Soon we were to have a visit from H.Q., and who should come to inspect us but Boom himself. We stood smartly to attention while the

"Voice" told us that we would be bombing Essen. "Of course some of you may not get back," he said.

This did not go down well; back came our fears; we all felt that to go to Essen meant we should not have the petrol to return.

This was our only visit from H.Q., and we went back to our happy, carefree life at once.[63]

No. 110 Squadron did not penetrate as far as Cologne, let alone Essen and the Ruhr, and the squadron's casualty rates demonstrated that sustained attacks by daylight on "special long range" objectives would be an expensive proposition for the Independent Force. Cipher wires from the GOC IF to the Air Ministry requesting replacements attest to the impact of casualties and wastage.

I.F.G. 116, 22 July 1918: In continuation of my I.F.G. 115 July 22nd. Weather perfect. More work would have been done but for following. One squadron B.H.P. D.H.9 and one squadron Rolls Royce D.H.4 on half work owing to shortage of machines. One squadron B.H.P. D.H.9 still out of action owing to shortage of machines.

I.F.G. 136, 31 July 1918: Regret to inform you that No. 99 Squadron (B.H.P. D.H.9) . . . lost seven machines. Only two returned. . . . Utmost importance to make this Squadron up to strength. Can special effort be made.

I.F.G. 180, 12 August 1918: . . . The fighting has been very heavy the last two days. The objective of the Squadron which bombed HAGENAU this morning was MANNHEIM; but owing to heavy fighting they were unable to get there.

I.F.G. 198, 16 August 1918: Regret to report have had to suspend operations by 104 Squadron owing to shortage of pilots.[64]

These confidential messages underscore the continuous disruption the Independent Force experienced whenever it attempted to raid targets in Germany.

Daylight losses were so serious that the GOC IF wrote to General Sykes on the matter in early August 1918.[65] The ubiquitous Major Lord Tiverton, a staff officer in FO3, analyzed the issue and proposed two solutions:

(1) The employment of escorting fighting machines.
(2) The adoption of large formations.[66]

In Tiverton's view, massed attacks appeared more desirable because the German counter to such large raids would in time require that "a constant supply of these enemy machines must flow into the area."[67] These German reinforcements would not then be available for use elsewhere. But the reverse was also true; that is, the first proposal (to supply escort planes for IF day attacks) would mean that British "machines and personnel must be diverted from other and possibly more useful work."[68] On long-range escort missions it would be "necessary to alter or redesign the fighters allocated, with possible interference with production or loss of efficiency."[69] Trenchard, however, never marshaled the forces necessary to mount formations on such a scale.

Some have argued that IF day attacks, despite their losses, did in fact force the Germans to divert valuable fighter strength from frontline duties to home defense. The validity of this claim, however, rests on the questionable accuracy of wartime intelligence estimates of German scout units that opposed IF operations.

In an earlier discussion, No. 3 Naval Wing's activities were cited as an example of how bombing results had to be measured indirectly. Results were gauged from efforts; that is, total sorties flown and bombs hauled supposedly provided a reliable index of the damage inflicted. Much the same phenomenon occurred in 1918, with respect to the somewhat grimmer parameters of aircrew casualties and enemy countermeasures. Mounting British losses were attributed to increased diversion of German aviation assets from the front to home defense.

Trenchard himself was convinced that such was the case. In his diary, he asserted that "British attacks forced the redistribution of a disproportionate part of German air strength to home defence duties."[70] Likewise, the official history concluded that one of the major effects of bombing was that it caused diversion of German assets.

> The bombing caused] a diversion of fighting squadrons, anti-aircraft guns and searchlights, and of a great amount of material and labor, to active and passive schemes of defense.[71]

This cause-and-effect assumption has never been seriously questioned. Neville Jones, writing in 1973, repeats the claim.[72] Historians have tended to accept the notion that casualties in the IF were due primarily to a comprehensive German air defense system and that maintenance of the system diverted scarce resources from the front.

In fact, however, German response to IF operations did not require the massive reallocation of valuable assets that wartime estimates assumed and historians accepted. M. J. D. Cooper, who has investigated this issue in considerable depth using German documents, concludes that the German buildup of air defenses received neither the priority nor the materials that British sources have postulated.

> In fact, the "330 first-class fighting aircraft" he [Neville Jones] and his predecessors have ranged against the 120 bombers of Trenchard's squadrons were originally the product of inflated R.A.F. intelligence summaries in 1918. These estimates placed the total number of home defence fighter units at 16, and vested each with a strength of 15 aircraft. German sources show that there were only 9 Kampfeinsitzerstaffelen in existence throughout the entire period (2 of them split into 2 independent sub-flights) with an average strength one quarter to one third under the British estimates. Until the last few months of the war, these units had to make do with an assortment of aging aircraft discarded by front-line fighter units. Only in September and October did the overstrained German aviation industry begin to meet the low-priority demand for modern home defence equipment. Finally, it must be pointed out that any large transfer of front-line fighter units southwards was undertaken primarily to meet the build-up of American air strength on the Western Front.[73]

Other studies confirm that German home defense needs never received particularly high priority at any time during hostilities. Consider, for example, this excerpt from a German authority's summarization of the relative importance of home defense versus frontline allocations.

> The number of "Kest" (Kampfeinsitzerstaffel) single seater fighter squadrons employed in home air defence could unfortunately be increased no further. Some of the squadrons in fact had to be sent to the front.[74]

While it is true that the German air arm, the *Kogenluft* (Kommandierenden General der Luftstreitkrafte), was reorganized during the war to include a unified command (Heimatluftschutz) dedicated to the aerial defense of the homeland, this adjustment occurred in October 1916, well before British long-range bombing efforts had coalesced.[75] When the German general staff determined their total military aviation requirements

for the 1918 offensives, home defense needs were not a significant consideration; in fact they were scarcely mentioned.[76]
Apparently most of the increased German emphasis resulted
from America's imminent entry into the fray. On 25 June
1917, Ludendorff reviewed the *Kogenluft's* proposals for aerial
expansion and forwarded them to the Prussian War Ministry.

> America's entry into the war compels a considerable strengthening of
> the air force by 1 March 1918. In order to be somewhat equal to the
> combined English-French-American air fleet, I order the formation of
> an absolute minimum of forty new fighter groups and seventeen new
> flight units.[77]

The prospect of bombardment by the RAF never constituted
much impetus for strengthening the aviation component of
Germany's *Amerika* program. Neither attrition nor the necessity for redeployment to counter the British strategic air threat
underlay German wartime aerial reorganization.

Aircrew inexperience, unreliable aircraft, and adverse
weather combined with enemy countermeasures to frustrate
the British long-range daylight bombing effort. These limiting
considerations of late 1918 correlate very closely with factors
that Noble Frankland and Sir Charles Webster identified as
constraints upon Bomber Command in the Second World War.

> Thus, the principal operational elements in the strategic air offensive
> are: first, the calibre of the crews, which is a question of selection,
> training, experience, leadership, and fighting spirit; secondly,
> performance of the aircraft and of the equipment and bases upon
> which they depend; thirdly, the weather, fourthly, the tactical methods
> adopted and fifthly, the nature of the enemy opposition.[78]

Analysis of Independent Force records would have led observers to the same conclusion 20 years earlier.

The impact of losses and wastage upon the activities of
Trenchard's command has not been previously studied in
much depth. For the most part, H. A. Jones' judgments in the
official history have been accepted as authoritative: "Of all
aeroplanes which set out, 3.9 percent never returned to their
aerodromes."[79] (This assertion is quite at odds with the record.) Webster and Frankland at one point consider that
losses in the daylight squadrons "were on the whole surprisingly small," citing them as only "3.9 per cent of the number
despatched."[80] These and other verdicts on IF operations in

the sixth volume of the official history, even with its 19-year hindsight, are too uncritical to be reliable. The official version ascribes to the bombing campaign a systematic, methodical guidance and strategic vision which did not in fact exist.

In the light of our later knowledge it would be difficult to suggest how the few independent bombing squadrons might have been more effectively employed.

After weighing all the contemporary factors Major-General Trenchard had to be sure that what he asked of his pilots and observers was something they could do and keep going. His aim was to avoid spectacular attacks with the danger or uncertainty that periods of inactivity during recovery would follow. . . . In this he was surely right, and his policy, judged by results was well suited to his belief.[81]

Careful analysis of the available documentation leads one to conclude exactly the opposite; that is, losses to the DH4 and DH9/9A squadrons of Trenchard's command demonstrated that sustained long-range day bombardment was manifestly an unrealizable goal.

The day component of the IF lost 257 aircrewmen in battle casualties alone between June and November 1918, 178 percent of total assigned strength at the Armistice. Total losses to these squadrons amounted to 407 flyers, the equivalent of nearly 12 full squadrons.[82]

Jones himself puts the total "wastage in missing aeroplanes" for daylight units between June and November 1918 at 89 machines: 18 DH4s, 54 DH9s, and 17 DH9As. He also tabulates 173 machines as wrecked: 51 DH4s, 94 DH9s, and 28 DH9As.[83] Considering that the day arm of the Independent Force accumulated approximately 21 squadron-months of operations during its existence, the average squadron wastage in machines amounted to 12.5 planes per month (262 machines/21 squadron-months of operation). At 18 planes per squadron at full complement, monthly wastage then averaged just under 70 percent. This loss rate eclipsed that of many hard-pressed scout squadrons on the Western Front.[84] The IF's daylight bombing campaign definitely cost dearly, in blood and in treasure.

Day bombing increased four-fold during 1918; yet the day effort diminished in comparison with night bombing. By September 1918, the Independent Force's night units had the potential to deliver 48,000 pounds of bombs in a single night.

The giant Handley Pages made the difference. Of the 10 assigned to each squadron, six were usually committed. With an average payload of 1,600 pounds, the six machines could lift a total of 9,600 pounds of bombs. By the end of August, with the upgrading of No. 100 Squadron, the night flyers could deliver four times the bombs their daylight colleagues could deliver.

During the first half of 1918, the single Handley Page squadron in the Nancy–Ochey sector, known first as "A" Naval, then No. 16, and finally as No. 216 Squadron, interpreted its offensive mission conservatively, not flying at all if conditions seemed doubtful.

> We used to bomb targets on the Rhine—but only on very fine nights as the Naval Air Wing only chose very fine cloudless nights for their raids.[85]

This outlook, which reflected No. 216's RNAS origins, conflicted with the RFC/RAF habit of flying whenever possible, taking risks, expecting losses, and hoping for the best. The Handley Page unit, the only night flying squadron capable of hauling substantial payloads on long-duration missions, sought to minimize tactical uncertainty.

No. 216's idiosyncratic attitude did not endear the squadron to the IF chain of command. Trenchard himself admonished Maj W. R. Read, who was preparing to take over No. 216 Squadron.

> "Well," he [Trenchard] said, "I have got you out here to take over 216 Squadron from Buss. They have got Naval ideas. They think they cannot fly at night if there is a cloud in the sky and they think they cannot do more than one raid in a night. You have got to get them out of those ideas."[86]

A week after taking over 216 Squadron, Read confided his philosophy to his diary:

> I think the question of moral[e] in a squadron is very important and if a squadron does a great deal of work without losing many machines it is doing as good work as a Sqdn. which is doing slightly better work but at a high cost of machines and personnel and consequently moral[e].

So my motto will be "be cautious without being faint hearted." And that put into practice will be a line of action which runs between R.A.F. and R.N.A.S. methods.[87]

Through July, the operational record of the Handley Page squadron during its tenure with Eighth Brigade and the Independent Force reflects this conservative perspective. Between 1 February and 30 June, No. 216 Squadron flew on 20 nights, compared to 31 occasions when their colleagues in No. 100 Squadron, flying shorter-ranged FEs, launched missions. During this five-month period, No. 216 received only three new Handley Pages—to replace one wrecked and two missing machines. No. 100 Squadron needed a total of 29 replacement FEs to replace six missing and 23 wrecked planes in the same interval.[88]

During July, when Trenchard's influence had begun to permeate the Independent Force, night flying began to increase, first in No. 216 and later in the three Handley Page squadrons that arrived in August. In July, No. 216 matched No. 100 Squadron, each unit flying on 12 nights. No. 216 lagged by just one night in August.

No. 97, a Handley Page unit that joined the IF in early August, managed to fly six missions from 19/20 August to the end of the month. A second new squadron, No. 215, which first flew with the IF on 22/23 August, launched four operations before month's end. Significantly, No. 216 was the only night squadron that did not participate in operations on the night of 22/23 August—a situation that seems to have been the motive for Trenchard's admonition to Read.[89] By the end of August, new Handley Pages had been sent to replace lost and wrecked machines.[90] Fourteen aircrewmen had been killed or wounded, or were missing, in night operations during the month; No. 216 had suffered no battle casualties.[91]

IF night squadrons sustained losses, but never at the rate that their day colleagues suffered. None of the Handley Page units was ever forced to stand down because of unacceptable losses. Table 1 gives the June–November battle casualties for the night squadrons.

Table 1
Battle Casualties, Night Squadrons, June–November 1918

A. No. 100 Squadron Battle Casualties

Month	KIA	WIA	MIA	Total	Percentage of Unit Strength
June	0	1	0	1	3.3%
July	0	0	0	0	0
August	0	0	0	0	0
September	0	0	2	2	6.7%
October	1	2	0	3	10.0%
November	0	0	0	0	0
Totals	1	3	2	6	20.0%

B. No. 216 Squadron Battle Casualties

Month	KIA	WIA	MIA	Total	Percentage of Unit Strength
June	0	0	0	0	0
July	0	0	3	3	10.0%
August	0	0	0	0	0
September	0	3	3	6	20.0%
October	0	0	0	0	0
November	0	0	0	0	0
Totals	0	3	6	9	30.0%

C. No. 97 Squadron Battle Casualties

Month	KIA	WIA	MIA	Total	Percentage of Unit Strength
August	1	0	9	10	33.3%
September	1	1	0	2	6.7%
October	0	0	0	0	0
November	0	0	0	0	0
Totals	2	1	9	12	40.0%

D. No. 215 Squadron Battle Casualties

Month	KIA	WIA	MIA	Total	Percentage of Unit Strength
August	0	1	3	4	13.3%
September	2	1	25	28	93.3%
October	0	1	3	4	13.3%
November	0	0	0	0	0
Totals	2	3	31	36	120.0%

E. No. 115 Squadron Battle Casualties

Month	KIA	WIA	MIA	Total	Percentage of Unit Strength
September	0	1	3	4	13.3%
October	0	0	0	00	0
November	0	0	0	0	0
Totals	0	1	3	4	13.3%

The operational strength of Independent Force more than tripled during August—a significant accomplishment. After the frustrations engendered by overly optimistic expansion schemes and aerodrome construction throughout the winter and spring, the arrival of these squadrons must have been most heartening. They appeared to be the harbinger of the long-anticipated massive bombing fleets. IF's operational capability ballooned from 21,600 pounds to 60,000 pounds in less than four weeks, and the temptation to quickly employ this armada proved to be irresistible. September's casualty rates illustrate the consequences of such precipitate action. (No. 215 Squadron, the hardest hit, lost 93.3 percent of its assigned strength that month.)

A detailed examination of night bombardment during September, the period in which the Independent Force realized its peak strength, shows not only the peculiar hazards of night operations but also their impact upon organizational policies and expectations. An increased force structure per se would not automatically translate into increased results, as IF planners learned from costly hindsight.

As September began, the long-range bomber force appeared to lack only a suitable opportunity. However, immediate employment of this newly enlarged force was delayed by two factors: (1) the requirement to support Allied offensives and (2) poor flying weather.

Being attached to ground commands was not a unique experience for the British long-range squadrons. From 1 April to 9 May 1918, No. 100 and No. 216, the night-flying units of Newall's Eighth Brigade, had deployed to the Villeseneux aerodrome (near Rheims). To help forestall any German offensive, the two squadrons had raided railway targets in the vicinity of Juniville, Amagne–Lucquy, and Asfeld, when weather permitted.[92] No. 55 Squadron, Newell's day unit, also supported the French ground plan by attacking railway targets in the area bordered by Metz–Sablon, Luxembourg, and Thionville.

In early September, the British bombing force was once again diverted to an army cooperation role. Trenchard's bombers supported the American offensive in the St. Mihiel Salient with aerodrome and rail attacks, mainly directed against the

Metz–Sablon railway triangle, between 12 and 17 September.[93] As with earlier efforts by Eighth Brigade, unfavorable weather limited the range and frequency of sorties. Later (23 to 26/27 September), IF raids would support the French and American offensive between Rheims and Verdun.

Weather likewise delayed significant long-range bombing efforts through the second week of September. The Independent Force preferred to raid by night during the week-long periods of full moons. September's moon would wax on 16/17 September, with 50 percent of full-moon brightness, and end on the evening of 23/24 September.[94] However, the RAF Summary of Air Intelligence lists no sorties between 8 and 11 September, owing to "unfavourable weather conditions." IF reports confirm the stand-down.[95] No. 216's commanding officer, Maj W. R. Read, details this spell of poor weather and provides insight into the mounting frustrations of his Handley Page crews.

> Sunday, 8 Sept. 1918: We are raiding Essen during the next moon. . . . I would like to be the first to get there, but Holley (a Flight Commander in No.216) has fixed his heart on getting there first and he jolly well deserves it. So I shall go later on.

> Tuesday, 10 Sept. 1918: General Trenchard is going to let Holley be the first one to get to Essen. Weather impossible. We have had rain high wind and low clouds all day.

> Wednesday, 11 Sept. 1918: A very bad day of strong wind and rain. No work was possible tonight.

> Thursday, 12 Sept. 1918: It rained a good deal of the time. Gen. Trenchard was very keen for a show to come off tonight if possible to help in the attack.[96]

In an attempted raid that Thursday evening, Read noted that "although wind was 10 to 15 m.p.h. on the ground," it reached "50 m.p.h. up aloft. It was also very gusty near the ground." Of 14 Handley Pages launched that evening, four could not locate any targets and two aborted—with engine trouble and an "observer coming over queer in the air."[97] Owing to adverse weather and one instance of engine trouble, none of the seven machines dispatched by No. 216 on 13/14 September managed to bomb assigned targets.[98]

The other night squadrons had similar luck. No. 215 Squadron lost two Handley Pages and had four machines abort with engine trouble on the 13th. On the 14th, Read noted that Holley had been confined to bed.

> Holley has influenza. He was sent to bed yesterday morning. He is feeling no better this morning. Jolly bad luck if he is feeling not fit for the Essen raid as Gen. Trenchard has promised that he shall be the first to get there.[99]

After a "very fine night's work" on the night of 15/16 September (four of No. 216's Handley Pages reached Karlsruhe and one flew two sorties against Morhange aerodrome and Metz-Sablon), the September moon period commenced. All five night squadrons prepared to take full advantage of the impending week of illumination.

W. R. Read's comments about Essen, reinforced by daylight squadron comments, leave little doubt that the impetus to launch maximum-strength attacks deep into Germany originated with Independent Force. Indeed, IF activities seem to have generated interest at all levels of the civil and military command. Trenchard's bombing force continued to receive its accustomed priority of support. On 6 August 1918, the War Office notified Field Marshal Haig, by "urgent and secret" letter, to transfer control of a Handley Page squadron to the Independent Force.

> With reference to War Office letter of the above number (O.B./1826) dated June 17th, 1918, I am commanded by the Army Council to say that the Air Ministry have now asked that No. 215 Squadron, Royal Air Force, which was temporarily placed at your disposal shall now be sent to the formation to which it was originally allotted, i.e. the Independent Force.
>
> In view of the value of the operations of this letter, in withdrawing enemy aircraft from the front as evidenced by the concentration of 40 machines against one of our raiding parties on July 31st (i.e., the mission in which No. 99 Squadron lost 7 of 12 machines to enemy action), I am to say that the Council propose to accede to this request, unless you have any strong objection to urge.[100]

No. 215 Squadron reached the IF base area on 19 August 1918.[101] Significantly, the unchallenged assumption that heavy friendly losses indicated a strongly reinforced German home defense system provided the rationale for this War Office directive. Rather than analyze Trenchard's casualty rates, authorities in London accepted his assertions that his forces could influence the overall course of the war.

That this misperception was not confined to the War Office emerges from a Foreign Office communication dated 10 September 1918, a time when IF aircraft were grounded by continued poor weather.

> The Under Secretary of State for Foreign Affairs presents his compliments to the Secretary of the Air Ministry and is directed by Mr. Secretary Balfour to state, for the information of the Air Council, that His Majesty's Minister at the Hague has reported that according to various sources the despondency in Germany is at the present moment intense: and that this would be greatly increased by air raids on German towns and that the moment would appear to demand the exercise of this method of warfare to its utmost extent.[102]

Copies of this communication were forwarded to Salmond and to Trenchard on 13 September 1918.[103]

Little doubt exists that Trenchard and the IF staff encouraged such widespread governmental and public faith in the efficacy of strategic bombing. In addition to news releases and official reports of No. 3 Naval Wing, 41st Wing, and Eighth Brigade, HQ IF devoted considerable attention and manpower to extolling its own activities. For example, HQ IF developed direct telephonic and telegraphic contacts with London. And in early July 1918, a lieutenant colonel in charge of "A.D. Signals, I.F., R.A.F." planned several enhancements to the patchwork system.[104] Initially, all IF signal circuits passed through a communications center at Chaumont. From there, telephone conversations were transmitted to London via American and British switchboards in Paris; telegraph messages were also routed to London through use of American facilities. Eventually, all telegrams passed directly from HQ IF to London. Telephone lines reserved for IF-London traffic were also established, with relay amplifiers sited at Paris, Haig's GHQ, and Calais. By late summer 1918, HQ IF enjoyed a communications system capability nearly equal to that of Haig's own headquarters.

Trenchard had an Army Printing and Stationery Service (APSS) unit assigned to his headquarters within three weeks of assuming control of the Independent Force.[105] This APSS organization comprised two officers, two noncommissioned officers, and 22 other ranks. In August 1918, an army major was assigned to this unit as deputy assistant director.[106]

Trenchard's initiatives to publicize his command succeeded. His dispatches and communiqués were well received in London, and were given widespread circulation. On 8 August 1918, the question of "action as to dispatches recording operations of the Independent Force, R.A.F. in France," was discussed at an Air Council session.

> The Secretary of State explained that despatches of this nature were a novel feature in the R.A.F. and that he desired to take the views of the Council as to how they should be handled in future, what the extent of the circulation should be, and how far they could be made public.
>
> It was decided that the reports should be circulated
> (i) to all members of the Air Council.
> (ii) to the Secretary of the War Cabinet.
> (iii) that circulation to Marshal Foch and other French generals should stand over till the forthcoming meeting of the Supreme War Council at Versailles, and
> (iv) that C.A.S. [i.e., Chief of the Air Staff] should revise the reports so that they could be published as a monthly communiqué without conveying any undesirable information to the enemy.[107]

On the day following this meeting, Lt Col J. A. H. Gammell, head of FO3, wrote to Lt Col E. B. Gordon, on Trenchard's staff at Autigny–la-Tour, with a proposed scheme of distribution for IF dispatches. In addition to the addresses suggested by the Air Council, Gammell included the King and the War Cabinet.

> We are out to binge the Independent Force for all we are worth, the opposition both inside and outside the building is considerable. I think a wide distribution of the despatches will help.[108]

Trenchard carefully monitored the extent to which IF operations remained in the public eye. In late August 1918, he requested notification if his "press communiqués" were not received.

> I should be glad if you would make arrangements that, in the event of the Press Communiqué not being received, a telegram is sent to me.
>
> Press Communiqué telegram No. I.F.G.220 of the 21st inst. reporting raid by one machine on DILLINGEN [Pattinson's above-cloud sortie] and night raids on three aerodromes did not appear to have been published in the "Times" of either the 22nd or 23rd.[109]

The strength of Trenchard's Independent Force grew significantly in the wake of his publicity campaign, and pressure for long-range attacks into Germany increased. Consequently, Trenchard directed his night squadrons to make the most of the September moon period. The flying activities of 16/17 September, and their aftermath, should be highlighted against this background.

For the period 6–12 September, Order No. 21 directed "Handley Pages to go to B.A.S.F. LUDWIGSHAVEN, MANNHEIM, and MAINZ," with Kaiserslautern designated as the alternate target for "the long-distance bombers."[110] The same order further stipulated that "the orders for long-distance bombing will also hold good until further notice." Weather, however, prevented implementation of this directive. IF operation orders for 12–14 September assigned close-in railway and aerodrome targets, but cautioned subordinate squadrons:

> These orders will not interfere with the special mission to SPEYERDORF. Pilots earmarked for this mission, and for the long-distance raid to ESSEN will be reserved as far as possible. (Order No. 23, 12 Sept. 1918)

> The above order will not interfere with the Special Mission to SPEYERDORF. Pilots earmarked for this, and for the long-distance raids to ESSEN, will be reserved as far as possible. (Order No. 24, 13 September 1918)[111]

HQ IF wished to have machines and aircrews available for special projects if conditions should improve. At Speyerdorf, specially equipped Handley Pages were to land on the enemy aerodrome, destroy German aircraft and field facilities with machine-gun fire, and then quickly depart. The operation order for 14 September directed that "the machines of No. 215 Squadron detailed for the SPEYERDORF operation will carry out their special reconnaissance."[112] These official extracts leave little doubt that missions to Speyerdorf and Essen would be carried out during the forthcoming moon.

Earlier in September, No. 216 Squadron's Handley Pages had had "additional petrol tanks to increase range" installed.[113]

> The increase of this latter meant that Essen could be attacked. Essen was always looked upon as the blue ribbon of bombing objectives.

Time and again there was a "Stand by" for Essen and as often the operation had to be cancelled owing to the treachery of the elements. The machines even started, and in one case a machine reached Treves on its journey.[114]

The squadron history also noted that reaching Essen was the object of "much secret competition" among the Handley Page crews.

When weather began to improve on 15 September, two day squadrons were directed to launch long-distance raids to the Rhine valley and beyond. No. 110 Squadron was to hit Mannheim; No. 55, Frankfurt.[115] However, No. 110 managed to penetrate only to Buhl while No. 55 bombed Stuttgart, well south of Frankfurt. Compared to the past week's conditions, the clearing weather presaged an intensive night-bombing effort.

Unfortunately, operation order files no longer contain HQ IF's assigned targets for night raids on 16/17 September, the first night scheduled to have 50 percent of full moon illumination. Order No. 31 for 16/17 September is missing, though 30 and 32 have survived.[116]

Approximate Results No. 84, covering 0400 16 September to 0400 17 September, prepared by Capt R. B. Bivar, the SO3 of the operations section of HQ IF Air Staff Branch, stated that four of the five night squadrons flew that night.[117] Nos. 97, 100, 115, and 216 Squadrons were listed; No. 215 Squadron was not mentioned. The Approximate Results provided this ancillary information:

1. WEATHER.
   Day—Weather fine, strong wind with certain amount of haze.
   Night—Visibility fair at first, but thick haze rising later, making visibility difficult.
2. MACHINES MISSING.
   Ten of our machines are missing.[118]

The loss of 10 Handley Pages, the equivalent of an entire squadron, received no further explication in this report; it is likely that no definite information was available at the time. Furthermore, this report marked the only time when that number of aircraft losses from this operation was ever admitted on an official IF return.

The intelligence summary transmitted to the Air Ministry on 19 September did not include loss data.[119] Concerning the weather on 16/17 September, the summary noted that visibility was "fairly good."

> Sky clear till about 4 a.m. Visibility fairly good. Strong westerly wind came up during the night.[120]

This unforeseen wind was to assume considerable significance in post-raid analyses and correspondence between HQ IF and London.

The weekly report from HQ IF, "Independent Force Communiqué No. 7," completed 21 September for 12–18 September 1918, amplified the night's events, somewhat altering meteorological conditions in the process.

> Night. 16/17th. - During the early part of the night it was very calm and clear, but high winds got up very quickly in the night.
>
> Machines of No. 97 Squadron bombed Lorquin and Frescaty.
>
> Machines of No. 115 Squadron bombed Metz–Sablon, dropping three and three–quarters tons of bombs on the railways.
>
> One machine of No. 100 Squadron made two trips to Frescaty Aerodrome.
>
> Machines of No. 216 Squadron bombed Frescaty and Boulay Aerodromes, and the railways at Mets, Merzig, and Treves.[121]

Neither the daily report nor this weekly return indicated that No. 215 Squadron had flown that night. Further, this weekly communiqué did not mention losses from night bombing on 16/17 September, though it noted that "two of our machines are missing" from the daylight mission on the 17th.[122] Much of this reticence concerning nighttime casualties undoubtedly stemmed from initial uncertainty, but there is also a perceptible undertone of official embarrassment.

Only seven Handley Pages were acknowledged lost in official channels, a figure that has been accepted ever since. The summary of air intelligence that was circulated to the King and the War Cabinet reported "seven of our machines failed to return."[123] Also of interest is the Air Ministry's fortnightly report to the War Cabinet concerning this particular mission:

> Three aerodromes./ Our machines attacked with bombs and machine gun fire. Good results were obtained.

METZ SABLON railways./ This target was very heavily attacked. Three fires were started.

TREVES railways./ Bombs were dropped all around the station.

FRANKFURT station./ This was also heavily attacked and bombs were dropped with good effect.

The night at first was calm but later high winds got up. 60 tons of bombs have been dropped in the last 3 days.

At present 7 of our machines have not been located.[124]

On 26 September 1918, in "Aircraft Work at the Front. Official Information," *Flight Magazine* presented an almost verbatim copy of the Air Ministry fortnightly report.

Headquarters, R.A.F. Independent Force. September 17th.

On the night 16th–17th our machines attacked three hostile aerodromes with bombs and machine-gun fire. Good results were obtained. The railways at Metz–Sablon and Treves were very heavily attacked, and three fires were started at Metz–Sablon. Bombs were dropped all round Treves station. The station at Frankfurt was also heavily attacked, and bombs were dropped with good effect. The night at first was calm, but later high winds got up. At present, seven of our machines have not been located. Sixty tons of bombs have been dropped in the last three days.[125]

Later, Trenchard's monthly dispatch to the Air Ministry discussed the 16/17 September missions under its "long distance raids" section, elaborating only slightly on the narratives previously disseminated.

(f) COLOGNE and BONN. On the night of the 16/17th September we lost 7 Handley Pages. Five of these, detailed for COLOGNE and MANNHEIM, were probably unable to return to our lines in the face of a strong south westerly wind which increased in velocity after the machines had left their aerodrome. One of these missing machines, with engine trouble, landed in Holland, having dropped his bombs at BONN. Unofficial German reports mention COLOGNE as being bombed during the night and of our machines being heard in the neighbourhood of DUSSELDORF.[126]

What Trenchard omitted from this report to the government was the fact that No. 215 Squadron, the Handley Page unit Haig had relinquished to the IF the month before, had also flown on 16/17 September. Of five No. 215 machines that left the ground at Xaffevillers aerodrome that evening, one aborted with engine trouble shortly after takeoff; the other four never returned.

No. 215 Sqdn.

5 machines left on operations. 1 Machine returned E.T., the other 4 machines failed to return.[127]

Interestingly, the typescript history of No. 215 Squadron does not cover the 16/17 September operation or its intended targets. The brief volume includes honors awarded and short biographies of key squadron personnel, but no casualty lists.[128]

However, a separate file of the unit's bomb raid reports, summaries, and intelligence reports contains the "Raid Orders Issued by O.C." for this particular mission.[129] This squadron raid summary confirms that assigned objectives included one machine each to Mannheim and Frescaty, and three Handley Pages tasked to hit Cologne.

DETAILS

3 machines left between 7.46 and 7.49 p.m. for Bombing Raid on Cologne, 2 machines failed to return. One machine experienced engine trouble, petrol leaking from rear tank in great quantities, and, after endeavouring for an hour to gain height, returned landing with bombs intact.

One machine left 7.50 p.m. for Bombing Raid on Frescaty, but failed to return.

One machine left 7.35 p.m. for Bombing Raid on Mannheim but failed to return.[130]

No. 215 Squadron lost 12 flyers the night of 16/17 September 1918.

Since HQ IF generally attempted to ascertain the fates of missing aviators, it is possible to establish overall casualties for 16/17 September.[131] No. 215 Squadron in fact had four aircraft go missing that night; tail numbers, names, ranks, and crew positions were all noted. Two aircrews became German prisoners of war while a third crew managed to crash-land on the friendly side of the lines. The fourth Handley Page (C.9727) had engine trouble and landed in Holland, where the crew were interned.[132] In a letter forwarded to the Air Ministry, the crew claimed that, though their assigned target had been Cologne, they had bombed the northwest section of Bonn;

they confirmed that the strong southwesterly wind had increased after takeoff. They "altered course for Holland" when they discovered that their "headway against the wind was very small, landing near Breda (25 miles southeast of Rotterdam) at 0130 17 September."[133]

Data gathered by the Air Intelligence staff at the Air Ministry during October included extracts from German newspapers of British air activity on 16/17 September. Aircraft had been heard southwest of Dusseldorf (north of Cologne), at Aachen (west of Cologne) and at Coblentz earlier in the evening.[134] Major Paul's notes show that he attributed all these incidents to machines from No. 215,[135] which strongly implies that No. 215's targets lay at least as deep as Cologne.

At least one Handley Page was heard near Dusseldorf, roughly midway between Cologne and Essen, the prize objective of the IF night squadrons. The official history notes simply that No. 215 Squadron lost two machines assigned to bomb Cologne, one tasked to hit Frescaty aerodrome, and one assigned to Mannheim.[136] Since Breda, where one Handley Page landed, lies north of Essen, it seems likely that many of the missing Handley Pages attempted to reach either Cologne or Essen that night.

Despite IF's selective narratives, all five of its night units flew on 16/17 September. Except for No. 97 Squadron, which had two machines abort with engine trouble, every Handley Page squadron suffered combat losses.[137] Because crashes on the friendly side of the lines and accidents were not included, actual aircraft wastage was considerably higher than the seven Handley Pages Trenchard chose to acknowledge.[138]

Trenchard's three cipher wires to the Air Ministry on 17 September, the day after the ill-starred operation, illuminate the means by which such unacceptable wastage can be reduced by administrative subterfuge.

G.O.C./172, 9 a.m. Regret to inform you that eight Handley Pages are missing on last night's raiding and two were wrecked. Can you possibly fill me up with machines and good pilots in time for this moon. Wire reply urgent.

I.F.C.326, afternoon. In continuation of Press Communique of to-day's date and my cipher wire of this morning. Of the eight machines reported missing one has been located completely wrecked on the side of the lines.

G.O.C./176, 9.05 p.m. It is possible that some of the seven missing machines have landed in HOLLAND. Five went to bomb COLOGNE and a very strong southerly wind got up. Please enquire and let me know.[139]

An independent check on these figures is possible, using the diary of Major Read, commanding No. 216 Squadron, who also flew that evening. His perspective of the operation and its aftermath differs considerably from the official version.

Read records that his squadron was tasked to send five Handley Pages to bomb Cologne and one to raid Frescaty aerodrome on 16/17 September.[140] Read left the ground at 2015 en route to Cologne, carrying one 550-pound bomb, eight 112-pound bombs, and eight and one-half hours of petrol. Read quickly realized that this condition would force a change in his objective.

Sgt. Keen [Read's observer] was not for going further than Mets on account of strong wind. However, I thought we could get to Treves in Germany and back on our petrol and so we went.[141]

Read's in-flight decision deserves amplification. Since a fully laden Handley Page cruised at somewhat less than 80 MPH, a 40 MPH southerly wind would considerably affect range calculations to targets north of IF aerodromes.[142] Cologne lay approximately 180 miles away, so a Handley Page boosted by a 40-MPH tail wind could reach the city within one and one-half hours, compared to two and one-fourth hours on a calm night. The homeward journey into the wind, however, would require three times as long, or four and one-half hours. Assuming perfect navigation, the round trip to Cologne on 16/17 September would require at least six hours—in a machine capable of flying a maximum of eight and one-half hours.

Tactical consideration and human error would extend the time aloft. Read, an experienced aviator, took nearly six hours for his round trip to Treves, a city located just halfway to Cologne.[143] His observer had misgivings over even that truncated journey. Under the prevailing circumstances, one can safely conclude that it would have been virtually impossible for any Handley Page to reach Cologne and return safely on

16/17 September. In fact, none of No. 216's five machines assigned to bomb Cologne had managed to do so; one was missing in action and one, which bombed Metz, crashed on landing back at Autreville.[144]

> Last night was disastrous for the Wing. Seven machines from the squadrons at Xaffevillers are missing and three machines were "write-offs" on landing through crashing.
>
> Counting our one missing and one crash it makes 12 Handley Pages lost . . . to say nothing of personnel.
>
> It was all caused through the bad night. The sky was clear enough but wind was very strong.[145]
>
> Last Sunday, when 8 machines were missing and three written off was the most disastrous day that the I.F. have had so far. It has steadied Wing's and Brigade's enthusiasm for flying on nights when weather is obviously doubtful.[146]

On 24 September, at the end of the moon period, Read wrote, "Tonight if it had looked fine we were sending 3 machines to Essen and 3 to Cologné."[147] The Handley Pages in fact never left the ground that night.

On 23 September, HQ IF, tempering its enthusiasm for long-range objectives, cautioned the line squadrons:

> 3. No attempt should be made to reach ESSEN by day unless the weather conditions are particularly favourable, and No's. 55 and 110 Squadrons can undertake the operation, flying at a good height.
> 4. It is possible that the projected attack on SPEYERDORF aerodrome may have to be postponed until the next full moon.[148]

The tone of this operation order stands in marked contrast to those promulgated just a few days earlier.

The prohibitive losses on 16/17 September seemed to dampen HQ IF's ardor for encouraging its Handley Pages to fly as far and as often as possible. For the rest of the month, the night squadrons were confined to targets considerably closer than the Rhine towns. Not until the last half of October (coinciding with the full moon of 18/19 October) did IF again schedule Essen as an assigned objective.[149] Weather, however, continued its dominance, forestalling these projected attacks; British bombers never reached the Krupp Works.

As the number and range of bombing sorties increased, losses rose proportionately. Unskilled aircrewmen, unreliable machines, adverse weather, and enemy countermeasures combined to severely limit the long-range bombing offensive. It seems very likely that these factors would have continued to constrain Trenchard's force, whether it eventually numbered nine squadrons or 90. Evaluation of the costs and accomplishments of the British long-range bombing campaign during 1918 requires, first of all, a reliable operational baseline.

No complete chronological summary has been available of Eighth Brigade and Independent Force between 1 February 1918 and the Armistice. The official history catalogs industrial targets primarily, and does not include weights of bombs dropped.[150] Further, it fails to list raids on German aerodromes, which accounted for nearly half the sorties flown by the Eighth Brigade and Independent Force during the last six months of hostilities.[151]

Compiling a more complete record of bombing activity has required data from numerous sources, cross-checked and collated. Records from Eighth Brigade and Independent Force, as well as returns from their subordinate units, intelligence summaries, and after-action reports, form the data skeleton; materials contained in Air Ministry staff files, unit histories, memoirs, and Cabinet records flesh out the chronology. Where possible, and in instances of ambiguity or conflict, information from the primary source (based on proximity or first-hand knowledge of the event) has been taken as authoritative.

The Rhine targets were of considerable interest to the War Cabinet and the Air Staff as "strategic objectives" throughout the campaign. Also in this group were the poison gas factories at "Mannheim." Blast furnaces ranked high in the bombing priorities of the French Air Service. "Miscellaneous" targets included industrial centers and urban areas, which later were to receive such prominent attention in the Air Ministry's final bombing report of January 1920.

It would appear that Trenchard's assumption of command did not inaugurate a significantly greater allocation of effort against any of these strategic targets. Despite the massive three-fold increase in Independent Force strength in the summer of 1918, the bomb total directed against these strategic targets in August actually decreased, reversing an upward trend evident since April. Part of this decline has usually been attributed to organizational turbulence as new units arrived in the IF area.

> During August No.100 Squadron, which was equipped with F.E.2b short-distance machines, commenced re-equipping with Handley Pages. While it was being re-equipped—which process took nearly the whole month—scarcely any work could be carried out by the squadron.[152]

Trenchard's apologia for the diminished effort directed against targets of strategic interest during August is somewhat inaccurate. In fact, No. 100 Squadron, which did not begin to convert to Handley Pages until 13 August, launched multiple-ship aerodrome raids, averaging approximately six machines each, on 14 successive nights between 11/12 and 30/31 August.[153] During the period in which the GOC IF claimed they had stood down to reequip, No. 100 Squadron had actually sustained a pace of operations unmatched by any other IF night unit.

For September, after No. 100 Squadron aircrews had completed their transition from FE2s to Handley Pages, and Nos. 92, 215, and 115 Squadrons had been established on station, the bomb total devoted to these key objectives barely surpassed what it had been in July. This strategic effort dropped steadily from September until the Armistice.

In any event, determining the size and importance of German industrial centers as bombing objectives did not greatly exercise HQ IF, despite Trenchard's assurances to Weir:

> My Intelligence Department provided me with the most thorough information on all targets such as gun factories, aeroplane factories, engine factories, poison-gas factories, etc., each target having a complete detailed and illustrated plan, and maps were prepared of every target that was within reach.[154]

Had such timely intelligence data been readily at hand at HQ IF, a request from the Air Intelligence Branch of the American Expeditionary Force, dated 18 October 1918, could have been promptly satisfied in the field. Asking for "information on German industries," the AEF G-2 sought "some data that will establish the relative size and importance of any industrial establishment," particularly "maps, general or detail, which will indicate the location of industries."[155] Instead of responding, Trenchard forwarded the request to Branch AI 1a at the Air Ministry.[156]

> It is probable that this information may not exist in the form required. If such be the case, any publications or reports that are at present in existence and which may give the desired data for any subject, or group of subjects, would be sufficient for the purpose.

> Can this information be forwarded to these Headquarters as soon as possible.[157]

Coming less than a month before the Armistice, this profession of ignorance concerning strategic objectives he had been explicitly directed to bomb suggests the minimal effort actually launched against such targets. Instead, Eighth Brigade and Independent Force devoted the bulk of their attention to enemy railways and aerodromes.

The final dispatch of the GOC IF noted that, "when it was impossible for squadrons to reach their objectives well in the interior of Germany," railways were first in order of importance.[158] Asserting that "the Germans were extremely short of rolling stock," Trenchard stated that such targets "were also fairly easy to find at night."[159]

On several occasions, French control of British bombing assets reinforced this aspect of the long-range campaign. Throughout April and the first third of May, Newall's squadrons operated against rail targets in support of the French offensive. In April, all Eighth Brigade bombs fell on the German railway system. Similar situations occurred again in September, when Trenchard's Independent Force cooperated in direct support of two Allied ground offensives by bombing enemy railways.

Neither Newall nor Trenchard was particularly reluctant to commit his squadron to ground cooperation missions of this sort. In fact, the GOC IF had repeatedly advocated such operations as the primary role of air forces. Concentration upon enemy railways also held other advantages, which will become evident later.

With respect to enemy aerodromes, German airfields received the overwhelming proportion of British attention and constituted the number one priority for the Independent Force during the campaign. That the abrupt surge and peak of this activity correspond almost exactly with Trenchard's tenure as GOC IF seems particularly significant.

Trenchard outlined his rationale for attacks on enemy aerodromes in his Final Dispatch to Weir on 1 January 1919. He based the decision on two points: "to prevent his [the enemy] attacking our aerodromes at night and by destroying his machines to render his attacks by day less efficacious."[160] As field commander, Trenchard would be naturally bound to protect his forces even if such protection might disrupt his assigned priorities. He defended his aerodrome campaign by citing the security his own airfields subsequently enjoyed.

> Of this amount (550 tons total) no less than 220–¼ tons were dropped on aerodromes. This large percentage was due to the necessity of preventing the enemy's bombing machines attacking our aerodromes and in order to destroy large numbers of the enemy's scouts on their aerodromes, and it was impracticable to deal with them on equal terms in the air. I think this large amount of bombing was thoroughly justified when it is taken into consideration that the enemy's attacks on our aerodromes were practically negligible, and not a single machine was destroyed by bombing during the period June 5th to Nov. 11th.[161]

By elaborating only upon the protection of IF airfields, Trenchard implies that the security of his rear area was of considerably greater concern than his loss rates. The official history endorses and amplifies this logic:

> When all is said, what remains true is that Major-General Trenchard's object was achieved. The aerodromes of the Independent Force day and night bombers were not seriously molested—of moral as well as of material importance—and the German defensive fighters, with some exceptions were unable to prevent the day bombers from attacking their distant objectives.[162]

A footnote on the same page as this quotation put IF losses from all causes at just 3.9 percent, a misleading statistic.[163] Given this unchallenged casualty claim and Trenchard's own refusal ever to discuss aircrew losses, securing his own aerodromes against German raids would emerge by default as the issue of greater import.[164]

Trenchard is correct when he asserts that his own airfields were seldom raided and little damaged during 1918. They were attacked just eight times between 12 July and 26 September, with negligible material damage and personnel losses of one killed and four wounded.[165] However, to ascribe this result solely to IF's campaign against German aerodromes begs the question.

British intelligence estimates consistently overrated the strengths and capabilities of German home defense units arrayed against Eighth Brigade and Independent Force. Further, when Major Paul's survey teams investigated the effects of bombing German airfields after the Armistice, findings were inconclusive at best.

> Unfortunately, the aerodromes situated in reconquered LORRAINE had been almost entirely dismantled by the resident civilians, and therefore little material damage was visible.

> On the whole one is forced to believe that, except on rare occasions, the actual destruction of hangars and installations has been moderate.[166]

The RAF field teams also discovered that, compared to wartime claims, material damages to all types of bombing targets were considerably less.

> [Damages] prove upon inspection to have been considerably less devastating than the photographs had led to believe. Similarly, bursts on aerodromes are difficult to gauge. A group of bombs close to a permanent hangar at HAGENAU were found to have caused much less damage than reports and photographs had seemed to indicate.[167]

Finally, as the Royal Canadian Air Force official historian concluded after examining German aerial archives, "nowhere in postwar German accounts of the air battle do losses from aerodrome bombing figure as a problem."[168] Trenchard's justification for bombing enemy aerodromes—that his own airfields were in consequence seldom attacked—smacks strongly of post hoc argument.

A much stronger case for concentrating on German aerodromes can be made for Trenchard's second point: to reduce the severity of enemy fighter attacks on his day bombers.

German countermeasures frequently stalled the British daylight offensive, inflicting losses that jeopardized the campaign's momentum. These casualties unquestionably constituted a more immediate and persistent problem than enemy raids on the IF base area. The relationship between mounting losses and frequent raids on German aerodromes is unmistakably evident. The GOC IF himself linked the two phenomena when he concluded a congratulatory telegram to the Handley Page crews on No. 216 Squadron with this exhortation:

> If mist not interfere with your operations, I hope that by bombing the enemy's Scout Aerodromes you will be able to exact due compensation for losses sustained by No. 99 Squadron today.[169]

Given the prohibitive casualties sustained by Trenchard's daylight component and the impressive poundage correspondingly dropped by his night-flying machines on enemy airfields, one must conclude that Trenchard was forced to resort to these airfield attacks in an attempt to reduce unacceptable IF losses in the air—not on the ground.

As bombing targets, aerodromes and railways alike possessed several attractive features. They were easily identifiable from the air, and they were not particularly heavily defended.[170] During 1918, Eighth Brigade and Independent Force squadrons attacked a total of 16 different enemy aerodromes. Of these, only three lay more than 30 miles from the front lines—the deepest not 45 miles behind the trenches—and they were raided fewer than 15 times.[171]

> Owing to the fact that many of them were situated within 40 miles of the lines, they formed useful instructional raids for young pilots; in spite of this fact, very few casualties were incurred on the raids.

> Roughly it took five machines to destroy one German aircraft on the ground. . . . We lost, on an average, one machine in three raids.[172]

Railways appealed for much the same reasons. The huge Metz–Sablon rail triangle lay just 12 miles behind the trenches.[173] Inexperienced aircrews could locate and identify such objectives without penetrating the German air defense system to any depth.

Even with this foreshortened targeting program, the pace of the British bombing campaign did not slacken. Several sources indicate that IF resources and personnel were continually pushed to their maximum.

In mid-September, Capt H. McClelland, the veteran Handley Page pilot reassigned to the Directorate of Flying Operations, forwarded a disturbing memorandum. Using figures from Trenchard's own monthly dispatches, McClelland demonstrated that, although the IF flying hour total for July exceeded that for June by 33 percent, the number of machines wrecked jumped by 67 percent—twice the flying rate.[174] Analyses for July and August revealed that, while flying hours had increased by just 13 percent, the rate of machines wrecked went up by 31 percent.[175]

> The increase in flying time to the increase of machines wrecked is altogether disproportionate and apparently would point to lack of organization in some respects.[176]

The following month, McClelland's chief informed the Director of Flying Operations, General Groves, that the Independent Force had wrecked 44 percent of its assigned machines in crashes during September and that a further 37 percent had gone missing in action.[177] (No. 5 Group, RAF, similarly equipped, had engaged in long raids from Dunkirk during the same month and lost just one DH9 and no Handley Pages.)[178]

In light of the marginal proficiency of his aircrews and the effectiveness of German air defenses, aerodromes and railways represented the only classes of targets Trenchard could hope to raid on a sustained basis. Targets just over the lines became increasingly attractive to replacement aircrews, inexperienced at navigation and facing natural hazards as well as enemy countermeasures. Daylight losses were such that the largest proportion of his night effort also had to be diverted to attack German aerodromes. Casualty rates became critical; losses dictated the types of objectives the Independent Force found itself able to raid effectively. Bomber aircrews did what they could, but it was generally a far cry from what HQ IF claimed they did.

Against these costs must be balanced the results actually achieved by the British bombing campaign during 1918.

Notes

1. J. M. Bruce, *The Aeroplanes of the Royal Flying Corps (Military Wing)* (London: Putnum, 1982), 74.

2. H. A. Jones, *War in the Air: Being the Story of the Part Played in the Great War by the Royal Air Force,* 6 vols. (Oxford: Clarendon Press, 1937), Appendix 18, between 130–31. By contrast, Bruce puts the Puma-powered DH9 service ceiling at 15,500 feet, two thousand feet below Jones' figure. See also Bruce, 77.

3. Bruce, 72.

4. J. E. A. Baldwin, "Experiences of Bombing with the Independent Force in 1918," in *A Selection of Lectures and Essays from the Work of Officers Attending the First Course at the Royal Air Force Staff College, 1921–1923* (London: Her Majesty's Stationery Office [HMSO], Air Ministry, December 1923), 11.

5. William Armstrong, *Pioneer Pilot* (London: Blandford Press, 1952), 34.

6. W. M. Lamberton, *Reconnaissance and Bomber Aircraft of the 1914–1918 War* (Warwick, England: Warwick Printing, 1962), 38.

7. Ibid., 74–75, 79.

8. War Diary of Eighth Brigade, Newall Papers, B392, Royal Air Force Museum (RAFM), Hendon, England.

9. Bruce, 72.

10. Ibid., 73.

11. As noted of 41st Wing, RFC operations, no reliable comprehensive chronological summary exists for the bombing campaign during 1918. Consequently, information has been compiled from a number of sources.

12. Lamberton, 40.

13. Bruce, 79.

14. Lamberton, 40; and Bruce, 81.

15. Jones, Appendix 27.

16. Lamberton, 36; Bruce, 49.

17. Baldwin, 2–4, 8, 10.

18. Jones, Appendix 12, facing 41.

19. Ibid.

20. Public Record Office (PRO), Air Ministry Records (AIR) 1/1972/204/273/1, Casualty Statistics, June–November 1918, IF Form A8 (Rew, England: Independent Force Press).

21. Ibid.

22. Ibid. Notation preprinted on IF Form A.8.

23. Quoted in Ralph R. Williams, "Navigation: From Dead Reckoning to Navstar GPS," *Air Force Magazine* 67, no. 12 (December 1984): 63.

24. 1 MFC 76/1/32, Trenchard Papers, Private Diary entry for 18 August 1918.

25. AIR 1/1972/204/273/1, data for No. 55 Squadron compiled from IF Form A.8 returns.

26. A. R. Kingsford, *Night Raiders of the Air: Being the Experience of a Night Flying Pilot Who Raided Hunland on Many dark Nights during the War*

(London: Hamilton, 1930), 170. One notable casualty was Capt W. E. Johns (author of the *Biggles* series) and his observer, 2d Lt A. E. Army, who were shot down on the raid to Hagenau aerodrome on 16 September 1918. See Peter Berresford Ellis and Piers Williams, *By Jove, Biggles! The Life of Captain W. E. Johns* (London: W. H. Allen, 1981), 86–87.

27. Imperial War Museum (IWM), "Miscellaneous," box 34, item 616, Aeroplane Diary, 1918, lists types and numbers of replacement machines.

28. War Diary of Eighth Brigade, date cited; and L. A. Pattinson, *History of 99 Squadron, Independent Force, Royal Air Force, March 1918–November 1918* (Cambridge, England: W. Heffer & Sons, 1920), 7.

29. AIR 1/1972/204/273/1, data for No. 99 Squadron compiled from IF Form A.8 returns.

30. Pattinson.

31. Ibid., 8.

32. Ibid., 13.

33. Ibid., 16–18.

34. Ibid., 19–24.

35. Ibid., 29.

36. Ibid., 29–30.

37. Alan Morris, *First of the Many: The Story of the Independent Force, RAF* (London: Jarrolds, 1968), 169–71.

38. Pattinson, 30.

39. IWM, box 34, item 616, Aeroplane Diary, dates cited.

40. Pattinson, 32.

41. War Diary of Eighth Brigade, entry for 15 August 1918.

42. Pattinson, 34.

43. Ibid.

44. AIR 1/1999/204/273/269, Report on the effects of Bombing German Blast Furnaces, Maj H. W. M. Paul, 26 February 1919, bomb-plot diagram facing p. 27.

45. Ibid., 52–53.

46. Ibid., 53.

47. Ibid., 54.

48. Pattinson, 56; and Jones, Appendix 15, 87.

49. Jones, Appendix 15, 55; and War diary of Eighth Brigade, date cited.

50. Pattinson, 55.

51. Ibid., 56.

52. IWM, box 34, item 616, Aeroplane Diary.

53. Ibid.

54. Ibid.

55. Ibid.

56. AIR 1/1972/204/273/1, date for No. 104 Squadron compiled from IF form A.8 returns.

57. Ibid.

58. AIR 1/1982/204/273/1, data for No. 110 Squadron compiled from IF Form A.8 returns.

59. Elwyn D. Bell, *Hyderabad Squadron: The Story of No. 110 (Hyderabad) Squadron, Royal Air Force* (London: Air Britain, 1972), 1.

60. Ibid., i, ii, and Appendix 4, list tail numbers and aircrew of missing machines.

61. AIR 1/2422/305/18/11, Trenchard to Weir, 23 June 1918.

62. Armstrong, 45.

63. Ibid., 46.

64. PRO, AIR 1/1997/204/273/252, GOC, IF to Air Ministry, Cipher Wires, 22 July–16 August 1918.

65. PRO, AIR 1/460/15/312/100, Trenchard to Sykes, 4 August 1918.

66. PRO, AIR 1/460/15/312/98, Notes on Defence of Bombing Squadrons Operating with Independent Force, 8 August 1918, folio 2.

67. Ibid.

68. Ibid.

69. Ibid.

70. MFC 76/1/32, Trenchard Papers, private diary, June–November 1918.

71. Jones, vol. 6, 153.

72. Neville Jones, *The Origins of Strategic Bombing: A Study of the Development of British Air Strategic Thought and Practice Up to 1918* (London: Eimber, 1973), 197.

73. Malcolm Cooper, "British Air Policy on the Western Front, 1914–1918" (PhD diss., Oxford University, 1982), 332–33.

74. AIR 1/711/27/13/2214, "Die Luftwacht" (October 1928), 54. Translated by Air Ministry A.7 (T) Section.

75. Alex Imrie, *Pictorial History of the German Army Service, 1914–1918* (London: Ian Allan, 1971), 39.

76. Ibid., 52–53.

77. Ludendorff to KM (War Ministry), no. 59034, 25 June 1917, in II no. 31576, 13 July 1917, IL 41/1 Military Archive, German Federal Republic, Freiburg. Quoted in John H. Morrow Jr., *German Air Power in World War I* (Lincoln, Nebr.: University of Nebraska, 1982), 95.

78. Sir Charles Webster and A. Noble Frankland, *The Strategic Air Offensive Against Germany, 1939–1945*, vol.1, *Preparation* (London: HMSO, 1961), 19.

79. H. A. Jones, vol. 6, 163n.

80. Webster and Frankland, 41, 44.

81. H. A. Jones, vol. 6, as cited.

82. AIR 1/1072/204/273/1, data compiled from IF Form A.8 returns.

83. H. A. Jones, Appendix 12, facing p. 41.

84. H. R. Brooke-Popham, "The Air Force," *Journal of the Royal United Services Institute (JRUSI)*, February 1920, 49.

85. IWM, 72/76/1, W. R. Read Papers, private diary no. 6, 36.

86. Ibid.

87. Ibid.

88. IWM, box 34, item 616, Aeroplane Diary, February–June 1918 data.

89. IWM, W. R. Read private diary no. 7, entry for 23 August 1918, notes that, "No. 216 should have gone to Cologne and Frankfurt last night but did not."

90. IWM, box 34, item 616, Aeroplane Diary, August 1918.

91. AIR 1/1972/204/273/1, data on losses compiled from IF Form A.8 returns.

92. Neville Jones, 191; and H. A. Jones, vol. 6, 134.

93. Neville Jones, 191; H. A. Jones, vol. 6, 148–49; Wise, 310–11; and Maurer Maurer, ed., *The U.S. Air Service in World War I*, vol. 3, *The Battle of St. Mihiel* (Maxwell Air Force Base [AFB], Ala.: Air Force Historical Research Agency, 1979), is devoted entirely to this five-day period; 717 lists the order of battle for participating Independent Force squadrons.

94. One must note how narrow in time this moonlight bombing window can be. Four days either side of the full moon, the approximate brightness falls to only one-third that for the full moon; at one week either side, to one-tenth or less. PRO, AIR 1/1997/204/273/257, Hydrographic Department of the Admiralty Moonlight Charts for Latitude 50° 30'N, Greenwich mean time, June–November 1918.

95. Summary of Air Intelligence, 6th series, A.I.1.a, Air Ministry, Bodleian Library, Oxford, dates cited.

96. IWM, W. R. Read private diary no. 7, dates cited.

97. Ibid., date cited.

98. Ibid., dates cited.

99. Ibid., date cited.

100. PRO, AIR 1/912/204/5/848, War Office to Haig, 6 August 1918.

101. Ibid., Haig to War Office, 10 August 1918.

102. AIR 1/912/204/5/848, Foreign Office, to Air Ministry, letter 153287/WG, 10 September 1918.

103. Ibid.; and Air Ministry to GOCs, RAF, and IF, 13 September 1918.

104. PRO, AIR 1/1997/204/273/255, Diagrams of Existing and Prospective Lines and Communications, IAF, Azelot Aerodrome, Air Depot Courban, and Note of Communications, IF and London, 23 July 1918.

105. PRO, AIR 1/1974/204/273/4, Haig, to War Office, letter OB/1873B, 30 June 1918.

106. Ibid.; and War Office, to Haig, letter 24 August 1918.

107. PRO, AIR 6/13, B.3199, Minutes of Air Council Meeting, Thursday, 8 August 1918.

108. AIR 1/416/15/312/104, Gammell, to Gordon, letter C4/38, 9 August 1918. "Binge" means "to enliven or pep up," as well as "to soak (a wooden vessel) so as to swell the wood and prevent leakage." *Supplement to the OED*, 1972, *Webster's Dictionary, Third Edition*, 1972.

109. AIR 1/461/15/212/104, Trenchard, to Air Ministry, letter C4/35, 27 August 1918.

110. PRO, AIR 1/1649/204/95/3, HQ, IF Operation Order No. 21.

111. Ibid., orders and dates cited.

112. AIR 1/1649/204/95/3, orders and dates as cited.

113. E. D. Harding et al., *History of Number 16 Squadron (known as "A" Naval Squadron) Royal Naval Air Service Renumbered 216 Squadron Independent Force Royal Air Force* (London: H. W. Hill & Son, 1923).

114. Ibid.

115. AIR 1/1649/204/95/3, HQ, IF Operation Order No. 30, 15 September 1918.

116. Ibid.

117. AIR 1/2085/207/5/2, Approximate Results No. 84, HQ, IF to Air Ministry, 17 September 1918. For Bivar's position see MFC 76/1/68 (Sheet 1 of 2), "Composition of Headquarters, Independent Force, Royal Air Force, Corrected to 8th October 1918. Confidential." Royal Air Force Museum, Hendon, HQ, IF, October 1918.

118. Ibid.

119. AIR 1/1986/204/273/112, Paul to Air Ministry, 19 September 1918.

120. Ibid.

121. AIR 1/2085/207/5/1, H.1., IF to Air Ministry, 21 September 1918.

122. Ibid.

123. Summary of Air Intelligence, 6th series, no. 16, 19 September 1918.

124. PRO, CAB 24/65, GT 5835, Air Ministry to War Cabinet, Report No. 7 for Fortnight Ended 28 September 1918.

125. *Flight*, 26 September 1918, 1099.

126. AIR 1/2085/207/5/1, Monthly Dispatch (IFG 79/5), Trenchard to Weir, 1 October 1918. Also available in CAB 24/69, GT 6234.

127. War Diary of Eighth Brigade, entry for 16/17 September 1918, Newall Papers, B392.

128. PRO, AIR 1/184/15/218/1, "History of No. 215 Squadron Royal Air Force (Late of No. 15 Squadron Royal Navy Air Service)."

129. PRO, AIR 1/1947/204/295/5, "No. 215 Sqdn. R.A.F. Bomb Raid Reports, Summaries, Intelligence Reports and Raid Orders Issued by O.C., April–November 1918," raid order for 16/17 September 1918.

130. Ibid.

131. PRO, AIR 1/1649/204/95/9, "VIII Brigade R.A.F. Correspondence and Reports on Casualties, September 1918 to February 1919."

132. Ibid.

133. PRO, AIR 1/1976/204/273/44, Handley Page which landed near Breda to Naval Attaché, British Legation, The Hague, letter, 1 October 1918.

134. Ibid., AI1b, Air Ministry, to HQ, IF(I), letter, 14 October 1918.

135. Ibid.

136. H. A. Jones, Appendix 13, 73–74.

137. AIR 1/1649/204/95/9, date cited.

138. *Aeroplane*, 8 January 1919, reprints this portion of Trenchard's Final Dispatch on p. 131; and H. A. Jones, vol. 6, 147.

139. AIR 1/1997/204/273/252, GOC, IF, to Air Ministry, cipher wires, 17 September 1918.

140. IWM, 72/76/2, W. R. Read private diary no. 7, entry for 17 September 1918.

141. Ibid., PRO, AIR 1/2104/207/36, *Results of Air Raids on Germany,* 3d ed., Directorate of Air Intelligence (DAI), no. 5, January 1920, 41 and map facing 40, indicate that six of Read's bombs hit the Hoff Brandy Distillery and straddled the rail line near the station in the western part of the city, without causing "much damage."

142. H. A. Jones, Appendix 27, 130–31, gives cruising speed of the Handley Page 0400 as 79.5 miles per hour, with bomb load.

143. IWM, 72/76/2, W.R. Read Papers, private diary no. 7, entry for 17 September 1918.

144. Ibid.

145. Ibid.

146. Ibid., date cited.

147. Ibid., date cited.

148. AIR 1/1649/204/95/3, HQ, IF Operation Order No. 32, 23 September 1918.

149. H. A. Jones, Appendix 13, 79, 81.

150. H. A. Jones, Appendix 13, "Industrial Targets Bombed by Squadrons of the 41st Wing and the Independent Force, October 1917–November 1918," 42–84.

151. Ibid.

152. Trenchard's Final Dispatch is reprinted in C. Gordon Burge, *The Annals of 100 Squadron* (London: Herbert Reach, 1919), 155–59; and *Aeroplane,* vol. 16, 8 January 1919, 129–31.

153. Burge, 13.

154. Burge, 157; and *Aeroplane,* 129.

155. PRO, AIR 1/1976/204/273/39, 18 October 1918.

156. Ibid., Trenchard to AI1a, 28 October 1918.

157. Ibid.

158. Burge, 158; and *Aeroplane,* 130. A study of the British program, conducted by the US Air Service in June 1918, concluded, "The great strategical importance of railway lines is indicated by the fact that about half of all bombing raids and nearly three-fourths of the long distance raids were directed against railways," *Statistical Analysis of Aerial Bombardment,* USAF Museum, Wright-Patterson AFB, Ohio, file L3-AA.

159. Burge, 158; and *Aeroplane,* 130.

160. Burge, *Squadron,* 157; and *Aeroplane,* 129–30.

161. Burge, *Squadron,* 158; and *Aeroplane,* 129–30.

162. H. A. Jones, vol. 6, 163.

163. Ibid.

164. On Trenchard's reticence, see Wise, 325–26.

165. PRO, AIR 1/1649/204/95/7, Report of Lt-Col commanding IF AA defences, n.d.

166. PRO, AIR 1/1998/204/273/263, Maj H. W. M. Paul to Air Ministry, Report of Allied Bombing Raids on Germany: Aerodromes and their Results, 26 February 1919.

167. RAF Hendon, Newall Papers, B395, Maj H. W. M. Paul to Air Ministry, Report of Allied bombing Raids on Germany: Railways, "Estimate of Material Results from the Reports of Pilots and Observers, and from Air Photographs," 26 February 1919. Paul's "Estimate" is not included in the PRO copy of this report (AIR 1/1998/204/273/262).

168. Wise, vol. 1, 325.

169. Trenchard to Maj W. R. Read, 31 July 1918. Quoted in PRO, AIR 1/184/15/219/1, typescript of No. 216 Squadron History. French raids on Germany aerodromes during this period had the same rationale. Concerning attacks on three enemy airfields on 25/26 September 1918, "These nighttime suppression raids made the ensuing daytime raids much safer by virtue of enemy aircraft eliminated on the ground." Peter Kilduff, "The History of Groupes de Bombardement 4 and 9," *Cross and Cockade Journal* 15, no.1 (Spring 1974): 21–22.

170. Kingsford; and Sqdn-Ldr W. A. McLaughy, "A Lecture on Night Flying," in *A Selection of Lectures and Essays from the Work of Officers Attending the First Course of the Royal Air Force Staff College, Cranwell, 1922–1923* (London: HMSO, AP 956, Air Ministry, December 1923), 34–36.

171. Wise, vol. 1, 288 (map).

172. Baldwin, 7.

173. Ibid.

174. AIR 1/461/15/312/107, SO3 to FO3, 17 September 1918.

175. Ibid.

176. Ibid.

177. AIR 1/461/15/312/107, FO3 to DFO, 15 October 1918.

178. Ibid.

Chapter 6

Postwar Assessments

Three broad themes characterized the British experience in planning and developing long-range bombing campaigns through 1917. Germany had held the early bombing initiative and the British were under considerable pressure to retaliate. Their response, however, was complicated by doctrinal differences between the War Office and the Admiralty; the War Office saw no need to build long-range bombers until adequate air support of ground forces had been provided.[1] Finally, interservice cooperation had been hampered for years by competition for aviation resources.

On 4 April 1916, the Admiralty presented to the War Cabinet a memorandum in which Rear Adm C. L. Vaughn-Lee claimed that Germany's Zeppelin raids against England demanded more than a purely defensive posture. He argued for a systematic attack to regain the initiative and inflict both direct and indirect damages on Germany.[2] A month later, having secured French cooperation in principle, the Admiralty began basing warplanes and aircrews near Luxeuil in southeastern France. This British unit—No. 3 Wing, Royal Naval Air Service—was to raid German munition works near the Rhine. These efforts, sporadic from the start, were discontinued in the spring of 1917 in order to reinforce the Royal Flying Corps on the Somme.[3]

Also from the start, determining the results of long-range bombing raids was difficult at best. The documentation sources were fragmentary and, often, contradictory. Such qualitative sources as aircrew observations, agents' reports, captured letters, and German newspaper articles necessitated caution in evaluation.[4]

References to "moral effect" began to appear in early spring 1917, before No. 3 Wing was disbanded. Admiralty bulletins devoted increasing attention to this concept of indirect damage: "It is reliably reported that the Allies' recent frequent aerial bombardments of objectives in the Saar Valley have caused panic among the workmen, and they refuse to carry on their work." This heartening information, published by the Admiralty, came just as severe pressure was being applied to transfer No. 3 Wing's assets to the RFC.[5]

The notion of indirect, or "moral," effects of the British bombing campaign picked up steam and speed thereafter, even within the Royal Flying Corps. By November 1917, General Trenchard was carrying the moral effect banner. His memorandum to the British Air Policy Committee that month formed the basis of the committee's own memorandum to the Supreme War Council.[6] The following passage was included, almost verbatim, in the Committee's report to the War Council:

> Long distance bombing will produce its maximum moral effect only if the visits are constantly repeated at short intervals so as to produce in each area bombed a sustained anxiety. It is this recurrent bombing, as opposed to isolated and spasmodic attacks, which interrupts industrial production and undermines public confidence. On the other hand, if the enemy were to succeed in destroying large numbers of our bombing machines, and above all, if they could interrupt the continuity of our bombing operations, their achievement (as the Allies' success against Zeppelins shows) would be an immense encouragement to them which would operate almost like a military victory.[7]

The United States had entered the war by this time, and Colonel Gorrell, chief of the Strategic Aviation Branch of the US Air Service in France, had also picked up the moral effect theme.[8] The Allies' considerations of moral effect helped to render their bombing efforts cost-effective and psychologically satisfying. Moral effect diminished uncertainty by making every bomb count, whether or not any material damage resulted.

The British seemed to project their own outrage under German air attack onto the German population. Any damage done to German morale was highly valued in England. Favorable public opinion on the home front was bolstered by claims of moral effect; these claims were therefore carefully nurtured by British air authorities. Few considered the opposite effect; that is, that the German populace would become habituated to the bombing threat.[9]

Let us now evaluate the claims put forth by the advocates of long-range bombing. The German collapse afforded Allied observers the opportunity to examine and analyze the results of RAF ordnance on enemy targets. To this end, the Air Ministry dispatched a group of experienced intelligence officers from the Independent Force into occupied territory west of the Rhine.

On 7 December 1918, less than a month after the Armistice, Major Paul and Lt W. J. T. Wright, Eighth Brigade and 83d Wing intelligence officers respectively, plus three other ranks, proceeded on this survey. A week later, Capt A. R. Ovens, another IF intelligence officer, joined the party.[10] They returned from this temporary duty on 20 January 1919, having spent six weeks gathering data on all targets up to the east bank of the Rhine. Major Paul's final report, submitted on 26 February 1919, contained some unexpected conclusions.

As submitted to the Air Ministry, the RAF field report ran to seven volumes. The first six, organized according to categories of targets, included a study of the development of German countermeasures to Allied bombing.[11] The last volume assessed the effects of British bombs and contained Paul's overall conclusions. Major Paul and his colleagues seem not to have made a systematic comparison of the dates of British missions to each target with corresponding German records showing the extent of bomb damage. However, considering the limitations imposed by lack of time and personnel, this RAF survey is remarkably complete.

As an experienced and capable intelligence officer who had served on Newall's staff since November 1917, Paul very likely touched a bureaucratic nerve when he submitted his findings in late February 1919. At any rate, his assessments were severely edited in the Air Ministry's final bombing report, "Results of Air Raids on Germany Carried out by the 8th Brigade and Independent Force, Royal Air Force," which appeared in January 1920 as the institutional judgment on the British bombing campaign.

Luckily, the Americans, though relative latecomers to the field, also conducted an extensive postwar survey on the effects of aerial bombardment. Twelve teams, each headed by a

US Air Service officer with two enlisted troops (photographer and chauffeur), visited 140 towns in occupied territory between early March and 20 May 1919. Like the RAF teams, the Americans sought information on these topics:

(1) Basic facts such as times, names of factories and their products, and whether the places were always bombed during each raid alert period.

(2) Material damage.

(3) Bombing of railways, including the lengths of time that trains had been delayed.

(4) Countermeasures.

(5) Moral effects, if any, of the raids.[12]

Except for the low priority given moral effect, the charter of the American teams paralleled that of their RAF counterparts who had traversed the same ground a few weeks earlier. Since only eight of the locations they visited had been bombed exclusively by the US Air Service, the Americans were in effect conducting their own inquiries into the strategic and tactical results of the Eighth Brigade and Independent Force.

Ironically, the completed American bombing survey, comprising two volumes, arrived at Tours too late to be included in the comprehensive index that the US Air Service had prepared for the 280-volume history of American wartime aviation that had been compiled.[13] Consequently, this bombing assessment has been overlooked for nearly half a century. One historian/editor used the history for more than 15 years before he unearthed the unindexed US Air Service bombing survey in July 1974.[14] It has since been consulted more frequently, though mostly as the predecessor of the US Strategic Bombing Survey conducted after World War II.

The value of the American survey as a supplementary authority to the evidence contained in the Paul report is obvious. In general, the two Allied field reports agree very closely. Like the RAF report, the American bombing survey provides an independent counterpoise to the Air Ministry's claims in its final bombing report of January 1920. In conjunction with the RAF survey, the US report comprises a powerful instrument for dissecting this official evaluation.

A structure of optimistic assumptions concerning the capabilities of strategic bombing had been erected during the war;

by mid-1918, most skeptics had acknowledged its potential. The impact of such contradictory information as that collected by RAF and US intelligence survey teams must be measured against this buffer of ingrained bureaucratic optimism.

The third edition of the Air Ministry's classified report, "Results of Air Raids on Germany Carried out by British Aircraft" (known also as AP 1225), which appeared in January 1920, has been generally accepted as the authoritative assessment of the bombing campaign.[15] However, the accuracy and objectivity of this postwar verdict must be considered with respect to its predecessors, the first and second editions of AP 1225. Major Boyle, the Air Intelligence staff officer who had analyzed strategic bombing during hostilities, supervised its evaluation after the war, even as he controlled access to the classified materials upon which the Air Ministry judgment was ultimately based. The wartime editions of AP 1225, produced by the same Air Staff directorate that compiled the final report, had firmly established an analytical precedent for the widely cited third edition.

Air Staff interest in determining and disseminating the results of strategic bombing first arose in mid-1918, after Trenchard had departed to command the Independent Force. On 28 June, General Groves, director of Flying Operations, wrote to General Sykes, the new chief of Air Staff:

> I have asked D.D.A.I. to make out a brief summary each month of the results obtained by strategic bomb attacks. This summary to be compiled under the heading of:
>
> (1) Moral effects.
> (2) Material effects.
>
> I think a summary of those lines will be of use as a guide for future action as strategic bombing develops, and also as a handy reference for furnishing information and reports.[16]

Sykes agreed, and the Directorate of Air Intelligence henceforth assumed responsibility for cataloging the effects of British bombing.

During 1918, two editions of AP 1225 appeared. Prepared by Section AI1B under Captain Boyle and printed in August and October, these wartime assessments relied heavily upon captured letters and agents' reports for details. The introduction to the second edition included a caution: "It should be remembered that the German censorship is very strict and that newspaper references to air raids are very scarce and incomplete."[17] Nonetheless, the wartime AP 1225 editions asserted that "the morale of the German population becomes lower as the range and power of our bombing squadrons increase." This positive tone echoed and reinforced the claims of other news releases, communiqués, and dispatches disseminated by London and HQ IF.

The RAF intelligence teams transmitted their findings to the Air Ministry, via Salmond's HQ, RAF in the field, on 26 February 1919.[18] The Air Ministry's AI1 Branch of the Directorate of Air Intelligence (DAI) then produced the third and final volume of AP 1225, purportedly based upon an evaluation of these firsthand findings. Most of the Directorate's efforts, however, appear to have been devoted to advocacy rather than accuracy.

Captain Boyle, head of Section AI1B, took over newly formed Section AI3C in November 1918. His six-man section, subordinate to the AI3 Branch ("Relations with Foreign Countries"), was responsible for collecting postwar data on "bomb targets," "results of raids," and "A.A. defences" for the Air Intelligence Directorate.[19] In June 1919, after Trenchard had again become chief of Air Staff, Boyle, now a major, headed the entire AI1 Branch, charged with "receipt and custody of intelligence papers," "all general intelligence questions," and "censorship."[20]

His Air Ministry staff assignments clearly indicate that Boyle oversaw the two wartime printings of AP 1225. He also headed the staff groups that sifted the RAF field survey after the Armistice to produce the third edition of the Air Ministry report in January 1920. His additional responsibility for postwar censorship, formerly entrusted to Branch AI6, "Censorship and Propaganda," also seems significant.

In contrast to the seven-volume RAF field survey, which grouped information by target category, the final report lists objectives alphabetically.[21] Its arrangement is useful to the civil servant or staff officer interested only in a particular target, but it hinders analysis of bombing effects upon classes of objectives; for example, railway systems, the chemical/munitions industry, or enemy blast furnace complexes. A four-page introduction, "Effects of Air Raids," precedes the table of contents listing specific targets.[22] This brief narrative, excerpted from RAF survey conclusions on the material and moral effects of British bombing, does not constitute a comprehensive assessment. In fact, very little substantive analysis of captured materials or cross-checking against RAF wartime records was undertaken prior to release of the final report.

Of seven appendices to the Air Ministry volume, six are simply edited portions of the RAF survey. They are primarily concerned with German active and passive countermeasures to British bombing. The last appendix, "Comparative Charts," details the scope of Eighth Brigade and Independent Force operations, down to the numbers of each type of bomb dropped per month.[23] The correlation between RAF *effort* and bombing *results*, based upon German documents and operational studies, or intelligence assessments compiled by RAF staff, appears somewhat sketchy.

All parties acknowledged that the limited capabilities of the British bombing squadrons precluded any hope of widespread or significant material results. Trenchard admitted as much in the final dispatch, citing the small size of his forces and "the limitations imported on long-range bombing by the weather" as his two major constraints.[24]

Privately, he had already concluded that IF's efforts were less than had been hoped for: "I am certain the damage done both to buildings and personnel is very small compared to any other form of war and the energy expended."[25] He also complained about IF's staff size.

> The more I think of it the more I think that if the Independent Force has glamour about it everybody thinks it is responsible for doing greater deeds than it has done, but at present the total result is an enormous increase of staff, personnel and work to carry it out.[26]

The findings of RAF and US Air Service bombing survey teams confirm this view.

Apart from isolated incidents that caused unexpectedly great damage (and received correspondingly greater coverage in AP 1225), the material results of Eighth Brigade and Independent Force air raids are unremarkable. The 17 May raid on Metz–Sablon, which caught a Kaiser honor guard in the open, and the 16 July raid on Thionville, which detonated an ammunition train, are notable exceptions.[27]

Site inspections by the RAF survey teams brought to light significant differences between even the moderate degree of damages expected and actual results. And Major Paul had pointed out the difficulties in assessing probable damage in daylight raids.

> The utmost a pilot or observer can do is to record where a bomb fell. If a large fire or explosion should result, this can be seen from the air, and is reported, but otherwise no estimate of the amount of damage is possible.

For night raids, Paul identified navigational imprecision as a contributing factor.

> How easy it is to mistake one locality for another in the dark, when operating over a large area, is proved by the number of cases which have come to light in which bombs were dropped on towns or railways miles away from the assigned objective, which escaped attack altogether. . . . It is manifestly impossible to attach much importance to reports unless it is reasonably certain that no mistake has been made in locating the objective. . . . Experience in the Independent Force would seem to indicate an invariable tendency to optimism both on the part of those reporting results from observation and of those estimating results from photographs.[28]

Major Paul reinforced his view that British estimates of damage caused by RAF bombs were overly optimistic in the "General Opinion of the Allied Bombs" section of the RAF field survey.

> In view of the above, and of what has previously been stated, under Railways, Blast Furnaces, Aerodromes and Industrial Centres, it cannot be said that our bombs have proved of more than moderate efficiency.
>
> Speaking generally, shooting has been moderate on the part of all.[29]

The US Air Service survey reached similar conclusions, including a tabular summary of the costs of direct and indirect material damage to each location in their final report. Their figures are almost identical to those in the RAF survey.[30]

In monetary terms, a recent appraisal estimates that the results of Allied bombing during 1918 inflicted damages to the value of less than one-tenth of 1 percent of German war expenditures.[31] AP 1225, the Air Ministry report of January 1920, presents detailed tables to verify that the Roechling works at Völklingen suffered a production shortfall of 15,803 tons of steel in 1918, owing mainly to air raid alarms. While considerable, this deficit represented less than 5 percent of the plant's 1913 production (over 340,000 tons)—a perspective the Air Ministry does not provide.[32] Material effects did not, however, constitute the main objective for the GOC IF.

> By attacking as many centres as could be reached, the moral effect was first of all very much greater, as no town felt safe, and it necessitated continued and thorough defensive measures on the part of the enemy to protect the many different localities over which my Force was operating.
>
> At present the moral effect of bombing stands undoubtedly to the material in proportion of 20 to 1, and therefore it was necessary to create the greatest moral effect possible.[33]

This emphasis on moral effect needs to be examined in detail. Upon becoming GOC IF in June 1918, Trenchard took pains to justify moral effect as a primary objective in his proposed concept of operations. This notion was not peculiar to Trenchard, however; it seems to have enjoyed considerable support within the Air Ministry from mid-1918 to the Armistice.

The importance of moral effect figures prominently in the two wartime editions of AP 1225. In August 1918, the introduction to the first edition noted that the German populace was unsettled and terrified.

> Letters captured on German prisoners show how unsettled and terrified is the German populace, and presumably the receipt of such letters has a demoralizing effect on the fighting value of the recipients.
>
> Though information as to results is increasingly hard to obtain, it is certain that the moral [sic] of the German population becomes lower as the range and power of our bombing squadrons increase.
>
> The accumulation of evidence from all quarters of Germany provide indisputable proof of the efficacy of air raids during the period under review.[34]

The second edition noted a similar "moral" effect in October 1918.

> In the period August–October, evidence has accumulated as to the immense moral effect of our air raids into Germany. To this a large number of letters found on captured prisoners bears witness. . . . Further, it should be remembered that the necessity of providing large numbers of anti-aircraft guns, searchlights, balloons, and home defence squadrons must prove a serious drain on Germany's resources.

> Though material damage is as yet slight when compared with moral effect, it is certain that the destruction of factories, and, consequently, loss of production will precede material damage.[35]

Boyle himself, in a four-page summary prepared after the Armistice but before publication of the third edition of AP 1225, contended that the British claims of damage were supported by photographs.

> In addition to captured letters, German press reports, and information from other reliable sources, a large number of photographs taken during and after raids show how effective the bomb dropping had been and give ample evidence of the damage done during both day and night raids.

> Apart from the material damage caused, the moral effect on munition workers, railway employees, and on the civilian population generally, has been enormous, an effect which, judging by captured letters, has made itself felt at the front.

> The loss of production caused by sleepless nights, terror of daylight raids, false air raid warnings, etc., is known to have been very great.[36]

From these Air Ministry analyses, the ascendancy of moral effect as the primary goal of the British bombing campaign becomes unmistakably evident.

Because of the lack of friendly intelligence available during wartime, the Air Ministry had to rely on enemy indicators to support their assertions. Boyle's staff habitually exploited agents' reports and captured letters as indices of enemy morale without ever questioning the reliability of such criteria. Extracts from civilian letters were assumed to represent accurately the extent to which air raids depressed morale within Germany. S. F. Wise, the RCAF official historian, noted the lack of follow-up.

> There seems to have been no follow-up. Since wartime intelligence is of necessity built up from such shreds of evidence, it is understandable that some weight—perhaps undue weight—was given

to this tiny sampling by those that were most concerned with the bombing offensive.[37]

After the Armistice, RAF survey teams failed to conclusively substantiate the depth of depression that had been ascribed to the German populace. Nevertheless, the third edition of AP 1225 subsequently reprinted, without further amplification or qualification, the assertions of its two wartime predecessors concerning the moral effects of bombing.

The Air Ministry group compiling the classified final report had little choice, however, since the IF survey teams confined their sources of evidence to materials from official German files.[38] The British teams viewed the opinions of German plant managers and civil officials with considerable skepticism. In nearly all cases, the Germans contended that air raids had had only minor impact upon civilian morale and productivity.[39]

A similar RAF survey team investigating the effects of bombing in the operational area of No. 5 Group, RAF, along the Belgian coast, adopted the same cautious approach. In its 12 March 1919 report to the Air Ministry, this group explicitly excluded the sorts of material upon which the January 1920 edition of AP 1225 was to rely so heavily: "Unverified reports of Agents during the war have not been accepted as evidence."[40]

The German citizenry in fact fretted about bombing effects more in terms of their individual pocketbooks than in terms of collective morale. In September 1918, an Air Ministry intelligence summary featured an extract from a recent issue of *Trierische Landeezeitung.*

> We, a city which has been the specially selected target of hostile aircraft, finally demand a definite statement that there does exist a legal claim to compensation for damage.

> Either: let it be seen that the criminal barbarity of these aerial attacks on the defenseless civil population ceases once and for all; Or: let the Government state that we can recover for all damage: damage done to property, and (which is the main thing) damage to life and limb.[41]

This aggrieved tone echoes that of any citizen confronting bureaucratic inefficiency. A month later, the intelligence summary printed a similar extract from a Frankfurt newspaper.[42]

These and other documents contradict the Air Ministry assertion that in Germany "the public generally remained calm, but as soon as casualties were caused, panic became general."[43] Demands for financial compensation impelled most of the outbursts from German civilians; IF ordnance did not seriously erode their will to resist. What the Air Ministry characterized as panic was mainly a demand for prompt payment of insurance claims.

Overall, the moral effect of Independent Force bombs was far less than the Air Ministry had assumed. The German experience paralleled that of British civilians facing Zeppelins and Gothas earlier in the war.

> As in Britain, there was considerable early unease among industrial workers because of bombing, but . . . ultimately most workers were able to build up mental defences against it.[44]

Trenchard made a similar linkage in his private diary.

> The moral effect is great—very great—but it gets less as the little material effect is seen. The chief moral effect is apparently to give the newspapers copy to say how wonderful we are, though it really does not affect the enemy as much as it affects our own people.[45]

In other words, raiding Germany raised British home-front morale proportionately more than it lowered the spirits of the enemy's civil population.

The chief practitioner of strategic bombing during 1918 thus concluded that moral effect, while useful, could not be logically touted as a decisive, or even significant, military result of his bombing campaign. When he was chief of the Air Staff once again between 1919 and 1929, Trenchard either forgot or chose to ignore this fundamental point.

The conclusions reached by the US Air Service bombing survey merit consideration. The evaluations provide a strong counterpoint to the Air Ministry's assessment.

> The greatest criticism to be brought against aerial bombardment (British-America did not have enough bombing aviation to warrant its employment other than without ground forces—France did not approve of this use of its bombing aviation) as carried out in the war of 1914–1918 is the lack of a predetermined program carefully calculated to destroy by successive raids those industries most vital in maintaining Germany's fighting forces. The evidence of this is seen in the wide area over which the bombing took place as well as the failure

of crippling, beyond a limited extent, any one factory or industry. (It might be well to add that in many conversations with officers of the British Independent Air Force there was a growing feeling of dissatisfaction against their bombing policy. It was the statement of these officers that they did not believe they were getting the best results possible and that while the wish and later the decision to "bomb something up there" might have appealed to one's sporting blood, it did not work with greatest efficiency against the German fighting machine. It was on the return of an American officer from a three day visit with the British that it was learned of the disgust held by a British bombing expert—who had achieved very good results in bombing submarines—of the inaccuracy of bombing by the British Independent Air Force and the unintelligent choice of targets.)

This investigation has decidedly shown that the enemy's morale was not sufficiently affected to handicap the enemy's fighting forces in the field. The policy as followed by the British and French in the present war of bombing a target once or twice and then skipping to another target is erroneous.

Bombing for moral effect alone such as took place over Cologne, Frankfurt, Bonn, and Wiesbaden, and which was probably the excuse for the wide spread of bombs over a town rather than their concentration on a factory, is not a productive means of bombing. The effect is legitimate and just as considerable when attained indirectly through the bombing of a factory.[46]

This independent assessment corroborates many of the criticisms presented earlier of organizational confusion and operational shortcomings in Eighth Brigade and Independent Force employment during 1918.

Against this general summary, a closer examination of the specific effects of the British long-range bombing campaign can proceed. This analysis will focus primarily upon the reliability of the postwar third edition of AP 1225, the classified final bombing report published by the Air Ministry in January 1920.

The Air Ministry's final report of January 1920 provides detailed information on 33 objectives raided by the British long-range force in 1918. The report includes brief extracts from British and German communiqués, aircrew reports, German bomb-plot plans, and photographs taken during and after the operation. Targets of considerable interest during hostilities, such as Cologne and the BASF/Oppau chemical and munitions complex at "Mannheim" (actually in Ludwigshafen), received proportionate coverage in AP 1225.[47] Information about raids on industrial centers made up the bulk of the Air Ministry's postwar publication.

On balance, the Air Ministry publication is sadly wanting. Serious discrepancies exist between the Air Ministry document and other records, primarily the RAF and US Air Service surveys and wartime returns from the field.

AP 1225 coverage of industrial centers, the largest target category, exemplifies these many factual inaccuracies. These objectives fall into one of two groups, determined by whether Allied postwar survey teams were able to visit the location in question.

The Air Ministry final report summarizes information on several industrial centers bombed by Eighth Brigade and Independent Force in 1918. RAF and US Air Service intelligence teams had visited nine centers immediately after the Armistice, and had independently assessed raid effects at those locations.

Bonn	Duren	Main (Mayence)
Coblenz	Kaiserslautern	Pirmasens
Cologne	Landau	Wiesbaden

AP 1225 includes a brief narrative on each target, based on wartime aircrew claims or German sources such as agents' reports, captured letters or news releases; aerial photographs; and bomb-plot plans derived from German records unearthed by the RAF survey teams.

The AP 1225 coverage of Cologne is typical for industrial objectives. Cologne, the report says, was raided on three occasions in 1918. It cites reports, aerial photographs, and bomb-plot plans in detailing these attacks. For the first raid (24/25 March), AP 1225 reprints a British wartime bulletin noting that "Half a ton of bombs were dropped by us on the railway station at Cologne, where a fire was started."[48] According to the Germans, however, no bomb damage occurred anywhere in the city on 24/25 March 1918.[49] Eighth Brigade wartime records for this mission related that the Handley Page crewmen encountered "mist and drifting fog banks" and twice lost their way.[50] The US Air Service survey team found that the Handley Page bombs fell on a pile of lumber in Deutz, across the Rhine from Cologne.[51]

Two raids on Kaiserslautern during October 1918 illustrate the same phenomenon: Local German authorities recorded no damage to targets that RAF crews claimed to have bombed. On 5 October, returning aircrews reported unobserved results; later in the month, they claimed significant results at their designated target. On the first raid, a formation of No. 110 Squadron DH9As, diverted from Cologne, bombed Kaiserslautern but could not observe the results. The squadron lost four machines to enemy action.[52]

The German bomb-plot plan of Kaiserslautern shows no bombs within its map coverage, which extends approximately two kilometers beyond the built-up area.[53] The US Air Service survey likewise lists no raids on Kaiserslautern between 25 September and 21 October 1918.[54]

Less than three weeks later, on the night of 23/24 October, No. 215 Squadron aircrews claimed to have dropped 3,748 pounds of bombs on Kaiserslautern. They claimed two direct hits on railway bridges.[55] Again, neither the RAF survey nor the US Air Service survey reveals any bomb damage.[56]

The Air Ministry report is also afflicted with a second type of discrepancy, revealed in its coverage of Cologne: Damage acknowledged by the Germans was not covered. On 16/17 September 1918, the night in which the IF lost an unprecedented number of Handley Pages, some of the missing aircraft had been ordered to raid Cologne.[57] The Air Ministry final report does not allude to this date, even though the German bomb-plot plan in the RAF survey clearly shows that one bomb or cluster of bombs hit the western outskirts of the city.[58] The Air Ministry AI1 Branch selectively transcribed the bomb-plot data onto another municipal map of Cologne, altering both scale and coverage in the process.[59]

This questionable technique recurs throughout AP 1225. In every one of 20 instances, despite the availability of German bomb-plot plans, the Air Ministry composed and substituted its own maps. In some instances, the report did not even provide revised versions.[60]

Other captured materials, however, are photographically reproduced from the RAF survey and included in AP 1225; for example, German photographs of bomb damage and IF diagrams of enemy air defenses. Clearly, the Air Ministry had the technical means to treat captured bomb-plot plans in a similar manner.

The scale and coverage of the revised maps in AP 1225 are oriented to exclude bombs that fell inaccurately. Blinds (unexploded ordnance) are neither indicated on these maps nor alluded to in the report, even though the Germans frequently referred to them and the RAF survey discussed them in detail.[61] For the Wiesbaden entry, the German bomb-plot plan is not reprinted, even in revised form; however, captured photographs dramatically portraying the effects of a 1,650-pound bomb are included.[62]

AP 1225 coverage of raid results at Pirmasens typifies the third category of discrepancy in the Air Ministry report. Here, the final report includes the results of two raids in which Pirmasens was neither the assigned objective nor the target that IF aircrews claimed to have bombed. On 21/22 August 1918, No. 216 Squadron dispatched two Handley Pages to raid the railways at Treves.[63] Though the aircrews reported bombing Treves from 7,000 feet on a clear night, German records in the RAF and US Air Service surveys show no damage in the vicinity of the city.[64] At Pirmasens, however, a cluster of six bombs fell on the southwest edge of town.[65] AP 1225 included these raid results in its revised bomb-plot plan.

On 30/31 October, No. 100 Squadron sent a Handley Page to raid the Burbach Works at Saarbrücken; No. 115 also launched a single machine, this one to bomb Baden.[66] Both aircrews reported unobserved results, owing to "thick mist and fog."[67] German bomb-plot plans indicate that neither the Burbach steel works nor the adjacent town of Saarbrücken suffered any damage on this night.[68] Since neither survey team visited Baden, possible results there remain unknown. Six bombs fell into the northeast part of Pirmasens, killing six people and causing 175,000 Marks damage.[69] The Air Ministry final report included this raid in its bomb-plot plan of Pirmasens.

On 5 October, a single machine of No. 110 Squadron claimed to have bombed Pirmasens as a target of opportunity, though with unobserved results.[70] The German bomb-plot plan and other records indicate that no bombs fell within three kilometers of the town that day.[71] The Air Ministry final report does not depict or summarize any aspect of this single-ship raid.[72]

The 20 February 1918 operation by No. 55 Squadron, in which Pirmasens was indeed the assigned target, is briefly summarized in the Air Ministry final report.[73] This summary virtually duplicates the description of the material and moral effects visited upon Pirmasens in the October 1918 edition of AP 1225.[74] In fact, this mission represents the only raid on Pirmasens for which AP 1225 included a narrative extract to supplement bomb-plot plan information.

In summary, the AP 1225 entries that evaluate raid results at these nine industrial centers exhibit serious deficiencies. The extent to which the Air Ministry classified report of January 1920 can be misleading is revealed in the failure of staff officers in the Air Intelligence Directorate to perform even the most rudimentary cross-checks with other pertinent data.

Although RAF bombing survey teams were unable to visit the following 11 industrial centers in Germany, the Air Ministry report covers them in some detail.

Darmstadt	Lahr	Stuttgart
Frankfurt	Oberndorf	Worms
Freiburg	Offenburg	Zweibrücken
Karlsruhe	Rottweil	

At eight of these localities (all but Darmstadt, Frankfurt, and Karlsruhe), the Air Ministry final report cautions that "this town was not visited by the Commission and the only information available is that received during hostilities."[75]

No British survey records exist to challenge or verify the wartime claims reprinted in the Air Ministry assessment. However, US survey teams were able to evaluate damage at Worms and Zweibrücken. The German materials they unearthed undercut Air Ministry conclusions at several points.

The Air Ministry's final report indicated only a single raid at Worms, that of 29/30 October 1918.[76] However, the Germans reported bomb damage on 15/16 August and 28/29 October.[77] In the first incident, six machines from No. 216 Squadron had been assigned objectives at Mannheim and Saarbrücken; according to the Germans, neither location sustained damage that night.[78] At Worms, the US Air Service investigators learned that two bombs "fell in the Rhine."[79]

On 28/29 October, two Handley Pages, each carrying a 1,650-pound bomb, claimed to have bombed Mannheim and Treves.[80] Neither city was hit on that date, according to German records; however, one bomb fell on a rail junction at Worms.[81]

On two of the three dates for which the Air Ministry report reprinted wartime damage claims at Zweibrücken, German records listed no damage anywhere in the town.[82] Further, on 19 February, when 11 DH4s of No. 55 Squadron claimed to have bombed Treves after being diverted by weather from Mannheim, eight bombs dropped on the hills outside Zweibrücken.[83]

These discrepancies, which can be discovered only by recourse to sources other than British records, are consistent with the type and magnitude of contradictions revealed in studies of targets for which postwar documentation is available. It seems safe to conclude that similar errors of fact exist in the final report's coverage of German industrial centers that were never visited by either survey group. The motives for including such uncorroborated analyses in the official evaluation are open to question, particularly in light of the final report's equivocal entries for Darmstadt, Frankfurt, and Karlsruhe.

As all three of these cities lay east of the Rhine and thus beyond the zone of Allied occupation, they were not inspected by the bombing surveys. The Americans noted that it was "impossible to go directly to Karlsruhe" and that "Frankfurt A.M. at the time investigated was not occupied by Allied troops."[84] AP 1225 does not mention the fact, though it had for other industrial targets, that confirmation was impossible to obtain. Its coverage, which includes numerous aerial photographs of these cities, conveys the impression that its evaluations can be taken as authoritative.

Further, for Frankfurt and Karlsruhe, the Air Ministry report not only omits the "not visited" disclaimer but also includes bomb-plot plans to accompany the narratives and aerial photographs.[85] These plans may have been imaginatively compiled from raid photographs and wartime claims; the diagram for Frankfurt depicts suspiciously tidy clusters of ordnance that contrast markedly with actual patterns of dispersion on authentic German bomb-plot plans.[86]

Air Ministry coverage of these 11 industrial targets relies entirely upon reprinted wartime claims. Such official conclusions are at best dubious, as is clear when one compares their versions of Worms and Zweibrücken with American survey findings.

Further, the slanted coverage of Darmstadt, Frankfurt, and Karlsruhe would lead one to believe that RAF survey parties did in fact obtain information that confirmed the Air Ministry final report. The origins and reliability of the official bomb-plot plans for the latter two targets are especially questionable, however, and one doubts that Eighth Brigade and Independent Force damage claims against the remaining targets in this unsurveyed group can be any more accurate.

In effect, the Air Intelligence Directorate's final report includes entries for more industrial targets (eleven) for which postwar information was unavailable than for locations (nine) actually visited by RAF survey teams after the Armistice. And data on these nine targets were not cross-checked or subjected to critical scrutiny, even though the materials were readily at hand. These 20 urban targets comprised nearly two-thirds of the total number of objectives covered individually in the Air Ministry classified report.

For other categories of bombing targets, the detailed explication of the discrepancies revealed in the Air Ministry accounts of industrial objectives is representative; that is, yielding appreciably neither more nor less errors than seem to exist elsewhere in official coverage.

Several points are nonetheless worth noting. At the huge BASF/Oppau chemical and munitions complex at Ludwigshafen, for example, the 10 raids enumerated in the Air Ministry final report are outnumbered by 11 occasions in which the same objective was claimed to have been hit; German plant managers recorded no bomb damage. The circumstances of the Burbach blast furnaces at Saarbrücken further illustrate this selective coverage. AP 1225 discusses six raids on Burbach while depicting only four on the accompanying bombplot plan—and other records indicate that on 12 occasions for which Eighth Brigade and IF aircrews claimed hits, the Germans recorded absolutely no casualties or damage to the works.[87] The Thionville rail yards and stations are listed as having been hit by British bombs on 21 occasions in the Air Ministry's final report, but the report does not mention a further 15 raids for which aircrews claimed hits when no damage was caused.[88]

The singular lack of results from the large bombs dropped by IF Handley Pages in the last weeks of hostilities is also illuminating, as is the final report's coverage of those attacks. On three nights in October, night squadrons dropped a total of eleven 1,650-pound bombs on enemy targets. At Kaiserslautern on 21/22 October and at Wiesbaden on 23/24 October, one bomb on each city caused damage that was photographed by local authorities. These photographs were prominently displayed in the Air Ministry's final report.[89] The remaining nine large bombs apparently caused no significant damage, as German records do not refer to any effects that would be expected from ordnance of this size. In fact, at five targets for which aircrews reported hits and damage, the Germans reported no damage at all. Major Paul himself admitted that no evidence of these hits could be found.

No trace of 1650 lbs. (bombs) having fallen on or near METZ–SABLONS, SAARBRUCKEN, or TREVES Stations can be traced. Judging from the colossal effects caused by these bombs at KAISERSLAUTERN and WIESBADEN, no difficulty would have been experienced in tracing those bombs had they fallen on the three objectives mentioned above.[90]

These incidents dramatically highlight the gap between actual and claimed bombing effects.

The January 1920 final bombing report lists a total of 228 missions against enemy targets it catalogs; Air Ministry coverage of the Metz–Sablon railway triangle alone accounts for 45 raids.[91]

Against this selective coverage, the scope of discrepancies becomes significant. On 66 occasions in which British aircrews claimed to have hit particular locations in 1918, German records indicate that no damage was sustained. On 23 dates when particular locations were assigned or claimed bombing targets, and German records substantiate damage, the final report does not include raid results. Finally, on 38 occasions when particular locations were neither assigned nor claimed as bombing targets but were in fact damaged, the final report listed the date and took credit for the results. These 127 discrepancies, which come to light only through comparison of operational returns and Allied survey materials, severely undercut acceptance of the Air Ministry final report on January 1920 as an authoritative evaluation of the effects of British strategic bombing.

Despite the availability of friendly and enemy materials after the Armistice on which to base a comprehensive analysis, the third edition of the official bombing report does not depart from the uncritical tones of its two wartime predecessors. It distorts the subject considerably, and must be approached from that perspective, rather than an objective assessment. It does little more than encapsulate and institutionalize the optimistic view of bombing that had been promoted during hostilities. Bureaucratic momentum and public confidence were strengthened, but nothing was learned.

Despite AP 1225's shortcomings, the Air Ministry continued to publicize its perspective after the Armistice. A Parliamentary paper, "Synopsis of British Air Effort during the War," reflects the official verdict.

On the 1st April, 1918, when the Royal Air Force came into being, the Air Ministry immediately recognized the great possibilities of a policy of strategic interception, as well as the opportunities for striking at the moral [sic] of the German nation. Every effort was made to build up and maintain in the field a powerful striking force to execute a series of systematic raids on the key munition and chemical factories of Germany. Accordingly, on the 8th June, 1918, the Independent Force, Royal Air Force, was constituted, and the 3 squadrons of the original 8th Brigade, R.F.C., were gradually increased to 10.

The effect, both morally and materially, of the raids on German territory carried out during the summer of 1918 can hardly be over-estimated. The utterances of the German press and public bear eloquent testimony to the results of the new policy, and it is known that the German High Command were compelled to recall at least 20 fighting squadrons from the Western Front, and to immobilize a large number of group troups [sic] to man anti-aircraft batteries and an elaborate system of searchlights. In fact, the policy was so successful that when the Armistice was signed on the 11th November, 1918, it was intended to increase the Independent Force to a total of 48 squadrons by the end of May 1919.[92]

The seemingly unlimited potential of airpower was officially beyond reproach. Trenchard himself secured a year's grace from Admiral Beatty and Field Marshal Sir Henry Wilson in which to lay the institutional foundations of his new service.[93]

The consequences of this self-delusion are significant. Had the Air Ministry and the postwar Royal Air Force, once again under Trenchard as chief of Air Staff, studied their own records, they could have determined the constraints that weather, navigational precision, sighting accuracy, and aircrew proficiency impose upon long-range bombardment. These limitations inhere quite apart from any complications induced by enemy countermeasures.

Though this introspection would have been painful, such a reappraisal presumably would have spurred efforts to minimize operational limitations through research, doctrine, and training. Whatever the policy, "execution had to conform to what was operationally possible . . . which in turn depended on advances in tactics and technology."[94] More importantly, RAF policies would have more realistically reflected its actual capabilities during the interwar years. Instead, the Royal Air Force claimed to be capable of the impossible. Its planners neglected basic programs; for example, training in long-range navigation and bombing accuracy.

RAF survival was at risk after the Armistice, however, partly as a result of cuts in military funding and partly to forestall Admiralty and War Office efforts to return aviation to subordinate, "cooperative" roles. The Royal Air Force therefore had to emphasize the importance of its unique role.

Strategic bombing, after all, is the heart of air power. It is strategic bombing which distinguishes air power from military and naval power by giving it a characteristic far beyond what it would otherwise have been, a mere adjunct of armies and navies.[95]

The Air Staff accordingly stressed that control of the air could be significant, even decisive, in future conflicts; it repeatedly

argued that a fundamental reevaluation of the relative contributions of each fighting service was necessary.

> Should an air attack coincide with an invasion, it will be met by the
> close defensive air forces both regular and territorial.

> This will not entail the provision of air forces on a stronger scale than
> is normally required to resist air attack: as in order to counter air
> attacks of the enemy it will be necessary to continuously attack his air
> bases. The temporary diversion of this long range offensive to meet the
> rare occasions when invasion or a raid is attempted will have little
> effect on the attainment of general aerial supremacy. The power of the
> Air Force in this respect is sufficiently great to justify its use as the
> chief weapon of defence and the transfer of the responsibility to the Air
> Ministry.[96]

The Royal Air Force hamstrung its own development and
staked its institutional existence during the lean years on the
assertion that bombers could play a significant, if not decisive,
role in any future general conflict. Home defense gradually
became equated to this untested ability.

> The material effect of an air raid may be great; its moral effect is
> undoubted. Continuous air raids, even in the form of a single hostile
> aeroplane overhead, have a great and cumulative effect on the
> national morale. Work over large areas is stopped or seriously
> impeded by day and night, trains are brought to a standstill, and a
> large proportion of the population takes refuge below ground. In short,
> in view of the effects which can be produced by an aerial attack, it is
> almost inconceivable that a nation in a position to undertake the same
> should prefer the difficulties and risks attendant upon a landing raid:
> the latter appears therefore to be a form of attack definitely less
> probable now than in 1914. It seems therefore that if any single
> control is to be adopted it should logically be vested in an Air
> Commander responsible to the Air Ministry.[97]

The Salisbury Committee (of the Committee for Imperial Defence) met in 1923 to consider in detail the exact relations
between the three fighting services. One of its primary tasks
was to determine "the standard to be aimed at for defining the
strength of the Air Force for purposes of Home and Imperial
Defence."[98] Trenchard testified before the Balfour Subcommittee, a body of the Salisbury Committee, in May and June. He
again emphasized the concept that defensive forces should
consist largely of long-range bombers.

261

> It is on the destruction of enemy industries and, above all, on the lowering of the morale of enemy nations caused by offensive bombing, that ultimate victory rests.[99]

To buttress his case, Trenchard asked the subcommittee to ponder the political consequences for Britain if enemy bombers attacked in a future war.

> In a democratic country like ours, power rests ultimately with the people, and war cannot be continued unless the bulk of the people will support it. If the people are subjected to sufficient bombing they will compel the Government to sue for peace.

> As the Air Staff have previously pointed out, not the least part of the menace presented by overwhelming air attack, is the possibility that forces of disorder may be loosed upon the country with consequences which would be difficult to foretell and certainly unpleasant to contemplate.[100]

In August 1923, the Balfour Subcommittee recommended establishing the Royal Air Force as an independent service.[101] The Chief of the Air Staff was to be placed on an equal footing with his colleagues of the Army and Navy by the creation of the Chiefs of Staff Committee.[102] These recommendations were later incorporated, without significant alteration, into the final report of the Salisbury Committee.

Classified Air Staff Memoranda (ASM) 11 and 11A soon appeared (August 1923 and March 1924) to promulgate the official philosophy concerning "Air Strategy and Home Defence," throughout the RAF. ASM 11 asserted that the main objective for direct attack by the RAF was "the true objective of all war—the moral [sic] of the enemy nation."[103] ASM 11A, intended "as a Supplement to No.11 with the objects of further explaining the Air Staff views," analyzed the objective and methods by which the strategic air offensive would be conducted.

> The forces employed . . . can be used in two ways. They can either bomb military objectives in populated areas from the beginning of the war, with the object of obtaining a decision by the moral effect which such attacks will produce, and by the serious dislocation of the normal life of the country; or, alternatively, they can be used in the first instance to attack enemy aerodromes with a view to gaining some measure of "air superiority" and, when this has been gained, can be changed over to the direct attack on the nation.

The latter alternative is the method which the lessons of military history seem to recommend, but the Air Staff are convinced that the former is the correct one.[104]

The Air Staff acknowledged civilian demands for protection, but stressed the need for bombers.

It may be stated as a principle that the bombing squadrons should be numerous as possible and the fighters as few as popular opinion and the necessity of defending vital objectives will permit.[105]

Thus was civilian morale under aerial bombardment officially established as the crucial objective of aerial warfare, an assertion that persisted well into the Second World War.[106] Writing in 1931, Squadron Leader John C. Slessor, summarized the potential of airpower.

It has been borne in on us during the war that our own historical security was in some measure a thing of the past, and in fact the establishment of the R.A.F. as a single Service in 1918 was largely the result of insistent demands by organized public opinion for adequate protection against air attacks on centres of population and industry.[107]

The Air Staff took no active steps in the interwar years to rectify this unsupported but almost universal misconception.

This government position represented merely a refinement of popular assumptions dating from the Great War about the efficacy and terrors of strategic bombing, assumptions engendered and reinforced by official reports, classified analyses, and public bulletins in the years before the Second World War.[108] Marshal of the Royal Air Force Sir John Slessor admitted in 1954 that the RAF had underestimated the tools required for airpower to fulfill its promise.

It is also quite true that, anyway until about the end of 1938, we very much over-estimated what our own bombers of the day would be able to do. We enormously underrated the number of bombs required to get a hit, the numbers and weight of bombs required to do fatal damage when we did get hits, the toughness and resilience of civilian moral [sic] under bombing, our ability to bomb unescorted by day—with no self-sealing tanks—the scientific and technical aids required, and all that sort of thing. . . . Where we went wrong in those pre-war years was not in our estimate of what air power could do when it had the tools, but in our estimate of the tools required to do the job.[109]

Such miscalculations meant that Royal Air Force flyers, especially those of Bomber Command, confronted virtually the identical set of practical difficulties, equipment shortcomings, and operational limitations in the first three years of World War II that their predecessors had encountered in the Great War—and with corresponding losses.

Notes

1. George K. Williams, "'The Shank of the Drill': Americans and Strategical Aviation in the Great War," *Journal of Strategic Studies* 19, no. 3 (London: Frank Cass Journals, September 1996): 381–431.

2. Ibid., 386.

3. Ibid.

4. Ibid., 387.

5. Ibid., 388.

6. Ibid., 418.

7. Ibid.

8. Ibid., 420–21.

9. Ibid., 423–24.

10. War diary of Eighth Brigade, entry for 7 December 1918, Newall Papers, B392.

11. Subjects of RAF bombing survey volumes and their PRO classifications are: AIR 1/1998/204/273/262, Railways (B395); 263, Aerodromes (B398); 264, Industrial Centers (B399); 266, Bombs and Conclusions (B401); AIR 1/1999/204/273/268, Chemicals/Munitions (B397); 296, Blast Furnaces (B396). RAF Hendon classifications follow subjects. They are used hereafter.

12. US Air Service bombing survey is reprinted in Maurer Maurer, ed., *The U.S. Air Services in World War I*, vol. 4, *Postwar Review* (Maxwell Air Force Base [AFB], Ala.: Air Force Historical Research Agency [AFHRA], 1979), 364–65. Hereafter, "US Bombing Survey."

13. Maurer Maurer, ed., *The U.S. Air Service in World War I*, vol. 1, *The Final Report and a Tactical History* (Maxwell AFB, Ala.: AFHRA, 1978), 1–14, summarizes the US Air Service history.

14. US Bombing Survey, 561.

15. PRO, AIR 1/2104/207/36, Results of Air Raids on Germany Carried Out by the Eighth Brigade and the Independent Force, RAF, January 1st–November 11th, 1918, AP 1225, 3d ed., DAI No. 5, Air Ministry, January 1920. Hereafter, "AP 1225, 3d ed."

16. PRO, AIR 1/460/15/312/99, DFO to CAS, 28 June 1918.

17. PRO, AIR 1/2104/107/36, AP 1225, 2d ed., DAI, Air Ministry, October 1918.

18. PRO, AIR 1/1998/204/273/262, letter no. FI 11a/a (inside front cover), HQ, RAF in the field to Air Ministry, 26 February 1919.

19. AIR 1/2087/207/8/37, Air Ministry List of Staff and Distribution of Duties, November 1918.

20. PRO, AIR 1/2087/207/8/37, Air Ministry Office Memorandum no. 105, 20 June 1919.

21. AP 1225, 3d ed.

22. Ibid., 1–4.

23. Ibid., fol. 65.

24. C. Gordon Burge, *The Annals of 100 Squadron* (London: Herbert Reiach, 1919), 156–57; and *Aeroplane*, 8 January 1919, 129.

25. MFC 76/1/32, Trenchard Papers, private diary entry for 18 August 1918.

26. Ibid., entry for 13 July 1918.

27. AP 1225, 3d ed., entries cited.

28. B395 (Railways), "Estimate of Material Results."

29. B401 (Bombs and Conclusions).

30. US Bombing Survey, 492–94.

31. S. F. Wise, *Canadian Airmen and the First World War:* vol. 1 *The Official History of the Royal Canadian Air Force* (Toronto: University of Toronto, 1980), 321.

32. AP 1225, 3d., 2; and Wise, 323.

33. Burge, 157; and *Aeroplane*, 8 January 1919, 129.

34. Reprinted in AP 1225, 3d ed., 1.

35. Ibid.

36. PRO, AIR 1/451/15/312/19, n.d.

37. Wise, 332.

38. B395 (Railways).

39. B396 (Blast Furnaces); B397 (Chemical/Munitions).

40. PRO, AIR 1/2115/207/56/1, Report of the Aircraft Bombing Committee Appointed by the Air Ministry to Inquire into the Effects of Bombing in Belgium and the Defensive Measures Taken by the Enemy Against It, 4.

41. Air Ministry, *Summary of Air Intelligence*, 6th series, no. 17 (London: Her Majesty's Stationery Office [HMSO], 20 September 1918).

42. Ibid., 7th series, no. 2, 1 October 1918.

43. AP 1225, 3d ed., 3.

44. Wise, 322.

45. MFC 76/1/32, Trenchard Papers, private diary entry for 18 August 1918.

46. US Bombing Survey, 501–2.

47. AP 1225, 3d ed., devotes 14 pages of text, maps, and photographs to Mannheim/Ludwigshafen and 6 pages to Cologne.

48. AP 1225, 7.

49. B399 (Industrial Centres), map of Cologne.

50. B392 (War Diary); PRO, AIR 1/2005/207/5/3, Approximate Results; and AIR 1/2266/209/70/26, Detailed Raid Reports, both at R.A.F. Hendon in B393 (Newall Papers) for dates cited. Hereafter, AR and DRR.

51. US Bombing Survey, 485.

52. B392 (War Diary); AR, date cited.

53. B399 (Industrial Centres), map of Kaiserslautern.

54. US Bombing Survey, 457.

55. B392 (War Diary); and AR, date cited.

56. B399 (Industrial Centers); and US Bombing Survey, 457.

57. B392 (War Diary).

58. B399 (Industrial Centers), map of Cologne.

59. Ibid. AP 1225, 3d ed., map of Cologne facing p. 8.

60. B396 (Blast Furnaces); AP 1225, 3d ed., 2–3.

61. B401 (Bombs and Conclusions).

62. AP 1225, 3d ed., p. 42 and facing page; B399 (Industrial Centers), map of Wiesbaden.

63. B392 (War Diary).

64. PRO, AIR 1/2085/207/5/1, IF Communiqué No. 3, HQ, IF, 24 August 1918; B399 (Industrial Centers); and US Bombing Survey, 418–32.

65. B401 (Bombs and Conclusions), map of Pirmasens.

66. B392 (War Diary).

67. IF Communiqué No. 13, HQ, IF, 2 November 1918.

68. B395 (Railways); B396 (Blast Furnaces); and US Bombing Survey, 438, 440.

69. B401 (Bombs and Conclusions); and US Bombing Survey, 456.

70. B392 (War Diary); and AR.

71. B401 (Bombs and Conclusions); and US Bombing Survey, 456.

72. AP 1225, 3d ed., p. 32 and facing map.

73. Ibid.

74. AP 1225, 2d ed.

75. AP 1225, 3d ed., locations cited.

76. Ibid., 42.

77. US Bombing Survey, 467.

78. B392 (War Diary); B397 (Chemical/Munitions); B395 (Railways); B396 (Blast Furnaces); B399 (Industrial Centers); and US Bombing Survey, 438–39.

79. US Bombing Survey, 467.

80. B392 (War Diary).

81. B395 (Railways); B397 (Chemical/Munitions); B399 (Industrial Centers); and US Bombing Survey, 467.

82. B392 (War Diary); and US Bombing Survey, 454–55.

83. Ibid.

84. US Bombing Survey, 460, 465.

85. AP 1225, 3d ed., maps facing p. 12, 16.

86. Ibid.

87. German records show that only five bombs dropped on the Burbach works during 1918 were "effective." The plant ran at half capacity (4 of 8 blast furnaces in operation) throughout hostilities. PRO, AIR

1/586/21/13/2240, Original German Reports on Raids in Germany, 1918–1919 (trans. Air Ministry AI1 [T], 24 April 1919).

88. Ibid.; at the Carlshuttle works, Thionville, "in the opinion of the officials of the Works, the results obtained, both material and moral, were not worth the expenditure of bombs."

89. AP 1225, 3d ed., photographs facing p. 15, 42.

90. B395 (Railways).

91. AP 1225, 3d ed.

92. *Parliamentary Papers, 1919*, xxxiii (589): Cmd. 100, "Synopsis of British Air Effort during the War," Air Ministry, April 1919.

93. Harford Montgomery Hyde, *British Air Policy Between the Wars, 1918–1939* (London: Heinemann, 1976), 65; and *Parliamentary Papers, 1919*, xxxiii (849): Cmd. 467, "Permanent Organization of the Royal Air Force," Air Ministry, 25 November 1919.

94. Sir James Butler, "Foreward" in A. Noble Frankland, *The Bombing Offensive Against Germany: Outlines and Perspectives* (London: Faber and Faber, 1965), 7.

95. Ibid., Frankland, "Introduction," 16.

96. PRO, AIR 9/69, "The Responsibilities of the Royal Air Force of the Future in the Defence of these Islands against Invasion," Air Staff, May 1921, folio 9.

97. Ibid.

98. *Parliamentary Papers 1924*, x (277): Cmd. 2029, "Report of the Sub-Committee of the Committee of Imperial Defence on National and Imperial Defence," January 1921.

99. PRO, AIR 8/67, "Elaboration of Air Staff Answers for CAS's Verbal Statement before the Committee," Air Staff, June 1923, tab 24.

100. Ibid., "The French Air Situation and its Effect on British Air Policy," 15 May 1923, tab 6.

101. *Parliamentary Papers, 1923*, xv (827): Cmd. 1938, "Recommendations of the National and Imperial Defence Committee as Approved by His Majesty's Government upon the Relations of the Army and the Air Force and the Coordination of the Defence Forces," CID, August 1923.

102. Ibid.

103. Air Staff Memorandum No. 11, "Air Strategy in Home Defence," August 1923.

104. Air Staff Memorandum No. 11A, March 1924.

105. Ibid.

106. Uri Bailer, *The Shadow of the Bomber: The Fear of Air Attack and British Politics, 1932–1939* (London: Royal Historical Society, 1980), assesses this mood for the years immediately preceding the Second World War. However, this attitude developed during 1917–1918, was entrenched by the Armistice and continued much in evidence during the twenties.

107. "The Development of the Royal Air Force," *Journal of the Royal United Services Institute (JRUSI)*, no. 502 (May 1931): 326.

108. For example, see PRO, AIR 5/165, "The Future of the Air Force in National and Imperial Defence," Air Staff, March 1921; *Parliamentary Papers, 1920*, vii (299); and Cmd. 1157, "Proceedings of the Air Conference, 1920," for Trenchard's comments on "Aspects of Service Aviation," October 1920.

109. Marshal of the Royal Air Force Sir John Slessor, "Air Power and the Future of War," *JRUSI* 99, no. 595 (August 1954): 345. Emphasis added.

APPENDIX

Operational Summary of Raids By British Long-Range Bombing Units (41st Wing, Eighth Brigade, Independent Forces, 17 October 1917 to 11 November 1918.

Compiled by
Steve Suddaby

DATE	DAY/NIGHT	SQN	TARGET LOCATION	TARGET DESCRIPTION	BOMBS DROPPED (LBS)	A/C LAUNCHED	A/C BOMBING	A/C MISSING
10/17/17	Day	55	Saarbrucken	Burbach Works-Blast Furn	1792	11	8	0
10/21/17	Day	55	Wadgassen & Bous	Factory & Railways	2464	11	11	1
10/24/17	Night	100	Saarbrucken, etc	Railway Jtn, Stn, Trains	3335	14	12	2
10/24/17	Night	216	Saarbrucken, etc	Burbach Works	9408	9	7	2
10/29/17	Night	100	Saarbrucken & others	Railways, Brdg, Trains	915	9	3	0
10/30/17	Day	55	Pirmasens	Boot Factory	2712	12	12	0
10/30/17	Night	100	Saar Valley	Fact, Furn, SteelWrks, Tm	3075	12	10	0
11/1/17	Day	55	Kaiserslautern	Munitions Factory	1362	12	6	0
12/5/17	Day	55	Saarbrucken & Zweibrucken	Factory, Town, Rail Station	2440	12	11	0
12/6/17	Day	55	Saarbrucken	Burbach Works	2406	12	11	0
12/11/17	Day	55	Pirmasens	Rail Junction	1594	12	7	0
12/24/17	Day	55	Mannheim	Lanz Co, Rail Jtn, BASF	2252	12	10	0
1/3/18	Night	100	Metz, Mazieres, Woippy	Furnaces & Railroads	1190	10	5	0
1/4/18	Night	100	5 Sites w/i 20 nm of Metz	Rail, Fact, Furnace	3020	9	8	0
1/5/18	Night	100	Conflans & Mars	Rail Jtn & Station	2260	9	6	0
1/5/18	Night	216	Courcelles	Rail Junction	1344	2	1	0
1/14/18	Day	55	Karlsruhe	Munition Works, Railways	2752	12	12	0
1/14/18	Night	100	Thionville	Steel Works, Rail Jtn	2195	8	6	0
1/16/18	Night	100	Orny	Rail Sidings & Searchlite	560	6	2	0
1/21/18	Night	100	Thionville, Bernsdorf, Falknbg	Factories & Rail Targets	3510	17	11	1
1/21/18	Night	216	Arnaville	Railway	1344	2	1	0
1/24/18	Night	100	Treves, Thionville, etc	Towns, Steel Works	2594	16	10	1
1/24/18	Night	216	Mannheim	BASF	2688	3	2	0
1/27/18	Day	55	Treves	Barracks & Station	1356	12	7	0
2/9/18	Night	100	Courcelles	Sidings & Station	962	6	3	1
2/12/18	Day	55	Offenburg	Barracks & Station	2838	12	12	0
2/16/18	Night	100	Conflans	Sidings & Station	1708	6	5	0
2/16/18	Night	216	Conflans	Rail (aborted raid)	0	1	0	0

271

DATE	DAY/ NIGHT	SQN	TARGET LOCATION	TARGET DESCRIPTION	BOMBS DROPPED (LBS)	A/C LAUNCHED	A/C BOMBING	A/C MISSING
2/17/18	Day	55	Mannheim	BASF (aborted raid)	0	12	0	0
2/17/18	Night	100	Conflans	Sidings & Station	2192	12	6	0
2/17/18	Night	216	Unknown	Unknown (aborted raid)	0	2	0	0
2/18/18	Day	55	Thionville & Treves	Rail Sidings, Gas Works	2176	10	9	0
2/18/18	Night	100	Treves & Thionville	Rail, Steel Wrks, Barracks	2856	10	10	1
2/18/18	Night	216	Unknown	Unknown (aborted raid)	0	3	0	0
2/19/18	Day	55	Treves	Barracks & Rail Stn	2486	12	11	1
2/19/18	Night	100	Saarbrucken	Unknown (aborted raid)	0	13	0	0
2/19/18	Night	216	Thionville	Rail Stn & Steel Works	2912	2	2	0
2/20/18	Day	55	Pirmasens	Rail Stn & Factories	1900	10	8	0
2/26/18	Night	100	Frescaty	Aerodrome	3144	11	9	0
2/26/18	Night	216	Treves	Rail Stn & Barracks	1344	2	1	0
3/6/18	Night	100	Frescaty	Aerodrome	395	6	1	0
3/9/18	Day	55	Mainz	Factories, Station, Bks	2532	12	11	0
3/10/18	Day	55	Stuttgart	Factories, Railways, Bks	2842	12	11	1
3/12/18	Day	55	Coblenz	Factories, Station, Bks	2450	11	9	0
3/13/18	Day	55	Freiburg	Munit Dump, Station, Bks	1984	9	8	3
3/16/18	Day	55	Zweibrucken	Railways & Barracks	1878	10	7	0
3/17/18	Day	55	Kaiserslauten	Factories, Stn, Sidings	2585	10	9	0
3/18/18	Day	55	Mannheim	BASF	2346	10	9	0
3/23/18	Night	100	Frescaty	Aerodrome	3088	16	11	0
3/23/18	Night	216	Conz	Sidings, Stn, Bridges	1120	2	1	0
3/24/18	Day	55	Ludwigshafen	BASF	3083	12	12	2
3/24/18	Night	100	Metz & Thionville	Metz-Luxembourg Railway	4773	19	14	0
3/24/18	Night	216	Cologne, Lux, Courcelles	Factory, Railway, Station	3584	4	3	0
3/27/18	Day	55	Metz	Rail Jtn & Sidings	2482	12	11	0
3/28/18	Day	55	Luxembourg	Railway Station	2706	12	12	0
4/5/18	Day	55	Luxembourg	Railways & Station	2464	11	11	1

DATE	DAY/NIGHT	SQN	TARGET LOCATION	TARGET DESCRIPTION	BOMBS DROPPED (LBS)	A/C LAUNCHED	A/C BOMBING	A/C MISSING
4/11/18	Day	55	Luxembourg	Railways & Station	2464	12	11	0
4/12/18	Day	55	Metz - Sablon	Railway Sidings & Station	2464	12	11	0
4/12/18	Night	100	Juniville	Railway Sidings & Station	1344	8	6	0
4/12/18	Night	216	Amagne-Lucquy, Juniville	Jtn, Sidings, Station	4032	3	3	0
4/19/18	Night	100	Juniville	Junction, Station	1568	10	6	0
4/19/18	Night	216	Juniville & Bethenville	Junction, Stn, Sidings	4704	4	3	0
4/20/18	Night	100	Chaulnes, Roye, Ham	Rail Stations & Junctions	2128	18	7	0
4/20/18	Night	216	Chaulnes	Rail Station & Sidings	3136	3	2	0
4/21/18	Night	100	Amagne-Lucquy, Juniville	Rail Station & Sidings	2688	9	9	0
5/2/18	Day	55	Thionville	Railways & Station	2476	12	11	0
5/2/18	Night	100	Amag-Luc, Juni, Warnevil	Railways & Station	2016	18	9	0
5/3/18	Day	55	Thionville	Carlshutte Wrks, Rail, Brdg	2688	12	12	0
5/3/18	Night	100	Juniville, Asfeld, Amag	Rail Lines & Sidings	2016	18	9	0
5/15/18	Day	55	Thionville	Junction & Rlwy Triangle	2688	12	12	0
5/16/18	Day	55	Saarbrucken	Rail Station & Sidings	2688	12	12	1
5/17/18	Day	55	Metz	Rail Station & Sidings	2688	12	12	0
5/17/18	Night	100	Metz, Metz-Sablon, Thionvil	Rail Stations & Works	2240	13	10	1
5/17/18	Night	216	Thionville	Rail Station	1344	2	1	0
5/18/18	Day	55	Cologne	Rail Station & Sidings	1392	6	6	0
5/20/18	Day	55	Landau	Rail Station & Barracks	2258	12	10	0
5/20/18	Night	100	Thionville, Metz-Sablon	Rail Stations	2464	14	11	0
5/20/18	Night	216	Thionville, M-S, Coblenz	Rail Stations & Barracks	7392	6	6	0
5/21/18	Day	55	Charleroi, Namur, M-S	Railways	2464	12	11	1
5/21/18	Day	99	Metz-Sablon	Rail Station & Sidings	1344	6	6	0
5/21/18	Night	100	Saarbrucken, Thionville	Rail Station & Sidings	3248	15	15	0
5/21/18	Night	216	Thionville, Karthaus	Rail Stations & Chemical	9084	7	7	1
5/22/18	Day	55	Kinkempolis	Rail Station	2464	12	11	0
5/22/18	Day	99	Metz-Sablon	Railway Triangle	1344	6	6	0

DATE	DAY/NIGHT	SQN	TARGET LOCATION	TARGET DESCRIPTION	BOMBS DROPPED (LBS)	A/C LAUNCHED	A/C BOMBING	A/C MISSING
5/22/18	Night	100	Kreuzwald, Spittel	Electrical Station, Rail	3408	12	12	0
5/22/18	Night	216	Kreuzwald, Mannheim	Elect Stn, BASF	6496	5	5	0
5/23/18	Day	99	Metz-Sablon	Rail Stn & Triangle	2464	12	11	0
5/24/18	Day	99	Hagendingen	Thyssen Blast Furnaces	1792	12	8	0
5/27/18	Day	99	Bensdorf	Rail Station & Sidings	2128	12	10	1
5/27/18	Night	100	Kreuzwald, Metz-Sablon	Elect Pwr Stn; Rail	3424	18	12	1
5/27/18	Night	216	Mann, Kreuz, Landau, Courcls	BASF, Pwr Stn, Rail	6720	8	5	0
5/28/18	Day	99	Bensdorf	Rail Stn & Sidings	2240	12	10	0
5/28/18	Night	100	Metz-Sablons	Rail Stn	864	5	3	1
5/29/18	Day	55	Thionville	Railways	2464	12	11	0
5/29/18	Day	99	Metz-Sablon	Railway Triangle	1344	12	6	0
5/30/18	Day	55	Thionville	Railways	2688	12	12	0
5/30/18	Day	99	Metz-Sablon	Railways	896	12	4	0
5/30/18	Night	100	Metz-Sablon	Rail Station	1728	7	6	0
5/30/18	Night	216	5 Locations	Rail Stations & Sidings	8552	7	7	0
5/31/18	Day	55	Karlsruhe	Rail Station & Workshops	2464	12	11	1
5/31/18	Day	99	Metz-Sablon	Railway Triangle	2240	11	11	0
5/31/18	Night	100	Thionville & Metz	Rail Station & Junction	3296	15	15	0
5/31/18	Night	216	Karthaus & Metz-Sablon	Rail Station & Triangle	5600	4	4	0
6/1/18	Day	55	Karthaus	Railway Stn	2240	12	11	1
6/1/18	Day	99	Metz-Sablon	Rail	1344	12	6	0
6/2/18	Day	99	Metz-Sablon	Rail	2240	12	10	0
6/3/18	Day	55	Luxembourg	Railways	1568	12	7	0
6/3/18	Night	100	Metz	Railways	454	6	2	0
6/4/18	Day	55	Treves & Conz	Railways & Barracks	2694	12	12	0
6/4/18	Day	99	Metz-Sablon	Triangle of Railways	2240	12	10	0
6/5/18	Night	100	Metz-Sablon	Railways	1649	7	7	0
6/5/18	Night	216	Metz & Thionville	Rail Stn & Sidings	9184	7	7	0

DATE	DAY/NIGHT	SQN	TARGET LOCATION	TARGET DESCRIPTION	BOMBS DROPPED (LBS)	A/C LAUNCHED	A/C BOMBING	A/C MISSING
6/6/18	Day	55	Coblenz	Factories, Stn, Barracks	2246	12	10	0
6/6/18	Day	99	Thionville	Rail Stn & Sidings	1120	11	5	0
6/6/18	Night	100	Thionville, M-S, Maizieres	Rail & Blast Furnace	2395	10	10	0
6/6/18	Night	216	Thionville, Moulin-les-Metz	Rail	8064	7	6	0
6/7/18	Day	55	Conz	Railways	1910	12	9	0
6/7/18	Day	99	Thionville	Rail Stn & Sidings	908	6	4	0
6/8/18	Day	55	Thionville	Rail Sidings	2698	12	11	0
6/8/18	Day	99	Hagendingen	Factories & Rail Stn	2046	12	9	0
6/8/18	Day	104	Metz-Sablon	Rail Stn	2040	12	9	0
6/9/18	Day	99	Dillingen	Factories & Station	2736	12	12	0
6/9/18	Day	104	Hagendingen	Railways & Factories	1362	12	6	0
6/12/18	Day	99	Metz-Sablon	Railway Triangle	2736	12	6	0
6/12/18	Day	104	Metz-Sablon	Railway Stn	2394	12	11	0
6/13/18	Day	55	Treves	Railways	2998	12	12	1
6/13/18	Day	99	Dillingen	Usines Dillenger Hutton W	2052	12	9	0
6/13/18	Day	104	Hagendingen	Railways & Factories	1828	12	8	0
6/23/18	Day	55	Metz-Sablon	Railways	2622	12	11	0
6/23/18	Day	99	Metz-Sablon	Railways	2736	12	12	0
6/23/18	Day	104	Metz-Sablon	Railways	2276	12	10	0
6/23/18	Night	100	Metz-Sablon	Railways	3938	14	12	0
6/24/18	Day	55	Metz-Sablon & Dillingen	Railways & Foundaries	2328	12	10	0
6/24/18	Day	99	Dillingen & Saarbrucken	Factories & Railways	2276	12	10	0
6/24/18	Day	104	Saarbrucken	Railway	2052	12	9	0
6/25/18	Day	55	Saarbrucken	Railways & Factories	2110	12	9	1
6/25/18	Day	99	Offenburg	Railway Stn & Barracks	2506	12	11	1
6/25/18	Day	104	Karlsruhe	Munitions Factories	1592	12	7	1
6/25/18	Night	100	Boulay	Aerodrome; Rail Jtn	4747	u/k	15	0
6/25/18	Night	216	Metz-Sablon	Rail Triangle & Stn	6720	6	5	0

DATE	DAY/NIGHT	SQN	TARGET LOCATION	TARGET DESCRIPTION	BOMBS DROPPED (LBS)	A/C LAUNCHED	A/C BOMBING	A/C MISSING
6/26/18	Day	55	Karlsruhe	Railway Workshops	2532	12	10	0
6/26/18	Day	99	Karlsruhe	Railway Stns & Factories	1362	12	6	0
6/26/18	Day	104	Karlsruhe	Railway Stn	684	12	3	1
6/26/18	Night	100	Boulay	Aerodrome	1860	u/k	6	0
6/26/18	Night	216	Boulay, Mannheim, Saarbrkn	Aerodrome, Rail, BASF	5376	4	4	0
6/27/18	Day	55	Thionville	Railway Workshops	2628	12	11	0
6/27/18	Day	99	Thionville	Railway Workshops & Stn	2506	12	11	1
6/27/18	Day	104	Thionville	Railway Workshops	1132	6	5	0
6/27/18	Night	100	Boulay, M-S, Contillon	Aerodrome, Rail, Train	1548	9	5	0
6/28/18	Day	104	Frescaty	Aerodrome	1856	u/k	9	0
6/29/18	Day	55	Mannheim	BASF	2364	11	10	0
6/29/18	Night	100	Frescaty, Boulay	Aerodromes	3804	12	12	0
6/29/18	Night	216	Mannheim, Thionville, M-S	BASF, Rail Targets	7952	7	6	0
6/30/18	Day	55	Hagenau	Aerodrome	1854	u/k	8	0
6/30/18	Day	99	Hagenau	Aerodrome	1362	u/k	6	0
6/30/18	Day	104	Landau	Rail Stn and Barracks	2276	11	9	1
6/30/18	Night	100	Boulay, Thionville, Remilly	Aerodrome, Rail	3944	u/k	14	0
6/30/18	Night	216	Mannheim	BASF, Rail Targets	9408	8	7	0
7/1/18	Day	55	Karthaus, Treves	Railway, Workshops, Stn	2420	12	11	0
7/1/18	Day	99	Karthaus	Railways & Workshops	1356	10	6	0
7/1/18	Day	104	Metz-Sablon	Railway Station	1362	10	4	2
7/1/18	Night	100	Boulay and Falkenburg	Aerodrome & Rail Stn	3292	u/k	14	0
7/1/18	Night	216	Mannheim & Thionville	BASF and Rail Works	6720	6	5	0
7/2/18	Day	55	Coblenz	Railway Sidings	2078	12	9	0
7/2/18	Day	99	Treves	Railway Stn	1368	9	6	0
7/5/18	Day	55	Coblenz	Railway Sidings	2610	12	11	0
7/5/18	Day	99	Saarbrucken	Stations & Factories	1312	6	6	0
7/5/18	Day	104	Barras	Village	908	6	4	0

DATE	DAY/NIGHT	SQN	TARGET LOCATION	TARGET DESCRIPTION	BOMBS DROPPED (LBS)	A/C LAUNCHED	A/C BOMBING	A/C MISSING
7/6/18	Day	55	Metz-Sablon	Railways	2774	12	12	0
7/6/18	Day	99	Metz-Sablon	Railways	1362	6	6	0
7/6/18	Day	104	Metz-Sablon	Railway Stn	1698	6	6	0
7/6/18	Night	100	Saarburg & Marne Canal	Rail Jtn, Convoy	2468	12	9	0
7/6/18	Night	216	Metz-Sablon	Railways	4032	8	3	0
7/7/18	Day	99	Kaiserslauten	Railways	1362	6	6	0
7/7/18	Day	104	Kaiserslauten	Rail Stn & Factories	1132	6	5	2
7/8/18	Day	55	S. Luxembourg	Railway	2784	12	12	0
7/8/18	Day	99	Buhl	Aerodrome	1272	u/k	6	0
7/8/18	Day	104	Buhl	Aerodrome	824	u/k	4	0
7/8/18	Day	104	Buhl	Aerodrome	824	u/k	4	0
7/8/18	Day	104	Buhl	Aerodrome	824	u/k	4	0
7/8/18	Night	100	Boulay, Vallieres, Falknbrg	Aerodrome, Trains	3132	u/k	11	0
7/8/18	Night	216	Freisdorf & Boulay	Aerodromes	3920	u/k	3	0
7/11/18	Day	55	Offenburg	Railways	2778	12	12	0
7/11/18	Night	100	Boulay, St Avold	Aerodromes, Village	2503	u/k	10	0
7/11/18	Night	216	Freisdorf, Boulay	Aerodromes	5376	u/k	4	0
7/12/18	Day	55	Saarbrucken	Railway Sidings	2314	12	10	0
7/15/18	Day	55	Offenburg	Railways	2504	12	11	0
7/15/18	Day	99	Buhl	Aerodrome	1592	u/k	7	0
7/16/18	Day	55	Thionville	Railways	1412	12	6	0
7/16/18	Day	99	Thionville	Railways	2718	12	12	0
7/16/18	Night	100	Hagendingen & Ham	Blast Furnaces & Rail Jtn	3064	14	12	0
7/16/18	Night	216	Saarbrucken & Dieuze	Burbach Works & Aerodrome	4032	7	3	0
7/17/18	Day	55	Thionville	Railways	2538	12	11	0
7/17/18	Day	99	Thionville	Railways	1350	12	6	0
7/18/18	Night	100	Boulay, Falkenburg	Village, Aerodrome, Rail	5190	u/k	11	0
7/18/18	Night	216	Saarbrucken, Mannheim	BASF, Blast Furnaces, Rail	7840	8	6	0

DATE	DAY/NIGHT	SQN	TARGET LOCATION	TARGET DESCRIPTION	BOMBS DROPPED (LBS)	A/C LAUNCHED	A/C BOMBING	A/C MISSING
7/19/18	Day	55	Oberndorf	Munition Works	1916	12	8	0
7/19/18	Night	100	Boulay, Freisdorf, Saar	Aerodromes, Rail	4868	u/k	14	0
7/19/18	Night	216	Mannheim & Saarbrucken	BASF, Lanz, GB, Burbach Wrks	6720	6	5	1
7/20/18	Day	55	Oberndorf	Munition Works	2548	12	11	2
7/20/18	Day	99	Offenburg	Railways	2270	12	10	1
7/21/18	Night	100	Boulay, Freisdorf	Aerodromes & Rail	5070	u/k	17	0
7/21/18	Night	216	Mannheim, Zweibrkn	BASF, Rail, Factory	5600	4	4	0
7/22/18	Day	55	Rottweil	Powder Factory	2302	12	10	0
7/22/18	Day	99	Offenburg	Rail Stn	2724	12	12	0
7/22/18	Night	100	Boulay and Lesse	Aerodrome, Village, Rail	3402	u/k	15	0
7/22/18	Night	216	Vahl Ebersing, Morhange	Aerodromes	2696	u/k	2	0
7/25/18	Night	100	Boulay, Freisdorf, Morhange	Aerodromes & 3 Trains	4768	u/k	17	0
7/25/18	Night	216	Offenburg, Boul	Rail and Aerodrome	11441	8	8	0
7/29/18	Night	100	Boulay, Morhange, Remilly	Aerodromes & Rail	2626	u/k	9	0
7/29/18	Night	216	Stuttgart	Fact, Rail, Aerodrome	9968	7	7	0
7/30/18	Day	55	Offenburg	Railway Sidings	2364	12	10	0
7/30/18	Day	99	Lahr	Rail Station	1810	12	8	1
7/30/18	Night	216	Stuttgart & Hagenau	Magneto Wrks, Town, Rail	6272	7	4	0
7/31/18	Day	55	Coblenz	Factories & Barracks	2358	12	10	0
7/31/18	Day	99	Saarbrucken	Rail Stn & Factories	1362	12	5	7
7/31/18	Day	104	Saarbrucken	Rail Sidings & Factories	2512	12	12	0
8/1/18	Day	55	Duren	Railways & Factories	2358	12	11	0
8/1/18	Day	104	Treves	Railways, Shops, Sidings	2282	12	10	1
8/8/18	Day	55	Wallingen	Wallingen Factory	2364	12	11	0
8/11/18	Day	55	Buhl and Metz-Sablon	Aerodrome & Rail Triangle	902	22	4	0
8/11/18	Day	104	Karlsruhe	Rail Station	2506	12	10	1
8/11/18	Night	100	Morhange	Aerodrome	624	2	2	0
8/11/18	Night	216	Buhl	Aerodrome	1344	1	1	0

DATE	DAY/NIGHT	SQN	TARGET LOCATION	TARGET DESCRIPTION	BOMBS DROPPED (LBS)	A/C LAUNCHED	A/C BOMBING	A/C MISSING
8/12/18	Day	55	Frankfurt	Rail, Chem Fact	2756	12	12	0
8/12/18	Day	104	Hagenau	Aerodrome	2500	11	11	2
8/12/18	Night	100	Dieuze, Morhange, Falkenburg	AAA, Rail, Aerodrome	3142	11	11	0
8/13/18	Day	55	Buhl	Aerodrome	2308	10	10	0
8/13/18	Day	104	Thionville	Rail Workshops	2500	12	11	3
8/13/18	Night	100	Buhl, Morh	Aerodromes, Rail, Furnace	2394	9	9	0
8/13/18	Night	216	Thionville	Rail Station	1207	4	1	0
8/14/18	Day	55	Offenburg	Rail Station & Sidings	2246	12	10	0
8/14/18	Night	100	Buhl	Aerodrome	3462	12	12	0
8/14/18	Night	216	Buhl, Saarbg, St Av	Aerodromes, Furnace, Rail	10976	8	8	0
8/15/18	Day	99	Boulay	Aerodrome	908	14	4	0
8/15/18	Day	104	Boulay	Aerodrome	2476	11	11	0
8/15/18	Night	100	Boulay, Freis, Buhl,	Aerodromes, Train	3120	10	10	0
8/15/18	Night	216	Boul, Mann, Saarbrkn, Buhl	Aerodromes, Fact, Furn	9632	10	8	0
8/16/18	Day	55	Darmstadt	Railways	2022	10	7	3
8/16/18	Night	100	Buhl, Boul, Morh, Remilly	Aerodromes, Rail Jtn	2359	8	7	0
8/16/18	Night	216	Boulay, Saarburg	Aerodrome, Rail Jtn	2464	7	2	0
8/17/18	Night	100	Freis, Morh, Boulay	Aerodromes	2808	11	9	1
8/17/18	Night	216	Saarburg, Forbach	Blk For, Furn, Aero,	8794	9	7	0
8/18/18	Night	100	Boulay, Morh,	Aerodromes, Villages, Rail	2184	7	7	1
8/18/18	Night	216	Saarbrucken, Buhl, Boulay	Rail, Burbach Wks, Aero	6832	5	5	0
8/19/18	Night	97	Metz-Sablon	Rail Triangle	4256	5	3	0
8/19/18	Night	100	Boulay, Morh, Avricourt	Aerodromes & Rail	2472	11	9	0
8/19/18	Night	216	Morhange, Boulay	Aerodromes	2464	2	2	0
8/20/18	Day	99	Dillengen	Blast Furnaces & Sidings	224	1	1	0
8/20/18	Night	97	Metz-Sablon, Buhl	Rail Triangle, Aerodrome	7616	5	5	0
8/20/18	Night	100	Boulay, Morhange	Aerodromes	2184	7	7	0
8/20/18	Night	216	Boulay	Aerodrome	2688	2	2	0

DATE	DAY/NIGHT	SQN	TARGET LOCATION	TARGET DESCRIPTION	BOMBS DROPPED (LBS)	A/C LAUNCHED	A/C BOMBING	A/C MISSING
8/21/18	Night	97	Buhl, Morhange, Lorquin	Aerodromes	8400	6	5	1
8/21/18	Night	100	Morhange, Buhl	Aerodromes	1872	6	6	0
8/21/18	Night	216	Colg, Frank, Boul, Treves	Rail Targets & Aerodrome	8594	8	7	0
8/22/18	Day	55	Coblenz, Whitlick	Railways, Factory, Village	2022	12	8	0
8/22/18	Day	99	Hagenau	Aerodrome	914	11	4	0
8/22/18	Day	104	Mannheim	Factories	2736	12	10	7
8/22/18	Night	97	Folpersweiler, Herzing	Aerodrome & Railway	3248	6	2	2
8/22/18	Night	100	Folper, Avrict, Saaralben	Aerod, Rail, Chem Factory	1872	9	6	0
8/22/18	Night	215	Folpersweiler	Aerodrome	14244	8	8	1
8/23/18	Day	55	Treves	Rail Station	2246	12	10	0
8/23/18	Day	99	Buhl	Aerodrome	2165	12	12	0
8/23/18	Night	100	Boulay	Aerodrome	2192	3	3	0
8/23/18	Night	215	Boulay, Ehrang	Aerodrome, Rail Jtn	10098	8	5	0
8/24/18	Night	216	Frankfurt, Boulay	Rail Stn, Aerodrome	2118	8	2	0
8/25/18	Day	55	Morhange, Luxembourg	Aerodrome, Rail & Triangle	2022	12	9	0
8/25/18	Day	99	Bettembourg	Railways	2730	12	12	0
8/25/18	Night	97	Boulay	Aerodrome	2542	6	3	0
8/25/18	Night	215	Mannheim, Boulay	BASF, Aerodrome	10335	6	5	0
8/27/18	Day	55	Conflans	Railway Sidings	2240	12	10	0
8/27/18	Day	99	Buhl	Aerodrome	1362	11	6	0
8/30/18	Day	55	Conflans, Thionville	Railways	2464	12	11	4
8/30/18	Day	99	Conflans, Doncourt	Railways, Aerodrome	2440	12	11	0
8/30/18	Night	97	Boulay, Morhange	Aerodromes	4220	7	3	1
8/30/18	Night	100	Boulay	Aerodrome	4072	5	5	0
8/30/18	Night	215	Boulay	Aerodrome	12352	8	6	0
8/30/18	Night	216	Boulay	Aerodrome	1568	8	1	0
9/2/18	Day	55	Buhl (0930 & 1520)	Aerodrome	4380	21	20	0
9/2/18	Day	99	Buhl (0900 & 1530)	Aerodrome	5222	24	23	0

DATE	DAY/NIGHT	SQN	TARGET LOCATION	TARGET DESCRIPTION	BOMBS DROPPED (LBS)	A/C LAUNCHED	A/C BOMBING	A/C MISSING
9/2/18	Day	104	Buhl (0925 & 1540)	Aerodrome	4328	24	21	0
9/2/18	Night	97	Buhl	Aerodrome	5654	5	5	0
9/2/18	Night	100	Boulay	Aerodrome	3024	2	2	0
9/2/18	Night	215	Buhl, Ehrang	Aerodrome, Rail Jtn	19528	11	9	0
9/2/18	Night	216	Saarbrkn, Boulay	Burbach Wks, Rail Stn, Aero	12137	8	8	0
9/3/18	Day	99	Morhange	Aerodrome	2496	11	11	0
9/3/18	Day	104	Morhange	Aerodrome	2736	12	12	0
9/3/18	Night	97	Boulay	Aerodrome	5573	4	4	0
9/3/18	Night	100	Morhange	Aerodrome	4704	3	3	0
9/3/18	Night	215	Morhange	Aerodrome	4084	2	2	0
9/3/18	Night	216	Morhange, Boulay	Aerodromes, Blast Furnaces	10956	7	7	0
9/4/18	Day	55	Buhl	Aerodrome	2022	9	9	0
9/4/18	Day	99	Morhange	Aerodrome	2246	10	10	0
9/4/18	Day	104	Morhange	Aerodrome	2960	13	13	0
9/6/18	Night	97	Lorquin	Aerodrome	3136	2	2	0
9/6/18	Night	100	Lorquin	Aerodrome	1456	1	1	0
9/6/18	Night	215	Lellingen	Aerodrome	2042	1	1	0
9/7/18	Day	55	Ehrang	Rail Jtn	1362	6	6	0
9/7/18	Day	99	Ludwigshafen	BASF	2422	12	11	1
9/7/18	Day	104	Mannheim	BASF	2270	12	10	3
9/12/18	Day	99	Courcelles, Orny, Verny	Rail Town	1350	6	6	0
9/12/18	Day	104	Champey	Railway	430	12	2	0
9/12/18	Night	97	Metz-Sablon, Courcelles	Railways	2900	2	2	0
9/12/18	Night	100	Metz-Sablon	Railways	1792	2	1	0
9/12/18	Night	215	Metz-Sablon	Railways	1668	2	1	0
9/12/18	Night	216	Metz-Sablon	Railways	6130	8	4	0
9/13/18	Day	99	Orny, Arnvl, Mt Park	Rail Jtn, Bridge, Transport	3596	28	16	2
9/13/18	Day	104	M-S, Arnvl, Mars, Orly	Railways, Orly Aerodrome	3064	14	14	0

281

DATE	DAY/NIGHT	SQN	TARGET LOCATION	TARGET DESCRIPTION	BOMBS DROPPED (LBS)	A/C LAUNCHED	A/C BOMBING	A/C MISSING
9/13/18	Night	100	Courcelles	Rail Jtn	1120	4	2	0
9/13/18	Night	215	Courcelles	Rail Jtn	4084	4	2	0
9/14/18	Day	55	Ehrang	Rail Jtn	2524	12	11	0
9/14/18	Day	99	Metz-Sablon, Buhl	Railways, Aerodrome	4092	23	18	1
9/14/18	Day	104	Metz-Sablon	Railways	3584	23	16	0
9/14/18	Day	110	Boulay	Aerodrome	2028	6	6	0
9/14/18	Night	97	M-S, Kaiser'n, Courcls	Railways	13522	11	9	0
9/14/18	Night	100	Metz-Sablon, Boulay	Railways, Aerodrome	5264	5	3	0
9/14/18	Night	215	Ehrang, Kaiser'n, Courcls	Railways	14295	13	9	2
9/14/18	Night	216	Courcls, Saarbg, M-S, Frescaty	Railways, Aerodrome	12076	11	8	1
9/15/18	Day	55	Stuttgart	Daimler Works	2058	12	9	0
9/15/18	Day	99	Metz-Sablon	Railways	2930	13	13	0
9/15/18	Day	104	Metz-Sablon	Railways	2706	12	12	3
9/15/18	Day	110	Buhl	Aerodrome	3030	10	10	0
9/15/18	Night	97	Lorqn, Morh, Mainz	Aerodromes, Rail	12396	11	9	0
9/15/18	Night	100	Lorquin, Buhl, Saarburg	Aerodromes, Convoy	5143	5	5	0
9/15/18	Night	215	Buhl, Karlsruhe	Aerodrome, Rail Stn, Docks	10210	6	5	0
9/15/18	Night	216	Karlsruhe, Morhange, M-S	Rail Stn & Docks, Aero	9711	6	6	0
9/16/18	Day	55	Mannheim	Rail Stn & Lanz Works	1138	6	5	1
9/16/18	Day	99	Hagenau	Aerodrome	2264	11	11	0
9/16/18	Day	110	Mannheim	Railways, Chem Factories	3266	12	11	2
9/16/18	Night	97	Frankfurt, Lorquin, Frescaty	Railway & Aerodromes	4350	5	3	0
9/16/18	Night	100	Frescaty	Zepp Shed & Aerodrome	3462	2	1	1
9/16/18	Night	115	Metz-Sablon	Railways	8176	8	6	1
9/16/18	Night	215	Cologne, Frescaty, Mannheim	Unknown	u/k	5	u/k	4
9/16/18	Night	216	5 locations	Aerodromes & Rail Stns	7138	6	5	1
9/20/18	Night	97	Buhl, Boul, Karlsruhe	Aerodromes, Gasworks	14033	9	9	0
9/20/18	Night	100	Mann, Karlsruhe, Saarbrkn	Lanz Wks, Gasworks, Blst Furn	4704	4	3	0

DATE	DAY/NIGHT	SQN	TARGET LOCATION	TARGET DESCRIPTION	BOMBS DROPPED (LBS)	A/C LAUNCHED	A/C BOMBING	A/C MISSING
9/20/18	Night	115	Morhange, Fontenay	Aerodomes	16128	10	10	1
9/20/18	Night	215	Frescaty	Aerodrome	6272	4	4	1
9/20/18	Night	216	Mannheim, Frescaty	Lanz Works, Aerodrome	10518	9	7	0
9/21/18	Night	97	Buhl	Aerodrome	9802	6	6	0
9/21/18	Night	100	Frescaty	Aerodrome	5376	3	3	0
9/21/18	Night	115	Morhange, Leiningen	Aerodrome, Rail Stn	4480	4	3	0
9/21/18	Night	215	Hagondange	Blast Furnaces	6126	3	3	0
9/21/18	Night	216	Rombach	Factories & Railroads	9174	6	6	3
9/25/18	Day	55	Kaiserslauten	Munitions Factories	2742	12	12	1
9/25/18	Day	99	Buhl	Aerodrome	1138	5	5	0
9/25/18	Day	104	Buhl	Aerodrome	1532	7	7	4
9/25/18	Day	110	Frankfurt	Works and Railways	3378	11	11	0
9/26/18	Day	55	Audun-le-Roman	Railways	1374	12	6	5
9/26/18	Day	99	Metz-Sablon	Railways	1362	10	6	1
9/26/18	Day	104	Metz-Sablon	Railways	2210	12	9	0
9/26/18	Night	97	Mezieres, Metz-Sablon	Railways	7355	6	5	0
9/26/18	Night	100	Thionville, Metz-Sablon	Railway Jtn, Railways	3238	2	2	0
9/26/18	Night	115	M-S, Thionvil, Plappeville	Railways, AAA, Aerodrome	3136	4	2	1
9/26/18	Night	215	Metz-Sablon, Frescaty	Railways, Aerodrome	6126	6	3	0
9/26/18	Night	216	Mezieres, Metz-Sablon	Railways	5926	8	4	0
9/30/18	Night	97	Foret-de-Sauvage, Mezieres	Railways	3461	8	2	0
9/30/18	Night	100	Saarbrucken	Burbach Works	1446	3	1	0
9/30/18	Night	215	Frescaty, Metz-Sablon	Aerodrome, Railways	4084	5	2	0
9/30/18	Night	216	Mezieres	Railways	0	4	0	0
10/1/18	Day	110	Treves, Luxembourg	Railway Stns	1686	12	6	0
10/3/18	Night	97	Metz-Sablon	Railways	1556	4	1	0
10/3/18	Night	100	Metz-Sablon, Morhange	Railways, Aerodrome	2892	5	2	0
10/3/18	Night	115	Metz-Sablon	Railways	1568	5	1	0

DATE	DAY/NIGHT	SQN	TARGET LOCATION	TARGET DESCRIPTION	BOMBS DROPPED (LBS)	A/C LAUNCHED	A/C BOMBING	A/C MISSING
10/3/18	Night	215	Frescaty	Aerodrome	2042	u/k	1	0
10/3/18	Night	216	Metz-Sablon	Railways	3014	7	2	0
10/5/18	Day	104	Metz-Sablon	Railways	2718	12	12	0
10/5/18	Day	110	Kaiserslautern, Pirmasens	Railways	2594	12	8	4
10/5/18	Night	97	Metz-S, Mezieres, Courcel's	Railways	7896	7	5	0
10/5/18	Night	100	Morhange, Saarbrkn, Mezieres	Aero, Burbach Wks, Rail	6476	4	4	0
10/5/18	Night	115	Thionville, Metz-Sablon	Railways	3136	5	2	0
10/5/18	Night	215	Frescaty	Aerodrome	4084	u/k	2	0
10/5/18	Night	216	Metz-Sablon	Railways	7504	7	5	0
10/9/18	Day	99	Metz-Sablon	Railways	2500	12	11	0
10/9/18	Day	104	Metz-Sablon	Railways	2942	13	13	0
10/9/18	Night	97	Metz-Sablon	Railways	5104	7	3	0
10/9/18	Night	100	Mezieres	Railways	2892	5	2	0
10/9/18	Night	115	Thionville, Morhange	Railways, Aerodrome	7728	6	5	0
10/9/18	Night	215	Metz-Sablon, Frescaty	Railways, Aerodrome	3860	4	2	0
10/9/18	Night	216	M-S, Mezieres, Thionvil	Rail and Karlschutte Wks	7942	8	6	0
10/10/18	Day	99	Metz-Sablon	Railways	1822	12	8	0
10/10/18	Day	104	Metz-Sablon	Railways	2724	12	12	0
10/10/18	Night	100	Thionville	Railways	1792	2	1	0
10/10/18	Night	115	Metz-Sablon, Longuyon	Railways	0	4	0	0
10/10/18	Night	215	Frescaty	Aerodrome	4084	u/k	2	0
10/10/18	Night	216	Mezieres, Rombach	Railways, Factories	3136	8	2	0
10/15/18	Day	55	Frescaty	Aerodrome	224	u/k	1	0
10/18/18	Day	99	Metz-Sablon	Railways	1816	12	8	0
10/18/18	Day	104	Metz-Sablon	Railways	2942	u/k	13	0
10/18/18	Night	100	Saarburg	Railways	1792	2	1	0
10/21/18	Day	55	Thionville	Railways	1592	12	7	0
10/21/18	Day	99	Metz-Sablon	Railways	2500	11	11	0

DATE	DAY/NIGHT	SQN	TARGET LOCATION	TARGET DESCRIPTION	BOMBS DROPPED (LBS)	A/C LAUNCHED	A/C BOMBING	A/C MISSING
10/21/18	Day	104	Metz-Sablon	Railways	3178	14	14	0
10/21/18	Day	110	Frankfurt	Railways & Factories	1592	13	5	7
10/21/18	Night	97	Kaiserslautern	Railways	5274	4	3	0
10/21/18	Night	100	Mezieres, Kaiserslautern	Railways	4989	6	3	0
10/23/18	Day	55	Metz-Sablon	Railways	2264	12	11	0
10/23/18	Day	99	Metz-Sablon	Railways	2500	12	11	0
10/23/18	Day	104	Metz-Sablon	Railways	2494	12	11	1
10/23/18	Night	97	Wiesbaden	Aerodrome	1750	6	1	0
10/23/18	Night	100	Saarbrucken, Metz	Railways, Burbach Works	6680	6	4	0
10/23/18	Night	215	Kaiserslautern, Saarbrkn	Rail Jtn & Stn	8208	6	4	0
10/23/18	Night	216	Mann, Saarbg, M-S, Coblentz	BASF, Blast Furn, Rail, Bridge	7882	9	5	0
10/27/18	Day	99	Frescaty	Aerodrome	1144	u/k	5	0
10/27/18	Day	104	Frescaty	Aerodrome	1810	u/k	8	0
10/28/18	Day	99	Morhange, Frescaty	Aerodromes	2842	u/k	12	0
10/28/18	Day	104	Morhange	Aerodrome	2942	u/k	13	0
10/28/18	Night	97	Mannheim	BASF	1874	5	1	0
10/28/18	Night	100	Longuyon	Rail Jtn	1446	7	1	0
10/28/18	Night	115	Thionville, Longuyon	Railways	3788	4	3	0
10/28/18	Night	215	Ecouviez	Railway Triangle	1446	9	1	0
10/28/18	Night	216	Treves, Thionvil, Saarbrkn	Railways, Factories	8634	8	6	0
10/29/18	Day	55	Longuyon	Railways	2264	12	10	0
10/29/18	Day	99	Longuyon	Railways	2736	12	12	0
10/29/18	Day	104	Jametz	Aerodrome	2942	u/k	13	1
10/29/18	Night	97	Hagenau, Mannheim	Aerodrome, BASF	3236	2	2	0
10/29/18	Night	100	Offenburg	Railway Jtn	3238	5	2	0
10/29/18	Night	215	Mann, Offenburg, Thionvil	BASF, Railway Jtns	4582	8	3	1
10/29/18	Night	216	Mannheim, Saarbrkn, Worms	Munitions Fact, Blst Furn	9408	8	6	0
10/30/18	Day	99	Buhl	Aerodrome	1144	u/k	5	0

DATE	DAY/NIGHT	SQN	TARGET LOCATION	TARGET DESCRIPTION	BOMBS DROPPED (LBS)	A/C LAUNCHED	A/C BOMBING	A/C MISSING
10/30/18	Night	100	Karlsruhe, Saarbrucken	Rail Wkshops, Burbach Wks	2892	3	2	0
10/30/18	Night	115	Baden, Morhange, Hagenau	Railways, Aerodromes	4012	3	3	0
10/31/18	Day	55	Bonn, Frescaty, Treves	Railways & Stn, Aerodrome	1810	12	8	0
10/31/18	Day	99	Buhl	Aerodrome	1592	u/k	7	0
10/31/18	Day	104	Buhl	Aerodrome	2028	u/k	9	0
11/2/18	Day	99	Avricourt	Railway Jtn	336	2	1	0
11/3/18	Day	55	Saarburg	Railway Sidings	1704	12	9	0
11/3/18	Day	99	Buhl, Lorquin	Aerodromes	2506	u/k	11	0
11/3/18	Day	104	Lorquin	Railway Sidings & Dump	2058	12	9	0
11/5/18	Day	110	Morhange	Aerodrome	2382	u/k	11	0
11/5/18	Night	97	Morhange	Aerodrome	1194	u/k	1	0
11/5/18	Night	100	Lellingen	Aerodrome	1547	u/k	1	0
11/5/18	Night	115	Dieuze, Frescaty	Railways, Aerodrome	2940	2	2	0
11/5/18	Night	215	Morhange	Aerodrome	1568	u/k	1	0
11/5/18	Night	216	Morhange	Aerodrome	1446	u/k	1	0
11/6/18	Day	55	Saarbrucken, Hattigny	Burbach Wks, Aerodrome	1368	6	6	1
11/6/18	Day	99	Buhl	Aerodrome	2302	u/k	10	1
11/6/18	Day	104	Buhl	Aerodrome	2506	u/k	11	2
11/9/18	Day	55	Bensdorf	Railway Stn	304	6	1	0
11/9/18	Day	99	Chateau Salins	Motor Transport, Railway	796	3	2	0
11/9/18	Day	104	Lorquin, Rachicourt	Rail Sidings,Tri, Dump	400	5	2	0
11/10/18	Day	55	Ehrang	Railway Sidings	2494	12	11	1
11/10/18	Day	99	Morhange	Aerodrome	1592	u/k	7	0
11/10/18	Day	104	Morhange	Aerodrome	1986	u/k	9	0
11/10/18	Day	110	Morhange	Aerodrome	2394	u/k	11	0
11/10/18	Night	97	Morhange	Aerodrome	1668	u/k	1	0
11/10/18	Night	100	Lellingen & Frescaty	Aerodromes	2212	u/k	2	0
11/10/18	Night	115	Morhange	Aerodrome	1668	u/k	1	0

DATE	DAY/NIGHT	SQN	TARGET LOCATION	TARGET DESCRIPTION	BOMBS DROPPED (LBS)	A/C LAUNCHED	A/C BOMBING	A/C MISSING
11/10/18	Night	215	Morhange & Frescaty	Aerodromes	3014	u/k	2	0
11/10/18	Night	216	Metz-Sablon, Frescaty	Railway, Aerodrome	3136	3	2	0

ABBREVIATIONS

Aero: Aerodrome
Amag: Amagne
Arnvl: Arnaville
Aurict: Auricourt
Bks: Barracks
Blst: Blast
Boul: Boulay
Brdg: Bridge
Chem: Chemical
Co: Company
Colg: Cologne
Courcls: Courcelles
Elect: Electric
Furn: Furnace
Fact: Factory
Falknbg: Falkenburg
Folper: Folpersweiler
Freis: Freisdorf
Jtn: Junction
Juni: Juniville
Kaiser'n: Kaiserslutern
Kreuz: Kreuzwald

Lorq: Lorquin
Luc: Lucquy
Lux: Luxembourg
M-S: Metz-Sablon
Mann: Mannheim
Morh: Morhange
Munit: Munitions
Offnbrg: Offenburg
Pwr: Power
Rlwy: Railway
Sab: Sablon
Saarbg: Saarburg
Saarbrkn: Saarbrucken
St Av: St Auold
Stn: Station
Thionvil: Thionville
Tri: Triangle
Trn: Train
Warnevil: Warneville
Wrks: Works
Zweibrkn: Zweibrucken

Bibliography

Manuscript Collections

Bodleian Library, Oxford.

Johnston Collection
Milner, Alfred. Papers

Imperial War Museum, London.

Puncher. Papers
Read, W. R. Papers
Wilkins, C. E. V. Papers

Royal Air Force Museum, Hendon, England.

Newall, C. L. N. Papers
1st Earl of Halsbury (Hardinge Stanley Giffard). Papers
Sykes, Frederick. Papers
Trenchard, Hugh M. Papers

United State Air Force Museum, Dayton, Ohio.

US Air Service Papers

Public Records and Documents, Unpublished

Public Record Office, Rew

Admiralty Records	ADM 1
Air Ministry Records	AIR 1
	AIR 2
	AIR 6
	AIR 8
	AIR 9
Cabinet Office Records	CAB 23
	CAB 24

Published

Books

Aders, Gebhard. *History of the German Night Fighter Force, 1917–1955*. London; New York: Jane's, 1979.

Air Ministry. *Bomb Sighting, with Short Account of Apparatus Now in Use*. A.P. 356. London: Her Majesty's Stationery Office (HMSO), November 1918.

———. *British Military Aircraft of World War One*. London: HMSO, 1976.

———. Air Historical Branch. *Members of the Air Council and Air Force Board of the Defence Council, 1918*. London: HMSO, September 1973.

———. *Notes on Night Reconnaissance and Bombing*. AP 387. London: HMSO, July 1918.

———. *Psychological Disorders in Flying Personnel of the Royal Air Force during the War, 1939–1945*. London: HMSO, 1947.

———. *A Selection of Lectures and Essays from the Work of Officers Attending the First Course at the Royal Air Force Staff College, 1921–1923*. A.P. 956. London: HMSO, December 1923.

———. *A Short History of the Royal Air Force*. AP 125. London: HMSO, September 1929.

———. *Summary of Air Intelligence*. Series 5–11. London: HMSO, 1918–19.

Allen, H. R. *The Legacy of Lord Trenchard*. London: Cassell, 1972.

Armstrong, William. *Pioneer Pilot*. London: Blandford Press, 1952.

Ashmore, Edward B. *Air Defence: An Account of Air Defence in England, 1914–1918*. London; New York: Longman, Green, and Co., 1929.

Baldwin, J. E. A. "Experiences of Bombing with the Independent Force in 1918." In *A Selection of Lectures and Essays from the Work of Officers Attending the First Course of the Royal Air Force Staff College, 1921–1923*. London: HMSO, Air Ministry, December 1923.

Baring, Maurice. *Flying Corps Headquarters, 1914–1918.* London: Bell, 1920.

Barnett, Correlli. *Britain and Her Army 1509–1970: A Military, Political and Social Survey.* London: Eyre Methuen, 1970.

Bartlett, C. P. O. *Bomber Pilot, 1916–1918.* London: Ian Allan, 1974.

Bell, Elwyn D. *Hyderabad Squadron: The Story of No. 110 (Hyderabad) Squadron, Royal Air Force.* London: Air Britain, 1972.

Bialer, Uri. *The Shadow of the Bomber: The Fear of Air Attack and British Politics, 1932–1939.* London: Royal Historical Society, 1980.

Blake, Robert, ed. *The Private Papers of Douglas Haig, 1914–1919: Being Selections from the Private Diary and Correspondence of Field-Marshal the Earl Haig of Bemersyde.* London: Eyre & Spottiswoode, 1952.

Bond, Brian. *War and Society in Europe, 1870–1970.* Bungay: England, Richard Clay, 1984.

————. *British Military Policy between the Two World Wars.* Oxford: Clarendon Press, 1980.

Boyle, Andrew P. *Trenchard.* London: Collins, 1962.

Bruce, J. M. *The Aeroplanes of the Royal Flying Corps (Military Wing).* London: Putnam, 1982.

Burge, C. Gordon. *The Annals of 100 Squadron.* London: Herbert Reiach, 1919.

Dane, Edmund. *The War Budget: A Photographic Record of the Great War.* London, 1917.

Davies, R. B. *Sailor in the Air.* London, 1967.

Dean, Sir Maurice. *The Royal Air Force and Two World Wars.* London: Cassell, 1979.

Ellis, Peter Berresford, and Piers Williams. *By Jove, Biggles! The Life of Captain W. E. Johns.* London: W. H. Allen, 1981.

Falls, Cyril. *Military Operations, France and Belgium, 1917.* London: Macmillan, 1940–48.

Fitzroy, Sir Almeric William. *Memoirs.* 2 vols. London: Hutchinson, 1923.

Frankland, A. Noble. *The Bombing Offensive against Germany: Outlines and Perspectives.* London: Faber and Faber, 1965.

Fredette, Raymond H. *The Sky on Fire; The First Battle of Britain, 1917–1918, and the Birth of the Royal Air Force.* London: Cassell, 1966.

Grey, C. G. *A History of the Air Ministry.* London: G. Allen & Unwin, 1940.

Groves, P. R. C. *Our Future in the Air by Brig Gen P. R. C. Groves: A Survey of the Vital Question of British Air Power.* London: Hutchinson, 1922.

Quinn, Paul. *British Strategy and Politics, 1914–1918.* Oxford: Clarendon, 1965.

Harding, E. D., et al. *A History of Number 16 Squadron (known as "A" Naval Squadron) Royal Naval Air Service Renumbered 216 Squadron Independent Force Royal Air Force.* London: H. W. Hill & Son, 1923.

Hart, Basil Henry Liddell. *Paris; or the Future of War.* London: Reagan Paul, 1925.

Higham, Robin David S. *Air Power: A Concise History.* London: MacDonald, 1973.

———. *Armed Forces in Peacetime: Britain, 1918–1940, A Case Study.* London: Foulis, 1962.

Hinsley, F. H. *British Intelligence in the Second World War: Its Influence on Strategy and Operations.* 3 vols. London: HMSO, 1979.

Hyde, Harford Montgomery. *British Air Policy Between the Wars, 1918–39.* London: Heinemann, 1976.

Imrie, Alex. *Pictorial History of the German Army Air Service, 1914–1918.* London: Ian Allan, 1971.

Jones, Henry A. *The War in the Air: Being the Story of the Part Played in the Great War by the Royal Air Force.* 5 vols and appendices. Oxford: Clarendon Press, 1922–37.

———. *Sir Walter Raleigh and the Air Force History: A Personal Recollection.* London: Cassell, 1922.

Jones, Neville. *The Origins of Strategic Bombing: A Study of the Development of British Air Strategic Thought and Practice up to 1918.* London: Kimber, 1973.

Joubert de la Ferte, Sir Philip Bennet. *The Third Service: The Story behind the Royal Air Force.* London: Thames and Hudson, 1955.

Kerr, Mark. *Land, Sea, and Air: Reminiscences of Mark Kerr.* London: Longman, Green, 1927.

Kingsford, A. R. *Night Raiders of the Air: Being the Experience of a Night Flying Pilot Who Raided Hunland on Many Dark Nights during the War.* London: Hamilton, 1930.

Lamberton, W. M. *Reconnaissance and Bomber Aircraft of the 1914–1918 War.* Warwick, England: Warwick Printing, 1962.

Lewis, Peter. *The British Bomber Since 1914: Fifty Years of Design and Development.* London: Putnam, 1967.

Livingston, G. *Hot Air in Cold Blood.* London: Selwyn & Blount, 1933.

MacIsaac, David. *Strategic Bombing in World War Two: The Story of the United States Strategic Bombing Survey.* New York: Garland Publishing, 1976.

"Manchester Guardian" History of the War. 9 vols. London: John Heywood, 1914–20.

Maurer, Maurer, ed. *The U.S. Air Service in World War I.* 4 vols. Maxwell Air Force Base (AFB), Ala.: Air Force Historical Research Agency (AFHRA), 1978–1979.

Maycock, R. *Doctors in the Air.* London: G. Allen & Unwin, 1957.

Miller, Leonard. *The Chronicles of 55 Squadron, R.F.C. and R.A.F.* London: Unwin, 1919.

Morison, Frank. *War on Great Cities: A Study of the Facts.* London: Faber and Faber, 1937.

Morris, Alan. *First of the Many: The Story of the Independent Force, RAF.* London: Jarrolds. 1968.

Morrow, John H., Jr. *German Air Power in World War I.* Lincoln, Nebr.: University of Nebraska, 1982.

Munson, Kenneth. *Bombers, 1914–1919.* London, 1968.

Moyes, Philip J. R. *Bomber Squadrons of the R.A.F. and their Aircraft.* London: Macdonald, 1964.

Neumann, Georg Paul, comp. *The German Air Force in the Great War.* Translated by J. E. Gordon. London: Hodder and Stoughton, 1920.

Parliamentary Papers, 1919, vol. xxxiii. Cmd. 100, "Synopsis of British Air Effort During the War."

———. Cmd. 467, "Note by the Secretary of State for Air on a Scheme Outlined by the Chief of the Air Staff for the Permanent Organization of the Royal Air Force."

———. 1920, vol. 8. Cmd. 1157, "Proceedings of the Air Conference, 1920."

———. 1920, vol. 11. Cmd. 1619, "Proceedings of the Second Air Conference Held on 7th and 8th February 1922."

———. 1923, vol. 9. Cmd. 1848, "Proceedings of the Third Air Conference Held on 6th and 7th February 1923."

———. 1923, vol. 15. Cmd.1938, "Recommendations of the National and Imperial Defence Committee as Approved by His Majesty's Government upons I—The Relations of the Navy and the Air Force [and] II—The Coordination of the Defence Forces."

———. 1924, vol. 10. Cmd. 2029, "Report of the Subcommittee of Imperial Defence on National and Imperial Defence."

———. 1926, vol. 8. Cmd. 2649, "Report of the Committee on the Amalgamation of Services Common to the Navy, Army and Air Force." [Signed 2 January 1923, not released until 22 April 1926.]

Pattinson, L. A. *History of 99 Squadron, Independent Force, Royal Air Force, March, 1918–November, 1918.* Cambridge, England: W. Heffer & Sons, 1920.

Penrose, Harold. *British Aviation: The Great War and Armistice, 1915–1919.* London: Putnam, 1969.

Pierce, W. O'D. *Air War, Its Technical and Social Aspects.* London: Waltz, 1937.

Powers, Barry D. *Strategy without Slide Rule: British Air Strategy, 1914–1939.* London: Groom Helm, 1976.

Raleigh, Sir Walter Alexander. *The War in the Air: Being the Story of the Part Played in the Great War by the Royal Air Force.* Vol. 1. Oxford: Clarendon Press, 1922.

Reader, William J. *Architect of Air Power: The Life of the First Viscount Weir of Eastwood, 1877–1959.* London: Collins, 1968.

Rhoads, Robert B. "Lessons Learned." In *Postwar Review*, ed. Maurer Maurer. Maxwell AFB, Ala.: AFHRA, 1978–79.

Robertson, Bruce. *The Army and Aviation A Pictorial History*. London: Cassell, 1981.

———. *Sopwith—The Man and His Aircraft*. Bedford, England: Sidney Press, 1970.

Roskill, Stephen W., ed. *Documents Relating to the Naval Air Service*. London: Navy Records Society, 1969.

———. *Hankey, Man of Secrets: 1877–1918*. Vol. 1. London: Collins, 1970.

Slessor, Sir John C. *Air Power and Armies by Wing Commander J. C. Slessor*. London: Oxford University Press, 1936.

———. *The Central Blue Recollections and Reflections*. London: Cassell, 1956.

Smythies, B. E. "Experiences During the War, 1914–1918." In *A Selection of Lectures and Essays from the Work of Officers Attending the First Course at the Royal Air Force Staff College, 1921–1923*. London: HMSO, Air Ministry, December 1923.

Spaight, J. M. *Air Power and the Cities*. London: Longmans, Green, 1930.

———. *Air Power and War Rights*. London: Longmans, Green, 1924.

———. *The Beginnings of Organised Air Power*. London: Longmans, Green, 1927.

Stewart, Oliver. *The Strategy and Tactics of Air Fighting*. London: Longmans, Green, 1925.

Sweetser, Arthur. *The American Air Service: A Record of Its Problems, Its Difficulties, Its Failures, and Its Final Achievements*. New York: D. Appleton, 1919.

Sykes, F. H. *Aviation in Peace and War*. London: Edward Arnold, 1922.

———. *From Many Angles: An Autobiography*. London: Harrap, 1942.

Symonds, C. P., and D. J. Williams. "Clinical and Statistical Study of Neurosis Precipitated by Flying Duties." *Flying Personnel Research Committee Report No. 547*. London: HMSO, August 1943, 9–42.

Technical Order 30-1-5. *Medical Officer's Guide.* Patterson Field, Ohio: US Army Air Forces Air Service Command.

Terraine, John A. *Impacts of War, 1914 and 1918.* London: Hutchinson, 1970.

———. *The Smoke and the Fire: Myths and Anti-Myths of War, 1861–1945.* London: Barrie & Jenkins, 1980.

———. *To Win a War: 1918, the Year of Victory.* London: Sidgwick & Jackson, 1978.

Till, Geoffrey. *Air Power and the Royal Navy, 1914–1945: A Historical Survey.* London: Jane's, 1979.

Thompson, James Clay. *Rolling Thunder: Understanding Policy and Program Failures.* Chapel Hill, N.C.: University of North Carolina, 1980.

Thomson, Lord. *Air Facts and Problems.* London: John Murray, 1927.

War Office. *Statistics of the Military Effort of the British during the Great War.* London: HMSO, March 1922.

———. *Daily Extracts of the Allied Press, Supplement.* 6 vols. London: HMSO, 1916–1919.

———. *Daily Extracts of the Enemy Press, Supplement.* London: HMSO, 1916–1919.

———. *Daily Extracts of the Foreign Press.* London: HMSO, 1916–1919.

Webster, Sir Charles, and Noble Frankland. *The Strategic Air Offensive Against Germany 1939–1945.* 4 vols. London: HMSO, 1961.

Winter, Denis. *The First of the Few: Fighter Pilots of the First World War.* London: Allen Lane, 1982.

Wise, S. F. *Canadian Airmen and the First World War: The Official History of the Royal Canadian Air Force.* Vol. 1. Toronto: University of Toronto, 1980.

Articles

Bird, W. D. "One Air Force or Three?" *Army Quarterly* 5, no. 2 (January 1923): 352–55.

———. "Thoughts on our Requirements in Relation to an Air Force." *Journal of the Royal United Services Institute (JRUSI)* 68, no. 470 (May 1923): 291–94.

Boyes, G. N. W. "The Advantages and Disadvantages of a Separate Air Force for the Royal Navy." *JRUSI* 69, no. 474 (May 1924): 276–305.

Brooke-Popham, H. R. "The Air Force." *JRUSI*, February 1920, 49.

Brune, Lester H. "An Effort to Regulate Aerial Bombing: The Hague Commission of Jurists, 1922–1923." *Aerospace Historian* 29, no. 3 (Fall 1982): 183–85.

Cooper, Malcolm. "The Development of Air Policy and Doctrine on the Western Front, 1914–1918." *Aerospace Historian* 8, no. 1 (March 1981): 38–51.

Edmonds, C. H. K. "Air Strategy." *JRUSI* 69, no. 474 (May 1924): 191–208.

Frankland, A. Noble. "The Air Offensive against Germany." *JRUSI* 117, no. 668 (December 1972): 66–67.

Jackson, Sir Louis. "Possibilities of the Next War." *JRUSI* 65, no. 457 (February 1920): 71–89.

Jones, H. A. "The Birth of the Royal Air Force." *JRUSI* 88, no. 529 (February 1938): 1–10.

Mackay, C. J. "The Influence in the Future of Aircraft upon Problems of Imperial Defence." *JRUSI* 67, no. 466 (May 1922): 274–310.

National Geographic Magazine 33, no. 1 (January 1918): 1–114, devoted to Allied aviation programs.

Norman, A. H. "The Advantages and Disadvantages of a Separate Air Force for the Royal Navy." *JRUSI* 69, no. 474 (May 1924): 264–75.

Patrick, Mason M. "Final Report of Chief of Air Service, A.E.F." *Air Service Information Circular (Aviation)* 2, no. 180 (15 February 1921).

Pearsall, Ronald. "Aero Engines of the First World War." *Royal Air Force Quarterly* 12, no. 3 (1972): 199–201.

Roskill, S. W. "The Ten Year Rule—The Historical Facts." *JRUSI* 117, no. 665 (March 1972): 69–71.

Slessor, Sir John C. "Air Power and the Future of War." *JRUSI* 99, no. 595 (August 1954): 343–58.

Smith, Malcolm. "A Matter of Faith: British Air Doctrine before 1939." *Journal of Contemporary History (JCH)* 15, no. 4 (October 1980): 423–42.

Smith, Melden E., Jr. "The Strategic Bombing Debate: The Second World War and Vietnam." *ICE* 12, no. 1 (January 1977): 175–91.

Stewart, O. "Air Forces in the Great War: Some Strategic Lessons." *JRUSI* 79, no. 514 (May 1934): 289–93.

Strauss, E. B. "The Psychological Effects of Bombing." *JRUSI* 74, no. 534 (May 1939): 269–82.

Sutton, B. E. "Some Aspects of the Work of the Royal Air Force with the B.E.F. in 1918." *JRUSI* 67, no. 466 (May 1922): 336–48.

Times, 18 October 1917, 6; 22 October 1917, 8; 31 October 1917, 6; 1 November 1917, 6; 6 December 1917, 6–7; 15 January 1918, 6–7; 26 January 1918, 6.

Walser, A. A. "The Influence of Aircraft on Problems of Imperial Defence." *Army Quarterly* 5, no. 1 (October 1922): 38–49.

Williams, Ralph R. "Navigation: From Dead Reckoning to Navstar GPS." *Air Force Magazine* 67, no. 12 (December 1984): 63.

Young, Robert J. "The Strategic Dream: French Air Doctrine in the Inter War Period, 1919–1939." *JCH* 9, no. 4 (October 1974): 57–76.

Unpublished

Cooper, Malcolm. "British Air Policy on the Western Front, 1914–1918." Oxford University, PhD thesis, 1982.

Inwood, S. "The Role of the Press in English Politics during the First World War, with Special Reference to the Period 1914–16." Oxford: PhD thesis, 1971.

Index

299

Aircrew shortages: 196
alleged redeployment of German fighter: 29
Allied bombing accuracy: 23
  cooperation was a two-edged sword: 79
  headquarters: 100
  investigators: 23
  occupation zone: 116
  Zone of Occupation: 18
American Air Service: 25, 50
  aviation units: 50
  bombing survey: 242
  Expeditionary Force: 225
  Expeditionary Force (AEF): 77
  intelligence personnel: 27
  intelligence teams: 113
  investigators: 119
  offensive in the St. Mihiel Salient: 211
  records: 77
  survey: 19
Anglo-French
  conference: 3
  cooperation: 1
AP 1225: 243, 249, 255
Approximate Results No. 84: 217
Armes, Lt Col R. J.: 148–149
Arnaville: 11
Arnaville and Wavreille as last-chance targets.: 57
assessments were severely edited: 241
Asturias: 11
attacking the enemy's morale: 52
Azelot aerodromes: 80

Bacon, Vice Adm Sir Reginald: 35
Bainville-sur-Madon : 77, 82
Baird, Maj J. C.: 134
Balfour Subcommittee: 261
Baring, Maurice: 79
battle casualties: 201
Beardmore-Halford-Pullinger (BHP) six-cylinder engine: 190
Beatty, Admiral: 260
Belgian coast: 37
BETTEMBOURG: 57

Bettoncourt: 202
Bivar, Capt R. B.: 217
blinds: 24
Blinds (unexploded ordnance): 254
Bomb damage: 115
bomb-aiming accuracy: 136
bombing
    accuracy: 122
    as a practical undertaking: 42
    performance: 122
    survey: 122
    surveys: 18
bombs failed to detonate: 24
Bonar Law: 146
Bosch magneto works: 165
Bous: 87
Boyle, A. P.: 74, 150
Breguets : 56
Briey: 57
Briey and Saarbrücken areas: 54
British Admiralty: 4
    aviation industry: 7
    casualties: 90
    daylight offensive: 229
    Expeditionary Force: 2
    intelligence estimates: 228
    liaison with the French War Ministry: 55
    survey party: 113
    survey team: 119
Brooke-Popham, Air Commodore: 90, 122
Burbach: 19
    works: 17, 95
    works at Saarbrcken: 44
Burge, Maj C. Gordon: 86

casualties and wastage: 203
casualty rates: 211
Cecil, Lord Robert: 134
Chambley : 11
Chief of the Air Staff (CAS): 51
Chief of the Imperial General Staff (CIGS): 15
Churchill, Winston: 134

German aerial attacks on London: 43
  archives: 30
  bomb-plot plan and other records: 255
  countermeasures: 229
  documents: 23
  emphasis resulted from America's imminent entry into the fray:
    206
  industrial records: 113
  Lys offensive: 144
  materials: 255
  morale: 26, 52
  naval bases: 35
  plant managers recorded no bomb damage: 257
  productivity along the Saar: 28
  records: 116, 252, 256
  war expenditures: 247
Gloucester Castle: 11
Gorrell, Lt Col Edgar S.: 77, 240
Gotha raid: 41
Gothas: 36–37
Groves concluded that Independent Force operations contravened
  military and political guidelines: 170
Groves, Brig Gen P. R. C.: 148, 163–64, 243

Hagendingen: 9–11, 22, 192
Haig: 11, 47, 58, 61, 62, 78
  and Trenchard bitterly inveighed against further production of
    the DH9: 190
  Field Marshal: 6, 14, 35, 213
  Sir Douglas: 5, 12, 37, 46, 48, 51, 74
Haig-Petain correspondence: 67
Halford, Frank: 191
Handley Page: 10, 11, 35, 43, 65, 76, 84, 89, 108, 166, 208
  night squadrons: 77
  squadrons: 189
  V1500: 158
Henderson, Brig Gen Sir David: 6, 35, 39
highest battle losses: 195
highest sick rate: 195
Hispano-Suiza model: 191
HQ RFC: 48
Hyderabad Squadron: 201

omission of any adverse data: 102
operational limitations: 264
  losses: 194
  srength of Independent Force: 211
Operations Division: 143
Oppau: 115
Ovens, Capt A. R.: 241
overall casualties for 16/17 September: 220

pact between Trenchard and Weir: 171
Paine, Commodore Godfrey: 11
panic during Gotha raids: 43
Pattinson's narrative underscores the organizational difficulties: 197
Paul, Maj H. W. M.: 18, 241
Pearson, Weetman Dickinson (Lord Cowdray): 39
perceptible undertone of official embarrassment: 218
perception of No. 3 Wing aircrews: 30
Petain: 59, 61, 74, 78, 157
photo interpretation: 100
Pirmasens: 87, 108,
poison gas factories: 224
policies of the Royal Flying Corps: 123
post hoc argument: 228
post-Armistice survey materials: 29
postwar bombing surveys: 29
  censorship: 244
  data: 20, 244
  German records: 21
  survey: 19, 114, 241
  survey teams: 22
practical difficulties: 264
preoccupation with morale: 28
presumption of moral effect: 26
priority of support to the Independent Force: 200
prohibitive losses: 223
questionable accuracy of wartime intelligence estimates: 204

RAF field survey: 244
  had underestimated the tools required: 263
  intelligence teams: 244
  survey: 242
Raid returns from No. 55 Squadron: 166

weight of British effort: 112
Weir: 144, 153–154, 178
   concept of strategic bombardment: 155
   patience wore thin: 145
Welchman, Capt P. E.: 198
Western Front: 5–6, 13, 37
Westphalia: 62
What Trenchard omitted: 219
Whitehall: 45, 47, 51, 66
Wilson, Field Marshal Sir Henry: 260
Wise, S. F.: 143, 248
Woippy: 63
Wright, Lt W. J. T.: 241

Xaffevillers: 80

Ypres offensive: 40

Zeppelin raids: 239
Zweibrucken: 62, 103